FLYING IN

My Adventures in Filmmaking

Gretchen McGowan

A POST HILL PRESS BOOK
ISBN: 979-8-89565-448-4
ISBN (eBook): 979-8-88845-863-1

Flying In:
My Adventures in Filmmaking

Cover design by Sara Mulvanny

All people, locations, events, and situations are portrayed to the best of the author's memory. While all of the events described are true, many names and identifying details have been changed to protect the privacy of the people involved.

Post Hill Press
New York • Nashville
posthillpress.com

Published in the United States of America
1 2 3 4 5 6 7 8 9 10

For Bob

"People who have not been in Narnia sometimes think that a thing cannot be good and terrible at the same time."

—C.S. LEWIS,
The Lion, the Witch and the Wardrobe

TABLE OF CONTENTS

THE TEASER

SAIGON, 1996

Caught in a gravel pothole, the tires spin, but the cab-driver hits the gas and we break free. In a smooth recovery, he pops in a cassette of the Bee Gees greatest hits. At first it feels like a mismatched soundtrack for this opening sequence. It's my third week in Saigon, and I'm still struggling to interpret the mysterious syllables of Vietnamese. As we speed through this city—a beehive wrapped in a sauna—the frenetic falsetto of Barry Gibb takes charge of the scene. *Night Fever* pulsates out the window as three Vespas whizz by.

If John Travolta tried to strut down these streets in Tony Manero's white disco suit, he'd be flattened. We accelerate toward a dizzying intersection, the point at which six roadways meet. No traffic lights, no cops whistling the right-of-way, just 500 vehicles hitting the circle at once and rotating—thankfully, in the same direction. Each driver endeavors to drift across, veering off to their exit, without killing or being killed. Cyclos, the manually pedaled rickshaws, keep pace with traditional bicycles. Deeply tanned, sinewy-muscled men carry one or two passengers in canopy-covered seats. Some carts just haul cargo, mangoes, and radios.

Every jolt of my body in the perilous security of the back seat reminds me that I am the luckiest person in the world. I get to travel around the globe on someone else's dime, plunked down into an alternate universe to make something from nothing.

To produce a film.

It's a daunting undertaking, often accompanied by a throbbing ache, a worry that I'm never doing enough, that I've forgotten something, that I'll throw the entire film off course. I'm sure every producer has this fear, the fear of underserving a film. But when we get it right, there's perfection on the screen for an audience to enjoy and a lump in your throat that won't dislodge, reminding you how hard you worked to make it happen.

I've been prepping in Vietnam for almost a month. Today, we're scouting magnificent locations within these city walls. Tonight, Sharon the production designer will arrive, triggering a round of crew hires and set construction. In two weeks, the cinematographer will fly in from New York. Then filming will begin.

But before most of this can happen, the money needs to land. Because right now, I'm subsisting on a zero balance in the film's bank account, and the remaining fumes in my personal account.

The cabdriver flips the Bee Gees cassette to the B-side. We've crossed three rivers and seven circles before we pull up to a concrete square donut of a building: Gai Phong Studio, my home for the next four months.

The studio owner's assistant waves me through the gates. I trail him into an underground hallway, past the main stage, through a gravel courtyard (the hole in the donut) and into the main production office, where a phone receiver dangles, waiting for me to grab it.

It's 10 p.m. in New York City, and there's no mincing of words around the grim news on an unexpected call. The film's financiers have balked, and they will no longer pay for the production. But they're not going to abandon me here (thanks!)—they're wiring money to keep us going for a month. Pre-production has been downgraded to a research expedition.

All the noise, joy, and horrors of trying to pull this movie towards production come to a full stop with one transatlantic call. The sound of the plug being pulled is just the click of the receiver back in the phone's cradle, but for me it's a deafening thud. The studio owner looks up from his desk as if he's heard the same thud. For him, it's the sound of lost revenue.

This is not the sexy side of making a movie.

Since Vietnam, I've worked on more than fifty films—mostly independent ones that are financed and produced outside of the studio system. For each of these movies that won awards, another two never made it to the first day of shooting. For each film you've seen, there are three you've never heard of. I've seen thousands of movies fall apart somewhere between the early development and the signatures on a contract. Despite the rigor, discipline, and excruciating amount of talent in the industry, it's shocking a movie gets made at all. Every three years, I've heard the indie film industry pronounced dead. But somehow they're still here, and so am I.

Even though I've helped make these movies, I've never told my own story. I've never told the stories of the crew and the teams of people who played leading roles in my life along the way, who gathered around the whir of a camera with me. Like most of them, my career didn't progress in a straight line, in chronological order. There was backtracking, and there were jagged leaps forward. There was arrested development, and the struggle to catch up to where I thought I should be.

If I'd spent my career making Hollywood blockbusters, I could tell you a more conventional story. A story about a rapid rise in the studio system and a *no-one-will-eat-lunch-with-you-in-this-town* demise. But those aren't the kinds of movies I work on, and that's not the kind of story I'm going to tell. When you make independent films, you roll up your sleeves and work with the money you have and the schedule you build.

It's a messy life, one that defies your circadian rhythm and lobs stones at your so-called love life. But these films breed strong friendships that last decades—twisted bonds rooted in survival. You work yourself to the bone until the job is done, and then you move on to the next gig.

The films I've worked on have disrupted every genre. They have flown me to Costa Rica, Jordan, Canada, Spain, and Germany. But for the most part, despite all of my global wandering, I've only tripped over myself. Along the way I've managed to piss off a Teamster, and I've worried Jim Jarmusch into thinking I'd been socked in the eye. I've begged royalty to release Brian De Palma's military uniforms for a war movie; I've denied Shelley Winters a pizza for breakfast; and I've had my identity stolen while filming eight thousand miles from home.

I'm not a household name by any stretch, but I'm more than just the scaffolding. And although filmmaking wasn't braided into my DNA, I found a way to hack into it and rearrange the strands.

| Chapter 1 |

THE SLICE OF LIFE

SOMEWHERE IN CALIFORNIA, SUMMER OF 1972

"Do not think," my oldest sister warned us between violent claps of thunder. "Do not even *think* about touching the sides of the tent during the storm."

Her flashlight glowed under her chin, and the rest of her was only lit up by intermittent lightning strikes. Everyone knew that when you pushed up against the edges, the tent would begin to leak. My sister lunged into another ghost story. This story was about a man with a golden arm and a crisp twenty-dollar bill. It terrified me every time she told it.

We were thousands of miles from home. By the morning it had rained sheets of water—biblical rains. I shape-shifted to fit my space and watched my three older sisters—twelve, ten, and eight years old—sprawled out in the tent next to me, hanging onto their last minutes of sleep.

"Let's go girls! Time to get a move on," my father barked in his impatient Navy tone.

He unzipped the orange tent that he and my mother shared. Their tent was newer and didn't leak. We lined up to brush our teeth, then for some reason chased that with a cup of Tang. The orange fuel of the astronauts would be good enough for us. I rolled up my wet sleeping bag and threw an envious glare at the RV next to us. It was barely 6 a.m. and they were still sleeping like a normal family should be.

We packed our bags and ourselves into our white Ford Fairlane, a station wagon that we nicknamed *The Coffin*. Aside from resembling a coffin or a white hearse, it broke down in ten of the forty states we drove through, gasping for air across each state line. It was roomy enough for our eight bony shoulders to bounce around in the back seat. There was no returning home to Philadelphia until Labor Day because we rented our house to another family for the summer. Until then, another girl—a stranger—was walking across my floorboards, sleeping soundly in my bed while we lived our nomadic life.

On the way out of San Diego, my father jerked the wheel south following signs for Tijuana. Cool aviator glasses, hands on ten and two. I thought he was movie star handsome. After a summer on the road, he had let his rust-red beard grow in, which was a contrast against his full head of dark brown hair.

During the last school year, he held my hand when he walked me to school, his other hand holding a brown briefcase. We walked the five blocks in complete silence. Maybe he had run out of stories to tell like the ones he told my sisters on that same walk. Instead, it was more like a private ritual, or maybe a meditation to preserve his energy for his poli-sci students. When he was sick and taken to the hospital, I snuck into his study to pick up clues about him. A tilted globe on its axis, a reel-to-reel deck to record speeches for his students, and stacks of American history books. I spun the globe and let my finger drag above the equator, landing in the middle of the Dead Sea.

"Look at the view! Girls!" Now, my father jumped out of the car at a rest stop with his Kodak Brownie motion picture camera, handing the binoculars over to my mother and panning his lens left to right. He ran hot and cold and we were caught in the bow waves of his moods. But when he clicked that Kodak camera on, he was somehow activated. He seemed genuinely happy. Maybe because he was building memories for us, providing proof of a smiling family baked into celluloid.

Back when he packed his army duffel to serve in the Korean War, he had thrown the Brownie in with a stack of 8 mm film. He documented the monotony on his auxiliary ship, a vessel large enough for a wet dock to repair smaller ships. He filmed endless semaphore practices and long shaky pans along South Korea's coastline. When the repaired ships left the dock, the main ship's empty bay was filled with water, serving double duty as a swimming pool for the troops. The guys were pretty good divers, each one mugging for the camera before leaping into the air. Once, he let someone else operate the Brownie. When he was in front of the lens, he made the perfect jackknife dive, leaving barely a splash.

Now my father flew past the turn that would take us toward the Grand Canyon and towards home. There was no air conditioning to bail us out of the heat. We rolled down the windows and let the dust blow in. We crept past armed agents, and I peeled my thighs away from the cheap upholstery, scooping sweat from under my knees. Each time we hit a bump, the cook stove clanked against the tent poles and one of us had to reach back to steady the gear.

I took in this new scene south of the border. Billboards advertised in Spanish, foreign but somehow familiar: *comida, cerveca, farmacia*. A donkey gave us a grunt before turning away. He was rope-drawn by horses, kicking up dirt where a sidewalk should be. It seemed like a world strictly for adults. I looked down an alley for a sign of anyone my age, but only a pack of stray dogs circled each other, marking their territory.

I was compelled to go further, to be pulled behind the curtain. On this camping trip, I had seen two hundred-foot geysers, presidents' profiles blasted into the mountainside of Mount Rushmore, and the parched massive lakes of Death Valley. And now here was Tijuana. I couldn't get my head around how we could just drive over an arbitrary line into another country. But just a few miles across that line, we made an abrupt U-turn returning to the north. Mexico, and the rest of the world—on my terms anyway—would have to wait because this traveling circus was going home.

Four used cars and five years later, my parents gave up their teaching jobs and we migrated from Philadelphia to the Berkshire foothills. In this tiny Massachusetts town, they took the opportunity to reinvent their lives. Maybe they thought my father's illness could evaporate here, far from the city sirens.

For us four girls our new home was a good place to get lost in the movies. At five dollars a car, our friends loaded into the bed of a pick-up truck and casually sped past the drive-in theater gate. *Paper Moon* played in a double feature with *The Bad News Bears*. Tatum O'Neal was about my age, but I sympathized with Walter Matthau. How was he going to train that scrappy group to win a baseball game? And was it even worth trying? But this was a Hollywood movie, so there was a guaranteed come-from-behind winning streak.

We returned for the double feature three times that week. At home, if you contorted the rabbit ears just right, you could watch *The Wizard of Oz* on our eight-inch black and white television set, but you had to imagine color saturating the screen when Dorothy's house landed on the witch.

On the raw October morning when my mother was supposed to bring my father home from the hospital again, I entered the door to his study. Across his desk, a row of unopened first aid kits, one for each of us. Out of reach on the top shelf—behind four fire extinguishers with their expiration tags dangling—the Brownie camera collected dust. I dug into a box of miniature spools of film, each one labeled in my father's blocky handwriting: *San Diego/Honeymoon, Yosemite, Summer of '72/'73, Korea,* and more *Korea* on the bigger spools. I thought about erecting the screen and threading up the projector for another home movie screening.

That's when the ambulance pulled into the driveway.

But my father wasn't in that ambulance; he never made it out of the hospital. My sisters and I watched from the living room window as my mother let herself out from the passenger side and steadied herself on the gravel. She reached up to adjust a hairpin in her bun in what seemed like slow motion, maybe buying time before looking up to us. The driver came around and hugged her. We knew the driver. We knew everyone in that town, and everyone knew us as the girls from Philly. City girls. Now they would know us as the four girls whose father died.

The world did not stop, and that surprised me. I lay in bed waiting for the tears to show up. I squinted at the wallpaper, memorizing the wild blue leaves clutching smaller blue flowers. I was barely eleven years old, what was supposed to come next? Maybe our lives would be easier without all the hospital visits and all the false hope of recovery, but what kind of monster was I to think that? I forced my eyes to well up, but it felt phony. Like Hollywood tears.

My father named me Gretchen. I always imagined it was because I was the last of four girls and he ran out of names. My sisters' more recognizable names were feminine and multisyllabic. But I was told that Gretchen translates to pearl, its true meaning in its strength. Years of tumultuous sea storms, intense pressure from the ocean above, crashed down upon the hearty oyster's shell, and all that chaos gave the tiny pearl within it its wisdom.

In the weeks that followed my father's death, I was told that I was brave and strong. And after so many times of being told how strong you are, you start to believe it. You carefully develop a new muscle in your brain, one with a low tolerance for your weaknesses. Finally, you deny that you have any weaknesses at all. What would I do with them anyway?

I lifted the lid on one of the neighbors' casserole dishes that covered the dining room table, probing at a top layer of toasted Special K cereal. So much food, so little appetite. Instead of a sympathy casserole, a friend in New York City offered us a roll of subway tokens and a week in her studio apartment near the United Nations building.

"Everyone gets two maps!" Our Manhattan friend was camera-ready at 7 a.m. as she handed out envelopes to the five of us. Had she trained in the Navy too, I wondered? "You've each got five dollars, an umbrella, and ten tokens. That's ten trips. Remember how I taught you to grab a bus transfer? *Always* get a bus transfer, you might need it later. Or you can give it to next guy if you don't need it."

I unfolded my map and sat in her window marking our location. If that building below us was the United Nations, then out the other window was the 59th Street Bridge reaching out towards Queens. The map's matrix of thick interwoven primary colors represented the train tracks that stretched all the way to the ocean in Coney Island, or farther north to the Bronx. With one token, an eleven-year-old could hop on a bus on any corner and travel to the end.

"Could we go to the World Trade Center?" I asked, looking downtown. I'd seen those twin towers in the movies, looming behind Robert Redford's paranoid phonebooth calls in *Three Days of the Condor* and rising in the background of Brooklyn's gritty streets in Al Pacino's *Dog*

Day Afternoon. The buildings had only been standing three years, but they were already iconic.

"It's the future!" A vendor yelled while he paced around the entrance of the UN in the November rain with an open umbrella fastened to his head. The umbrella kept the rain off his face, but the water dripped in a tight circle around him. "Secret's out, don't miss it!" he stage whispered down First Avenue.

Hundreds of commuters plowed past him, but if anyone listened, they didn't act like it. A shot of adrenaline hit me, fueled by the city smells of diesel and donuts. I turned west and walked alone block after block, entirely in charge of my direction. I shared the sidewalk with New York's international diplomats, eccentrics, and fur-adorned socialites. I would have dropped everything in Massachusetts for this New York City life. Because in one burst—one jolt from the city's pulse—I felt decades older than my eleven years.

As a college freshman on the pre-med track in Ohio, I worked the dining hall salad bar in an apron and clogs (in that pocket of fashion in the '80s when clogs were not cool). My biology lab partner, Tania, sat with our classmates at our unofficial lunch table, her brown curls piled high in an unruly bun. She threw me funny faces in solidarity while I Windexed the sneezeguard and refilled the crouton buckets. But the scarlet "F" was burned into my forehead: *Financial Aid Situation*, Ivory tower gatecrasher.

Library work was the next level up in Dante's circles of financial aid employment. I stamped due dates into each book from my rolling stool at the front desk. I was hyper-aware of the seating arrangement for each friend and every crush. It would have been a good place to study chemistry and calculus if I weren't so distracted by the theater of the student body. The administration imposed a hulking magnetic detector at the front entrance which seemed like overkill; was there really a book theft problem? With a thin metal probe, I pulled sticky magnetic strips through each book spine, working my way through the Dewey Decimal system.

Tania showed up at my library desk modelling a tool belt. Her parents were both doctors. Between them, at least eight letters in degrees after their names. I wondered what they would make of Tania now, in her utilitarian belt funded by their liberal arts tuition dollars.

"It's for the theater," THEE-a-tah, she pronounced it, framing her curls with her palm, Rita Hayworth style. "I'm hanging lights. But the cool thing: they're teaching me how to run the lighting board." My shoulders slumped in jealousy as I quickly drew a metal strip through the spine of another book.

Tania pulled a folded pale blue playscript from her back pocket and slapped it on the desk, *Charlie's Aunt*. "You should read it while you're confined to this habitat," she joked, as if my book magnetizing skills could be repurposed in the finer arts. "Come down and hang from the catwalk with me."

I acted in high school, but I was perennially cast as the middle-aged aunt in a tight bun or an awestruck teenager in pajamas, singing—no shouting—out the obnoxious first lines of *Bye Bye Birdie* into a pink telephone receiver. More often, I watched from the wings, clutching my clarinet and memorizing every line. We had no room downstage for an actual pit orchestra, so they moved us to the wings, rebranded as the *armpit* band.

The college's theater was built into a raked hillside on the south edge of campus. It housed the stage where Paul Newman had performed in *The Taming of the Shrew* and rigged lights for *Ghost*. With a wrench tied to my beltloop, I perched from the trusses high above the actors during a tech run-through. The lighting designer shouted cues from the panels as I tweaked the angle on a Fresnel lens and swapped out gels.

"Let's go—drama club photo." Someone with authority, the stage manager, whistled for me to come down from the catwalk. I wasn't a member; I was just hanging out. But it was too late, I was already pulled into the frame. The cooler-than-thou seniors—the ones who played the starring roles and directed plays—held court in their own clique in the back row. The tech crew knelt in the front row and the prop team snuck in sideways.

"Say: *Opening Night*!" the photographer cued us.

In this space, Shakespeare and the Aristotle were revered, but we were encouraged to play with the surreal and the grotesque, the Brechts and the Pirandellos. We memorized the dexterous dialogue of Marsha Norman, Lillian Hellman, and Harold Pinter.

I dragged the dorm hallway phone into the lounge, pulling out my calling card to dial home. While the phone rang on my mother's end, I sat on the carpet and picked the loose bits of fuzz and set it aside, creating a neat pile of anxiety.

"Calculus was easy until it got hard," I told my mother, just as I'd scripted it. "Same with embryology." There was a theme here: I was missing the second semester gene. More than once, I had fallen asleep during the 8 a.m. embryology lecture. I tried to prop my eyes open, but as soon as the lights dimmed and the projector's screen slid towards the floor, I nodded into my notebook. On the screen, the daughter cells split in two exploding into life's beginnings. Mitosis, it turned out, set me into deep hypnosis. There were other students who were killing it in biology lab; future doctors who would build brilliant teams and cure melanoma. Maybe my dropping out would give someone else that chance.

"So, I've been giving it a lot of thought, the pre-med thing?" I said, straightening my posture against the wall. I was the youngest daughter, the last hope to master the sciences and right all the wrongs. A drama major was not going to erase all of my father's hospital visits. And now I was opting for the exit ramp.

"Mm hmm?" Groceries were being unbagged; I could hear the familiar squeak of the vegetable drawer and the muffled switch of the phone receiver to her other ear.

"There's a deadline next week. I need to declare my major," then, in not quite the refined way I'd rehearsed it, "I'm switching to drama." Thud.

"I think that's great," she said, without missing a beat. "I can see it, and I can see you like the classes. I say, *why not*?!"

Why not? With two simple words, I was given permission to change my entire trajectory. Or maybe I'd just worn her out. She'd singlehandedly put four daughters through college, and I was the free-range one. The one who had let herself in the door alone after school and made dinner. In the last years of high school, we began to feel more like friends—equals even—shedding the clichéd frictions of mother and daughter.

I spent the final semesters of school at the theater, where the outsiders were insiders cordoned off in two buildings of their own. For Tania, theater was a college hobby, something to kill time between psychology and microeconomics. But for me, it was home. I wrote plays, acted (badly) and directed. And, while it wasn't the exit ramp I thought it would be, it was all practice for what would come next.

| Chapter 2 |

THE URBAN FANTASY

NEW YORK CITY, 1987

I reported for spy duty in neutral street clothes, as directed. It was on the 20th floor of the Starrett-Lehigh building, a massive hunk of bricks, mortar and glass that consumed the entire block. The building's freight elevators were so giant that they could lift Mack trucks to the rooftop. The steam radiators clanked but the room was icy cold with a few chairs scattered around, as if the last tenant had left in a hurry. When we were asked to line up for roll call, a dozen middle-aged men shouted out their names. And then there was me.

With a hundred dollars and an L.L. Bean duffel bag, I landed in New York City with a nanny job on West 99th Street. Mine was a cobbled together existence, the result of circled ads in the Village Voice. Far removed from the entertainment world, I had two children in my charge early mornings and late afternoons. I found supplemental work as a cater-waiter, a pre-school teacher, a temp, and a spy.

I surveyed my fellow spies as they leaned against the windowsills, arms folded, and ankles crossed. They were wearing white socks with white Nike shoes. They shook the same unfiltered cigarettes to the top of the pack. In unison, they exhaled bitter smoke.

"Chanel everybody!" our boss clapped his hands and shouted into our cement chamber. It was louder than anybody needed him to be. "Today is all about Chanel." He held up a photo of a handbag with two interlocking golden C's, their backs to each other in a petulant tug of war. At the top of the bag, there was a matching gold thick woven chain that was too cold for a bare hand to grasp in subzero weather. "Exhibit A everyone, take it in. Commit it to memory."

The point wasn't to arrest the sellers of these bags, that was too easy. We were directed to find the knock-offs and sniff out a trail to the source. This mission was sponsored by the brand that was tired of being ripped off. We piled into a van and drove down the West Side Highway while taking instruction on how to stealthily "shop" for the sponsored brand, whether that was fake Gucci bags or Rolex watches. For today, we would track only Chanel rip-offs.

When we pulled into a side alley behind Canal Street, the boss handed me a blank notepad and nudged me out of the van and into the chaos. I thought of the hours I had spent on our Philadelphia corner as an eight-year-old, hiding behind the azaleas and writing down license plates of cars that turned down our street. But this was Chinatown, not my Philly backyard, and I might as well have flown across two oceans. A waft of perfumed smoke caught in my throat, its source a line-up of incense sticks lit atop a tapestry-covered card table. If I could bottle this angst—the six lanes of charging Canal Street traffic, the fish carcasses gaping sideways on ice and intimidating vegetables—I could release it later as in incantation to transport anyone back to New York City circa 1988.

Now, my first vendor suspect snuck down Mercer Street, looking over his shoulder. The shimmer of the coveted golden interlocking Cs poked their head out of the trash bag he carried. The rip-offs were looking more real than the original. I was hot on his trail, but I tried to act like a casual stroller or a curious tourist.

In fact, my invisibility made me feel invincible on Canal Street. I was a 5'6" with henna-red hair, dressed in post-collegiate rethreads. I could be anybody. I lunged towards the corner pay phones, and a rush of adrenaline tingled up through my fingertips when I dialed into the Starrett-Lehigh office.

In the van, the boss raised my arm like a boxing champ, soliciting a reluctant round of applause from the guys and a cocky chill from me. The guys snorted at my beginner's luck, but the boss handed me an envelope of crisp twenty-dollar bills: $180 cash. Courtesy of Coco Chanel.

On weekday mornings, I taught pre-school in Riverside Park. I arrived before the parents and their miniature four-year-olds, early enough to chase the rats away by stomping around the playground and its bordering boulders. Mornings were fingerpaints and sidewalk chalk and I had to throw my clothes in the wash and find another outfit for the second leg of the day, when I'd distribute my resume at Off-Off Broadway theaters. This community was already lousy with unpaid college interns with jobs that dead-ended where they started. I could hold out for a job copying scripts and fetching bog-water coffee, but paid work in the theater wasn't a step ladder for people like me. The unconnected, the daughter of nobody in the business.

All these jobs afforded me one thing: the ability to live in Manhattan. Each street was a reminder of someone else's giant success in literature or cinema. It was an inspiration, but it could also be a drag when your own reality.

One night after pounding that pavement, I jogged up to Central Park's high chain-link fence and began to run around the path, slowly gaining speed. I chased the ghosts of the reservoir that leapt out ahead of me. Around the northwest corner, Dustin Hoffman ran the loop hard in *Marathon Man*. Of course, after this scene he'd be writhing in pain in a dentist's chair unable to answer the probing question, *Is It Safe?*

My friend Anne waited for me on the sticky floors of an Amsterdam Avenue bar. She pointed to the pint in front of her, code for *you look like you need one of these*. Just off work at her advertising job, Anne was at ease in a silk blouse and a pencil skirt. I was more comfortable in jeans and a black T-shirt. Before 8 p.m., beer on tap was half-price and free popcorn and chicken wings could stand in for a square meal. Happiness for a whole hour or more if the bartender was kind. But when Anne's friend Sarah blew in, our fifteen minutes of one-on-one conversation was over. Sarah's arm gestures slurped all the oxygen from the room. I was awestruck.

Sarah was saying something about *a provenance*. Something about how many Q-tips she'd been through while cleaning up a painting. This was *real* work, I thought, important work. Groups of school children would gather around to appreciate her opus. Patrons would pay good money to see this restoration. Like Anne's advertising work where she was making her mark on billboards and boardrooms, this would be Sarah's indelible creation.

"What's the solution?" I asked, without articulating what I meant.

"What solution?" Sarah didn't look up; she was struggling to ignite her Bic. *Click, click, click,* she fixated on the spark that refused to become a flame.

"I mean, what do you dip the Q-tips in when you're cleaning the painting?"

Sarah laughed and slowly stuck out her tongue, pierced with two silver balls.

"Saliva! My own saliva," she said. "That's the secret." And finally, a flame. She took a drag on her cigarette and looked up, as if noticing me for the first time.

"Gretchen," she quizzed me, "that's a name like Heidi, isn't it? It's like, I imagine you running through a field in the Irish countryside. Picking potatoes," she said, looking up to an imaginary landscape behind the bartender, and then to Anne for collusion. "Am I right?"

I caught my reflection in the bar's mirror, my face now in a heated blush.

"Pulling," I finally said. "You don't pick potatoes; you dig them up. Then you pull them out." I mimed pushing a shovel into the earth, but she'd already turned away to flick her cigarette ash.

"See! Right there," she pointed at me. "I wouldn't have known that. But you do." She waited a beat, then there was more.

"Nothing bad's ever happened to you, has it?" she asked. *Badzever. Bad's* like it ended in a "z."

She seemed to be saying *you're not New York enough. You're soft.*

This was true, I was still madly in love with the city. After starting the spy job in Chinatown, I had quickly learned the three tenets of walking its streets: avoid extended eye contact, stay to the right (except to avoid subway grates and manholes), and above all, act bored. If you could yawn your way down Broadway like every other New Yorker, you could belong. The first two were easy, but the third mandate was impossible. Only a fool could be bored in New York City.

I shot a glance at Sarah, by now she'd moved back to her favorite subject, herself. But she'd already touched a nerve. Would I ever carve out a New York life that didn't tether me to a hairnet or a photocopier, or to someone else's brood?

I wanted a career, not just a job. I wanted to be Melanie Griffith in *Working Girl,* whisked across the New York harbor, and reclaiming her ideas. I wanted to be Robert Redford at the crosswalk, holding back traffic after an uptown heist in *The Hot Rock,* or Jill Clayburgh in *An Unmarried Woman,* balancing that giant framed canvas. Owning it.

✈

The next Saturday, I hit Canal Street again in sub-freezing temperatures. I blew on my hands and stomped my feet, watching the knock-off vendors hustle. They moved like cats, setting up shop on a blanket in an instant. The break-down was even faster. Corners of the cloth pulled taught to form a sack and hoisted over their backs. Then performing the disappearing act into a crowd of tourists. These men grew eyes in the back of their heads by creating a network. They looked out for one another. If our spies were spotted or sensed, all it took was a quick-coded whistle, a hand signal or a nod, and the goods were cleared.

I had no business here. I didn't care about these brands. I didn't care about saving corporations from their copycats. Truth be told, I'd had my own stint at shoplifting: every twelve-year-old's right-of-passage in a pre-security-camera world. It began with tipping lip gloss into my bag and deteriorated to lifting a pair of shorts that I thought the world owed me. I was the fraud here. And for ten dollars an hour, I could do better.

The Village Voice came to the rescue again. I showed up to meet a couple in their '60s who supported their film-making habit with Manhattan real estate. Their Chelsea walls were covered with framed posters of films they had made and the awards they had won. Films about Isaac Bashevis Singer and Earl Scruggs for PBS shows.

Before the spy gig, the owner's growling temper would have intimidated me. But now I prepared to fudge dictation, deploying a self-taught shorthand. I ditched the nanny work and embraced every odd job at this tiny company. I ran the office, scheduled the plumber, and drafted the leases. I picked up the crew, pulled focus on camera lenses, and loaded fresh film stock. My real estate to-do list blended so closely with the film work that the two jobs were indistinguishable. What was filmmaking anyway, but a list of things to do?

The closest I came to a life in theater was at Sardi's, the famous Broadway restaurant. At an opening night party, we filmed an *American Masters* scene near a panel of framed caricature drawings of past and present Broadway stars. I grabbed a sun-gun lamp and bounced light off the wall, trying not to blind Neil Simon.

And that's when I met Toby. She was a freelance film editor brought in to edit the Neil Simon documentary. She was a Hampshire College graduate, one of the disciples of the documentary photographer Jerome Liebling. Toby grabbed a rubber band and threw a long mane of curls up on top of her head. She took a seat at the editing flatbed like a concert pianist, seamlessly pulled select shots, and assembled elegant scenes within minutes.

From Toby, I learned how to synchronize film dailies and how to run an editing room. I mastered the art of threading the film through a flatbed (this one had the brand name *Steenbeck*, but those in the know used Steenbeck as shorthand for an editing flat bed, like *Kleenex* is to tissue). I learned how to operate the other hulking steel machines around the office like the squawk box, the rewind table, and an eight-foot-tall sound transfer deck, a machine I operated while balancing on a metal folding chair. I walked down Seventh Avenue and Madison Square Park, recording sounds into a reel-to-reel deck (a *Nagra*). Then I brought these field recordings back to the office, closed the closet door behind me, and transferred those New York sounds to magnetic stock. Toby showed me how to stitch the new sound effects into the reels on the flat bed, matching the effect to a corresponding image on screen.

All this led up to one jittery morning: a screening for The Executives. Rotating the Steenbeck's power wheel to begin the first reel was a sacred act. The viewing was not to be interrupted until the last frame rolled out. We overdosed on coffee while watching the executives take notes throughout the rough cut. Each time they scribbled in their notebooks I was sure they would miss a pivotal string of frames; a key transition they would need to grasp the film's brilliance.

When we were left alone with the list of notes, Toby worked like a detective deciphering the intent between the lines. If there was a comment about a character's trip to the Rockaways, she sensed it wasn't about the trip itself. It was something just before or just after that was off. The note had validity but not specificity. We didn't cut out the whole scene. We found the snag in the story that was throwing the rest out of whack.

There's that one person for everyone; the one who nudges the rook out of its corner. I can trace everything else in my career—everything good anyway—to just two degrees of separation away from Toby.

It was Toby who connected me to the lobster shift gig, synchronizing dailies for *Making Do the Right Thing*.

I had entered the life of a freelancer; fending for jobs without the safety net of a regular paycheck. I reported at night to a second floor set of offices above a Popeye's fast food chicken shop. My machine faced Times Square, overlooking downtown across the center of the universe. On the flatbed's screen, bigotry smoldered during the hottest summer on record in Brooklyn. The cast wiped sweat from their foreheads and when I reversed the film through the flatbed's sprockets, they wiped it back. Sweat on, sweat off, until I got the synchronization right. I cut out the excess magnetic stock and spliced it back together, bringing the picture and audio in synchronization with each other.

St. Claire Bourne, the director of this behind-the-scenes feature, hovered over me as the picture's celluloid ran through the sprockets. He loved every frame of it, spotting the potential of each frame. But his legacy and his hulking presence made me nervous, and my fingers shook over the splicer. It was tricky to sync dailies in a command performance.

On the last night of filming, the dailies arrived in a pile of white lab boxes. My work was cut out for me. Mr. Bourne threw his leather bag over his shoulder and said goodnight. I was left alone in his room full of Steenbecks. I pulled up the window sash to let in some hot Popeye's air and took my seat at the flatbed—the way Toby had done. I kicked off my shoes to feel the cool linoleum floor. Two mice ran over my feet.

Now that I subscribed to a freelancing life, there were long dry spells of no film work. I grabbed at anything I could to make the rent, squeezing into panty hose and heading to Wall Street for temp work. There was cater-waitering for large events and grueling double shifts. I tried to consider it an adventure; research for my film career. New York was not yet a company town, and it was a while before a film career would sustain me.

It was only a slight upgrade to be kneeling on the concrete basement of Fox Movietone's film archive. Dust bunnies flew by like tumbleweeds while I flipped through a card catalog. I bit down on my pencil and pulled index cards from the card catalog. I transcribed library code references for 16mm prints of the footage I'd been searching for. The clerk handed me a packet of VHS tapes and I crossed town toward the main public library to scroll through microfilms.

I was told this was the catch-all job of *Associate Producing*: driving the crew to set, setting up lights, fetching coffee, and picking up cigarette butts after wrap. Sometimes the role was like professional stalking. Sweating out cold calls to prestigious people, and hoping they'd take pity on me when I stuttered out my pre-interview questions.

With the interview secured and the location locked, I escorted Abba Eban up to the mezzanine of a Flushing Meadows ice rink. I unwrapped Mr. Eban, the former foreign minister of Israel, from a burrito of warming clothes and propped him up next to a portable heater. I stood behind the camera while he reminisced about his 1947 victory for Israel. This icy box, so unassuming and utilitarian, had been the temporary home for the United Nations at that pivotal time.

With a close study, an associate producer could become a mini-expert in just about anything. If October brought

Buckminster Fuller or Tiananmen Square, November might bring bluegrass music, Hunter S. Thompson or a director's deep personal dive into the dating lives of middle-aged singles.

Within one crosstown block, the temperature dropped five degrees and the sidewalk seized into a slick sheet of ice. I could not be late. I could be underqualified, overanxious, and underdressed, but I could not be late. The interview was big: a line producing gig on an independent feature film. Richard Miller, the producer, had chosen to meet at the Square Diner, a greasy spoon vestige of a louder and grittier cobble-stoned Tribeca. If no one pulled the emergency cord on the subway train (again), I could make the trip in twenty minutes. I boarded a crowded downtown train just before the doors closed and glanced at my watch. New York's staccato pace turned a ride into a race.

While we hurtled through midtown, I hung from a metal strap leaning over two male passengers. One studied *The New York Times*, folded into a three-column origami. The other propped open the *New York Post*, his nose planted in the seam. Could one of these two be Richard? Was he a *Post* guy or a *Times* guy? The two men's shoulders jostled around in a synchronized dance at the train's will, their fingers stained in press ink. I rebalanced my feet and leaned over the tabloid.

"*Why me*!" Nancy Kerrigan sprawled in the rink and grabbed her knee. Her Olympic dreams were destroyed by a tire iron or a nightstick. I couldn't get the angle on her front-page story; I had an easier view of the bold-faced names on *Page Six*. The *Post* reader glared up at me and shook his paper. I snapped back to my own space, checking my watch.

At 14th Street, the *Post* guy pressed his necktie into his throat and rose to leave, leaving his paper behind. Now I had to pretend I didn't want to pick it up. No one took the seat, no one reached for the paper. It just sat there, all fifty cents of it. Its unapologetic celebrity worship, its punster headlines, and its salacious gossip columns claiming what movie star was spotted at Bar Pitti. But when the conductor announced my stop unintelligibly, I snatched the paper and buried it in my bag.

I reached the diner five minutes early and inhaled sharply before pulling the metal door handle. The spare five minutes would give me time to straighten out the damage my hat had done under there.

Act qualified, I reminded myself. But Richard had arrived even earlier. He waved me over from a table covered in notebooks and photo folders.

We shared a grilled cheese sandwich and a few familial exchanges to warm up for the interview. Fifteen minutes into the niceties, the bell on the diner door gave an icy ding and a couple took a seat in the booth behind us. When the cold blast passed, Richard handed me the script. I held it up and admired the clean simplicity of the cover page and its title: *Heavy*. The jitters in my hand might have been the caffeine or the cold, but I knew it was my nerves kicking in.

"Rachel said I should hire you," he said. "She said you're the one." Rachel was my friend and Richard's Columbia classmate. But Rachel had a flair for hyperbole, and she'd inflated my qualifications.

"She said that?" Incredulous, I tried not to let my inflection rise as this was not the moment to flaunt my inexperience. Underselling myself is a quality I inherited from my father.

I was not meant to be at the Square Diner interviewing for this job. There were no full feature films on my resume. No famous father or aunt in the spotlight. And with scrappy, mostly documentary work in my background, I was clearly out of step with the NYU and Columbia film school grads.

"Apparently Rachel's a big fan—from your work on her bluegrass documentary," Richard said. "So look, we need to get started right away. I know it's not much money, but I need help. Call me as soon as you've read it?" Richard would produce and James Mangold, the writer, would direct. It was their first feature film, but they were card-carrying members of an Ivy League graduate program. I imagined that film students like this were honor bound, that they created a lifetime collaboration in school, impenetrable to the rest of us.

I unbuckled my leather satchel and dropped the script in, pushing the *Post* to the bottom, now an embarrassing tagalong. The satchel was the armor I wore to give others confidence in me. My consignment shop, navy pea coat wouldn't reveal any expertise. But the satchel said, *trust me, I know what I'm doing.*

In my apartment, I lay on my bed with my legs up the wall to take in the script. On the first read, I forgot to pay attention to any production challenges. The script's sparse dialogue and brief stage directions reminded me of Pinter plays, rich with subtext and just a touch of exposition. "You're as big as an ox and no one sees you. I am the same way, I am loud and no one hears me, but when I whisper everyone looks around like something happened." James's characters were at once recognizable and sympathetic, simple only on the surface. I grabbed a pen and began to read again from the front cover, this time trying not to get distracted by the story and its characters. Now I had to sort out how to go about filming this movie.

I let my pen drive into the page, leaving a circle of useless blotchy dots. Where to begin? Fictional scripts were not the blueprint I knew. The job of line producing would be multi-faceted; I needed to read from the perspective of each of these roles. On one pass I read as a lawyer, and the next pass I read as an accountant. Then I read as a scheduler, location scout, and storyteller.

I had a paralyzing fear of screwing it up, but I dialed Richard's number and accepted the job. It was like falling in love; it had to be me.

It was still icy when I crossed Amsterdam and claimed the window seat in the Shakespeare & Company bookshop overlooking Broadway. I pulled all the relevant books from the shelves and leafed through them, thirsty for knowledge.

Hollywood fit neatly on a full two shelves, stories of decadence and big budget productions. Fatty Arbuckle's salacious—and ultimately deadly—romp through Hollywood starlets, and Julia Phillips dramatic downfall in the studio hierarchy. Hollywood films were greenlit and financed by the studio's deep pockets. They had their own machine to develop the scripts and churn out the marketing. It was no longer the old studio system of stock actors on exclusive contracts, but their big, sweeping, romantic comedies still attracted a top-tier cast. And I consumed the studio's movie culture as much as anyone, from the red carpet's swooping searchlights on premiere nights to the last kernels of popcorn in the bucket.

But it was 1993 and there were few books about the pioneering generation of independent film. It occupied a small corner of the store's bookshelf. There were no plastic action figures or lunchbox campaigns for these films. These were independently financed projects. Sometimes financed by a wealthy individual, and sometimes by a cadre of Wall Street financiers. Indies didn't try to make a diminutive version of the Hollywood film; films that performed well because the studio formula was plugged in and played. Instead, independent films took risks and broke rules. The characters were every shade of grey, nothing absolute evil or heart-of-gold good. And even though the budgets were micro and the schedules were challenged, there was no big studio executive hovering over the production, controlling the script, the cast, and the director. The independent film could attract attention at a festival premiere and an acquisition by a distributor.

Often, the finished indie film was fed back into that same studio machine.

I worked my way through *Spike Lee's Gotta Have It,* a memoir about the making of his first feature film. Spike Lee struggled to save money for a typewriter. He was convinced that as soon as he got one he would write the script that would raise the budget. Turns out, his was the script that would change the landscape of independent film. The urgency of his diary (and the fact that I'd seen the movie) assured the reader he'd get it done.

I moved into the hardwood floor aisles where I creased the pages of *The Film Director's Team,* a play-by-play manual on scene breakdown and how to assemble the results into a shooting schedule. I was researching what a line producer actually did and they seemed to be describing everything I was able to do. Aside from the basics of budgeting, scheduling, casting, hiring, and forecasting, the job seemed to boil down to one essential talent: rallying every department to achieve the director's interpretation of the script. On time and on budget. It was that simple.

The bookstore manager recognized me, and I smiled up when he pointed to my pile. He slid a pencil from behind his ear and jutted a hip forward.

"You know, you've got to *read* these books to learn this stuff. You can't sit on them and learn it osmotically." I removed two paperbacks from the seat of my pants.

He moved on and said nothing else for now. A warning. They appreciated an avid reader, but they weren't thrilled when a researcher pawed through the stacks for over an hour. The cheap customer would either sneak out without a purchase or spread her crumpled bills on the counter for the least expensive book.

At twenty-eight years old, most of my friends from college were now married, with robust bank accounts. They were producing children. In a split screen against my life, I pictured Tania and her husband buying Baby Björn's and circling a highchair. She would probably never see *Heavy*; it wouldn't be a blip on her entertainment radar. My escape to a remote location to make this small film was just another way of delaying the adulthood she'd already conquered.

I put the books back and pulled out the plastic lifeboat, my Mastercard. There was some wiggle room left on my limit and if there was one thing I needed before we left for rural New York, it was an upgrade to a down coat.

Acting the part, dressing the part, I prepared to meet the players—the rest the team Richard had already hired.

| Chapter 3 |

THE GENRE-DEFYING FILM

ELDRED, NEW YORK, 1994

Somebody's gotta roll up their sleeves and do the work.

—Shelley Winters as Dolly in *Heavy*

There's a wonderful scene in Peter Weir's film, *Witness*, that must be seen on the big screen. "I hear you're a carpenter," Kelly McGillis's suitor challenges Harrison Ford's character, just before the climactic sequence unfolds. It is cinema perfection: the synchronized division of labor, the assembled beams hoisted skyward and nailed into place, John Seale's exquisite cinematography. The music. It was filmed in Amish country in Lancaster, Pennsylvania. Even if Weir had cut out Harrison Ford's inimitable backward glances, the brewing romance, and the danger; the beauty of the scene would have worked. For these characters, everything else was set aside, every grudge and every fear. Nothing was more important than raising that barn.

Ten years later and three and a half hours northwest of that barn raising location, our crew unloaded from a van like prisoners on leave. We traveled three hours northwest of New York City and arrived at the vacant diner, our main location in Eldred. It was just a small town along the Delaware River, but this is where it would all happen. Adjacent to the diner, a former general store's wooden steps led up to its weather-beaten porch. I imagined the setting in its former glory being the hangout for townspeople on Sunday mornings. They'd grab a hefty *New York Times*, a gallon of milk, and sit on the railing sharing gossip with their neighbors.

Now it would be our production office. The snow had been plowed up to the side of the store, shoving icicles onto the sills of the second story's windows. It was hard to imagine these dense mounds of snow melting by the time we would leave town in eight weeks. All eyes were on that first day of principal photography.

Our first mission was to haggle for RV campers. On a scrappy, low-budget independent film like *Heavy,* we wouldn't be able to rent streamlined movie campers for our cast. We needed a creative solution, and we needed to find it locally. I had the logistics down and the negotiating power. But when I needed a partner to be sure those RVs would show up at our diner location, Diana was the one to make it happen.

As the film's location manager, Diana had already been in Eldred for three weeks, and she had made quick work. She met the town garage owner when he hooked a chain around the tow ball of her car and pulled her out of a snowbank. The garage owner introduced her to the Eldred Diner manager who, in turn, set her up with the owner of the Eldred Preserve fishing inn. I wondered if it was Diana's ingenuity that landed her in that snowbank in the first place.

Diana unfolded a map and circled the RV destinations, choreographing the afternoon's schedule. I popped the trunk and cleared her passenger seat, displacing her box of Kodak film rolls, glue sticks, and location folders. She had pasted together panorama photo collages of every interior and exterior location she researched. When we pulled up along the *Trailers for Sale* sign by the river, I could already see the owner's daughter behind the cash register. She white knuckled the edge of the counter, preparing for the movie people.

"She played Ado Annie in *Oklahoma!*," the owner said, throwing a thumb over his shoulder to indicate his daughter. "Here's the review, up on the board." The local newspaper's article was tacked into a cork board with rusting metal push pins. The edges near the photo of Ado Annie curled up at the edges.

"Dad, don't," the daughter gave her best Clara Bow, rolling her eyes back so hard only the whites were visible. "They don't wanna hear it."

"The thing is, there are so few extra roles on this film," I said. "The director chooses the cast, then there's the Screen Actors Guild..."

"SAG?" he said, cutting me off with the acronym. "Oh, we know all about SAG. She'll join." He knew about the guilds, the meal breaks, and even the intricacies of how residual payments worked.

Offering a role was a negotiating tool, but it wasn't where I wanted to start. I wondered if we should move on to the next RV lot; one with no strings attached.

Something about the way Ado Annie ducked out from behind the counter and struck a pose made me smile. Diana snapped her photo and jotted down her details. Maybe Jim, the director, could feature her in a booth at Dolly's Tavern, tucked behind Liv Tyler and Evan Dando.

"I'm sure we'll find something for her," I said.

The owner grabbed a series of keys from a set of hooks along the wood paneling. He had a parking lot full of rigs. He was ready to show them all, but the ones lined up by the river road looked just fine to us. We bumbled around the numbers and the dates, who would service the trailers, and how often. Then I invited them to have lunch with the cast and crew on the first day of filming. We had a deal.

I flipped through the cassette tapes in Diana's glove box: *The Fine Young Cannibals*, *The Crash Test Dummies*, and a new band, new to me anyway, *Radiohead*. I popped that one in and Diana rewound to cue up *Prove Yourself*. Sliding off the well-traveled highway, we merged onto a quieter bypass that hugged the river. We passed Pond Eddy and a few other hamlets that were named after the water eddies that hid behind rocks while fighting the current.

The lines blurred on a tiny feature like *Heavy* and each job description fit into a neat box. On the documentaries, these roles had blended, and I'd do whatever I had to in order to move the film along. Now there was a department assigned to each of those missions, which meant letting go of the details. I was still responsible for them in the big picture. Diana had her own job to do and if I micromanaged her, I would probably miss a land mine of my own.

Mike opened his knife and cut the strings to the neon sign rigged to the top of his truck. Jim and Diana had made the deal with this principal location, but it was Mike, the production designer, who would need to make every detail reflect the characters and the story. Now he was ready for the unveiling: our first look at the work his crew had done in Dolly's Tavern.

Mike flipped a panel of light switches behind the bar, setting the stage.

What had been blank walls and a deteriorating kitchen was now a fully functioning pizza tavern. It was a complete transformation from the original location photos sitting in Diana's car. You could just about hear the silverware clinking and the background murmur of a Thursday night crowd. If you squinted, you might see an airborne round of pizza dough.

"I can't dress that angle, I'm out of money," Mike pointed towards a bare corner without diner booths or Bud-Lite signs. "But it works for Jim and Big Mike." Big Mike was the cinematographer. Together, they decided on which angles to show and which sides of the room would need set decoration.

"It's fantastic—Jim's going to love it," I said. "It's like our home base: it stays dressed for the run of show." If it snowed or rained for our exterior scenes, the diner would be our cover set—our contingency plan.

I pushed through the swinging doors by the pizza slot wall and the set piece shifted forward. These walls could "fly"—we could pull them aside and move them back in place quickly, giving us more camera angles and better lens options in an otherwise tight space. All of the hard work from the intricate bric-a-brac, down to the light switch plate in the shape of a dancing chef was temporary and it would eventually be struck. Twenty cubic yards of dumpster would clunk down outside the building and in a far less time than it took to build, and with far less elegant tools, the set would be demolished.

"Sometimes, they just don't come out," Trish sighed and nodded toward the RV.

"Well, he can't just not come out," I was incredulous. "What should I do, call his rep?" Day One, first scene up, and one of our actors pouted in his trailer. We were all being grown-ups here. Couldn't he put the drama on the screen and pretend to be a grown up too?

"It's too early to call his agent." Trish looked at her watch and ran a sleep-deprived calculation. "It's 3 a.m. in LA."

Technically, I was Trish's boss. She had been a seasoned location manager on real movies, big films with meaty budgets. Now she was hired as the film's production manager. Trish came with all the right gear. Those of us still figuring out if this could be a career hadn't made the investment in REI or EMS paraphernalia. But Trish had it all: Gore-tex for rain, Columbia fleece under a North Face down coat for windy subzero exteriors. Neo boot covers for snow. Trish had the latest computer with all the Microsoft and the Movie Magic software. And she had binders, all her paperwork painstakingly hole-punched with color dividers into three loops. Those binders had Hollywood wisdom; a plan for every jam we could get into, but even they couldn't solve this one.

"He's probably waiting for you to come in," Trish said. "It's about attention, it always is." I could see this was true and I didn't envy Jim the director. He made over ten thousand decisions each day, and with so many demands, it was impossible to spread his attention evenly among his cast. Inevitably, someone would feel like the unloved child.

"Well, I'm not going in, I'll knock but I'm not going in," I wasn't going to humor him. "Oh yeah, you're going in," Trish laughed, pointed me in the direction of the trailer, and jogged back to set. She had better things to do.

It turned out I was good at getting people out of trailers. I don't remember exactly what I said or what I promised, but I left the trailer with my dignity intact and the actor behind me.

Trish and I thrived on making a good deal, negotiating hard for equipment, locations, catering, and hotels. We had coaxed crew members to join us. At three hundred dollars a week, plus per diem, no one was getting rich. And the location was not exotic and warm, but Trish and I sold the experience with some creative phrasing:

You know that place where they shoot all the car commercials? That beautiful winding river road? That's where we are. You should come!

And, if that didn't work: *Don't you need a break from the chaos? The horns and sirens of the city? It's so quiet up here, you can hear yourself think.* The same pitch, catered to the cash-strapped: *If you can sublet your apartment, the salary's not all that bad.*

Few of us were professionals. Most were under thirty and had been given a career boost into higher positions than we'd ever held. We were amateurs working on a level playing field. Most meals and all transportation were covered by the production, so the per diem allowance was more of a laundry and beer fund.

But here I was, in charge. No fellow crew member would guess I was living off high-interest credit card advances. Or that I was three years behind on my personal taxes.

"OK, people, listen up!" Priscilla whistled through her teeth to get the crew's attention. "Week two of filming, day one at Dolly's Tavern. So, guess what time it is?" Each day of filming at a new location is supposed to start with safety guidelines dictated by the first assistant director. I knew the insurance company required us to have them, especially if we had stunts or special effects. I knew only because I'd read it in a book when I squatted on the floor of Shakespeare & Company. Priscilla's instructions only got half the attention of half the crew, like a flight attendant's futile seatbelt charade. Most of the crew leaned back with folded arms preoccupied by what some other crew member thought of them. Or they tinkered with a C-stand and sandbags, trying to get a jump start. Time was precious, but so was safety, I thought.

When my father's cancer had been in remission, he'd taken firm control of our safety. He conducted fire drills for his four daughters, and by the time I was eight, I could grab a kitchen chair by its seat and slam the legs through a window. The most empowering step was sweeping the legs around the edges of the window, clockwise, to remove uneven shards of glass, then pushing your mattress through for a padded landing. I've never had to do it, but I played out this fictitious scenario whenever I entered a new room and planned my escape route.

I stepped outside to meet the production assistant (PA) who was driving the film to Manhattan. The PA was responsible for getting the filmed footage to the lab for overnight development and printing. He had just a few hours to meet the cut-off for the night's processing bath. I patted the roof of the car with my palm as he drove off. A good luck gesture for his precious cargo: three valuable days of film dailies. Then a hand landed on my shoulder, and I turned toward another PA as his walkie-talkie cackled.

"You're needed on set," he said.

"OK, be there in a sec."

"I have eyes on her outside," he said, referring to me in the third person as he reported his find into his microphone. "She's flying in."

And I did fly in, right to Priscilla's side. Anything could *fly in* to set, a vital prop or a human. If the line producer was requested, it was often for the delivery of impending doom: a slowed down schedule, a problem with an actor, or the decision to invade the meal break (a meal penalty violation—something we never liked to invade—not because of the cost but out of respect for a tired and hungry crew).

"We didn't get that tracking shot this morning," Priscilla said, the thin veneer of a raised eyebrow covering her panic. Then she turned her back to the camera to be more discreet, "I thought we'd pick up speed once we moved into Dolly's, but it's like treading water in cold molasses here."

The hustle in the room belied our slow progress. The prop master reset knives and forks for a close-up. The grips leveled the last stretch of steel track alongside the bar, with wedges of wood in various shapes shoved in for support. They sprayed down the tracks with a can of lemon Pledge for a smooth dolly move. For a few minutes, the waxy fake citrus of Pledge choked the air. But it was gone just as quickly, evaporating through the cracks of the drafty tavern. The rest of the crew grew restless. If they hadn't started smoking yet, they wandered outside to bum a cigarette. Not yet committed enough to buy their own packs.

Priscilla rested her hands on her hips, watching the prop assistant refill muddy cups of coffee to their original continuity lines. This woman scared me a bit. She was someone who could commandeer the juke box and feed it quarters, picking the next twelve songs that you would have to endure. But in this environment, she was laser focused on the schedule, swapping scene strips around in her head.

"Let's see if we can do this," Priscilla handed me her chicken scratch in the margins of the call sheet. I rolled up the paper as if it were the baton in a relay race and ran for the production office, banging out her notes into the strip board on the computer. A new manifesto.

Priscilla had the toughest job on set. On a low-budget film like *Heavy,* the schedule and budget had been drafted early in pre-production, long before we could afford to bring a first assistant director on board. We extracted the scenes from the script, reflecting every element on camera and behind it: cast, props, special equipment, time of day, interior or exterior, and a sentence describing what happened in the scene. Then the two-hundred-page behemoth, the anti-creative distillation of the script, was converted into strips of numbers and lines. We stacked the strips in a logical order, with day breaks, adding up to the number of filming days that matched our budget. This puzzle became our bible; the shooting schedule. We patted ourselves on the back for this achievement. Congratulations, we had created a feasible film shoot schedule. The problem was that it only existed in a vacuum.

Enter reality, all the variables we couldn't have foreseen earlier. Shelley Winters had to consolidate her work into a two-week period. Liv Tyler was wrapping another film and wouldn't arrive for rehearsals until four days before principal photography. It turned out that our lead actor didn't drive, so we'd have to rig a process trailer for daytime driving shots, or maybe even hire a driving double. For night driving shots, we would park the car in a roomy a garage, and have grips rocking the car while the actor sat behind the wheel, and electricians flew fake headlamps by the windows to imitate movement of passing cars. This was the poor man's process. (Green screen wasn't yet a solution for low-budget projects. It was still a photochemical optical process that was too expensive for us to composite the images together in post-production.)

The dream schedule was abandoned, and we shifted to the new plan. It was all on Priscilla to pull it off. If we didn't *make our day* (shoot all the scenes and pages we'd listed on the call sheet) we would have to start cutting or consolidating scenes and dropping shots. Or we'd have to extend the number of filming days.

It was no surprise Priscilla was the first to befriend the local bartender. She carved out a spot opposite the beer taps. On cue, the barkeep slid an ashtray her way. She exhaled a cloud of grey stress releasing her deepest breath of the day.

At the other end of the bar, Richard, Trish, and I took a hard look at four sheets of paper that boiled down our financial status. We had to make the call: a two-week extension of filming. If I had seen it coming sooner, I could have started conversations with key crew members, ensuring their commitment to stay longer. Now we would lose some crew and I would need to recruit help for the final leg. It seemed I could solve problems as they came up, but I couldn't see far enough down the road to prevent them.

The clammy river air penetrated my bones as I zipped my jacket up to my chin. With all our production assistants out on urgent missions, I had delegated myself to drive Shelley Winters to set. But Shelley wasn't ready to leave, and she would not be rushed. Shelley Winters's iconic contribution to The Industry, even just quantified in the number of days she had served on film sets, sneezed at the cumulative experience of our entire crew. I was not going to rush seasoned talent like Shelley.

I made up for lost time on the familiar roads and we were just fifteen minutes late when we made the last turn over the bridge.

"I'm hungry!" Shelley yelped from the back seat.

"Just a few minutes away Shelley," I said. "Priscilla says they've got your breakfast standing by."

"Well, I'm hungry now!" she blew through her pouted lips. We passed a pizza shop, its gate pulled down at 6 a.m., and her eyes lit up. "Pizza! Pizza for breakfast!" She was joking, right? "Gretchen. If you don't stop for pizza right now, I'm going to tell Jim he should fire you!" Her command was served in old Hollywood style. If a whine and a song had a baby, it was Shelley's voice.

Fire me, really? Do it, I wanted to say. If I got fired, I could sleep. I could sink into the tragic discomfort of my futon in New York and salvage normalcy. I snapped out of it and remained calm, conjuring up the image of Shelley hanging from a chandelier, her pivotal *Poseidon Adventure* scene. All was lost on the capsized cruise ship, but she hung on to a light fixture for dear life. I expected she wished all of us had memorized her blonde bombshell performance in *The South Sea Sinner*. But for us the chandelier stunt was indelible.

We rounded another corner to see one adult with seven children trailing behind, balancing the asphalt where the edge of the road dropped off.

"Who's the pied piper?" Shelley let out a belly laugh. By now, she knew who the pied piper was. He was the cinematographer, Big Mike, the one making sure she was well-lit. His brood had come to see Daddy at work.

Right after threatening my job over her pizza pie craving, Shelley was out the door and whisked to set by an assistant director. Shelley didn't get me fired. She'd already shifted into character, and I was just the driver. I'm not sure she knew I was the line producer or even what a line producer was supposed to do. But then again, I didn't really know either.

An hour later, I volunteered for the next hotel cast shuttle that would deliver Deborah Harry to set. The day's set emergencies wound down, and the sun warmed us up as I hugged the curves of the river road.

Debbie's tiny terrier scratched itself back to the rear window and stretched out for a sunbath. Deborah Harry, rock star. The icon of New York cool and the lead singer of Blondie, was in my back seat. Debbie Harry, whose *Call Me* had glamorized the telephone receiver the way the Beatles had iconized the Abbey Road crosswalk. There she was, larger than life with cheekbones like sails, fitting squarely in the shape of my rearview mirror, rocking the back seat of a Saturn rental.

"Nice outfit," Debbie gave me a nod of approval. "I like it."

"Thanks!" I pointed both thumbs back at my green pantsuit, no one's idea of the right threads for set. But it was comfortable, and I liked its buttons that were shaped like long wooden beer barrels. "Canal Street," I said, regretting it the moment it came out of me.

Canal Street? Debbie didn't care about the provenance, the *origin* of the pantsuit. She didn't want one of her own. When something is so loud and wrong that you can't look away, you need to say *something*.

The crew set up for another scene and the cast retreated to their trailers, except Debbie and Joe Grifasi, who seemed to like the energy of our young crew.

"Come run lines with me," Joe tugged my arm. "I'm feeling rusty."

The porch in the back of the diner was loaded with sandbags and carts, but there was enough room for two milk crates, forming a makeshift break room. We settled into the cadence of running lines. I read dryly, careful not to impose any kind of tone on Debbie's character. Joe didn't sit on his crate; he was happier pacing three feet of splintering floorboards. Otherwise, the words might evaporate.

When we re-entered the set, I saw Jan, the sound mixer, adjusting knobs and flicking switches on her Seussian cart. I thought the best seat in the house was next to Jan, watching the scene play out on her black and white reference monitor. Jan used both hands to loan me a headset to listen to the recording from the actors' microphones. She gave me a stern look in the eye to acknowledge that I had accepted these headphones; a visual contract with a commitment to return them before I ran off set again. I clipped the receiver to my belt, *McGowan* scrawled in sharpie on silver tape over the leather encasement. Even though the tape would be replaced with another producer's name on the next show, seeing my name gave me temporary comfort. Now the crisp frequency of actors' voices transmitted directly to my ears. Every sibilance, sigh, and pop was audible here, unadulterated by background noise. Joe's mic was hot, but he ran lines aloud to himself. The rest of the world shut down sonically, the crew going silent as they moved around the camera for last looks.

It was going to get loud. We crammed into my cabin at the fishing motel where sweat, smoke, and exhaustion mingled with beer. A long week deserved a Saturday night game of truth or dare. It was a stupid game, but there was no HBO so we made our own entertainment.

The grip and the hairstylist sat on opposites sides of the room, further evidence they were sleeping together, I thought. Or had they broken up? There were other affairs more obvious than those two, and I counted five suspected pairings so far. I was one of them, but I kept it quiet. At least, I thought I did.

A joint resembling a shedding cigar circulated the group. The next dare was up. The grips were challenged to run around the hotel's fishing pond in their underwear. The three of them rose to take the dare; choosing truth was not a consideration. In this smoke-clogged fishing cabin, the world was small and everything was fair game.

We devolved further after more beers and a female technician was dared to kiss a woman in the room. I rolled my eyes, thinking this was not the sophisticated version of spin the bottle they had sold me. I must have been the first female in her eyeline. I wasn't her direct manager, I thought, justifying the act before it was the act.

The kiss was less than two seconds and then we burst out laughing, gulping at a beer to chase it away. Another two seconds and the blood rose to my face: *Have I completely fucked up? Would the crew lose respect for me now?* To be fair, we were in my hotel room, I didn't have the option of walking away. They would have lost more respect for me if I shushed them and kicked them out. But then the grips challenged the electric department to another lap around the grounds and we rallied them out the door. The kiss was already forgotten.

We shot our final scene at the Culinary Institute of America, the other CIA. It was a long-distance company move to the Hudson River. Our equipment truck—held together with Bondo, road salt, and gaffer's tape—coughed its way across the state. We wouldn't need its generator here, but we did need the equipment. And then the truck just needed to make it back to the city before it melted into a puddle of metal and wheels.

There were several courtyards within the CIA, all of them crowded with chain smoking student chefs in tall white hats. Our character's scenes in these grounds were written as his emancipation—he'd finally been released from the chains of his Shelley Winters-like mother. He was free from tossing pizzas and destined for higher cuisine. If this had been a musical, a big dance number would be choreographed here. White toques would fly in the air as the chefs-in-training circled a pinwheel of Dutch ovens.

Most of us returned to the city, and groups of us planned to grab dinner or drinks together every so often. Some relationships would persist for a few weeks. We were taking bets that one couple might even marry (we were right). But most of the magic had ended on location and the intensity of the close-knit bonds died out. Until the spark was relit on the next merry-go-round.

When I had worked in the theater, our troupe had moved like a singular unit eating midnight meals on the apron of the stage. We would shout out lines from the play—now well-worn grooves in our brains—not quite ready to let the suspended reality go. The morning after the final performance would be bleak, a loss of routine and family. With no place to report to. But on a film production, there was no real satisfaction of completion with a final performance. We had literally raised the barn, and now it was in the hands of the director and the editor.

Now, I shut the front door to my apartment, leaving the unraveled cult on the other side. Back into the quotidian grind of replacing the toilet paper roll and feeding the cat. I collected my take-out trash and threw it down the hallway incinerator. That's when the chill of failure caught up with me.

What had I done wrong? What could I have done better? I was left to reckon with a laundry list of faults I couldn't see in the thick of production. There had been the talent agents, I was terrified of them. They spoke over me and didn't give me room to negotiate. But of all the things that still mystified me about feature filmmaking, the numbers were the most confounding. It wasn't the calculations; that part was simple math. It was the projections, the ability to forecast the resources needed to get through the film. This missing link could only come from experience. What I needed was access to a bigger film, to get inside and see the machinations from a professional.

| Chapter 4 |

THE HEIST

NEW YORK CITY, 1994

"Nobody walks to the bank, not on my watch," Joey leaned out of his gas-guzzling Suburban window and wagged a finger at me. He had the physique of a bodyguard and the face of a teenager. On his shirt lapel was a button he wore every day: RELAX! IT'S ONLY A MOVIE.

Whatever you do, don't mention the puppets, I reminded myself. Joey had to be the one who brought them up first.

"Oh, I'm good," I said, continuing to walk, sure that I'd defied some unwritten law as soon as I said it.

Joey waved me towards the passenger seat. "Get in."

Who was I to argue with a teamster? I had been going to the bank without an escort all my life, but I'd never withdrawn ten thousand dollars in cash before. I could walk across SoHo and back, carrying a backpack of bills, no one the wiser about its contents. But if I did that, I'd miss Joey's company and the opportunity to learn about his puppet side-hustle. We stuck to the normal banter about traffic and the teamster mantra: *a half-full tank is an empty tank*.

A friend had offered me this production accounting job on *Bullet,* a studio film featuring Mickey Rourke's character out on parole and ready to raise hell. But the job was self-inflicted punishment. I knew I couldn't line produce again until I understood the numbers. The first place the numbers won out: salary. *Bullet* paid more than twice what I'd earned on *Heavy*.

Joey drove across Prince Street, and I snuck a look into the back seat hoping to catch sight of the puppet suitcase, some hint of the magic. I eyed the glove compartment, maybe he stowed them there?

A Teamster, I quickly learned, was an essential element whenever someone (X) or something (Y) had to move from point A to point B. In this case, X was me leaving the production office (point A) to retrieve the cash (the Y) for the bank (point B). Then back to point A safely.

Joey tuned his radio to 1010 WINS for its traffic report with a background soundtrack of clattering typewriters and telex machines. The voice reported on a United Nations summit which meant gridlock in the city, even a full forty blocks from the diplomatic chaos.

Inside the bank, Joey stood by the door like a bouncer. His feet were set apart in a Martial Arts defensive stance. He nodded to me as if to say *OK, kid, get the dough*. The teller set me up in a back booth to count denominations. I could do this on my own without Joey's help. I lay out stacks of per diem for the out-of-town cast, then I prepared envelopes for crew who liked their salaries in cash. Who did they think they were fooling? The net amount was right there on the paystub, with the taxes already deducted. Why did these sweet, green bills have more value than a check? Was it about trust, a concern that the production was a fly-by-night operation handing out bad checks? I held up a couple of crisp and newly minted fifty-dollar bills; enough to burn a hole in your pocket on a Friday afternoon. I could see the appeal of cash on the barrel head.

When Joey's SUV brought us eastbound on the cross-town return, we had Spring Street to ourselves. He escorted me back to my office where I locked most of the cash up in the Sentry Safe. While I counted out the rations, Joey took a seat on the pleather chair, and launched into *The Story*. Finally, I'd hear about the puppets. His passion flared from his nostrils and every pore on his face came to life. He introduced a horse, a family, and a few townspeople. I began to ask about the plot line, but Joey held up a hand—he didn't entertain questions. His presentation was polished, and I would learn more by keeping my mouth shut.

"On this next show, we're doing something new. Let me show you...." Joey's excitement was interrupted by the spastic buzzing and blinking of his pager. He tilted up the pager's face from his belt and sighed when he recognized the number. "It's the set. I gotta go." He rose to the call, but pointed a playful finger at me. "Next time, we'll talk costumes."

I pictured Joey driving rigs around the ribbons of the city's highways, daydreaming about the continuing saga on his stage. He might have been the only uncloseted puppeteer on this production, but he was not the only crew member with a side hustle.

My office was on the 4th floor of a Cass Gilbert building on Lafayette Street, tucked at the end of a labyrinth of rooms, the same hallowed halls where MAD Magazine had been published. From Alfred E. Neuman's toothy grin on the front cover to its back cover's fold-in image, MAD had delivered all the necessary snark that wasn't fit to print. Now, in this same office, the production manager and I handled over $4 million in just eight weeks.

I opened the window for some post-rain ozone and Nirvana's acoustic *About a Girl* reverbed around the brick alley. Someone across the courtyard was mourning the loss of Kurt Cobain. Before letting the song finish, the needle was picked up and dropped in the same *About a Girl* groove. No shame in a good song played twice.

By the fifth replay of *About a Girl,* the best boy grip had popped in and taken refuge on the pleather chair. Between sorting his hardware receipts for rope sash and matte knife blades, I learned he was an art major-turned-sculptor on the side. But gripping squared with the rent, so he chased every work tip. Another technician painted murals on the pull-down security gates for boutique shops in the East Village. The scenic artists painted house exteriors during their hiatus. Waiting for your next gig would not pay the bills.

Just when I thought I was in the clear to get some work done, Mickey Rourke's assistant hung up his coat and took up residence in the pleather chair, again. He gave a play-by-play of the new scenes in his own side hustle, a fantasy screenplay. He hadn't written anything down—it was confined to his head where it marinated, because working for Mickey was a twenty-four/seven commitment.

My office hideaway put me in the unexpected role of crew counselor. I thought about swapping out the pleather chair. Maybe if my visitors weren't so comfortable, they wouldn't spill the long versions of their stories. I learned to listen for the *moment of settle,* when their backbones relaxed, and they made an indentation into the seat. Even when I gave a subtle glance to my bare wrist, (wasn't this the international sign for *lots to do!?*) they didn't take the hint. But I knew that a chance to share these stories was a break from the feral conditions and punishing hours of the film set. I wouldn't visit set again until Thursday's payday, so I took in the news of its messengers.

Nirvana kicked in again on the next day when the high-angled fall sun hit the courtyard. *About a Girl* on a loop, but it was more like a sweet hum; a dirge for his suicide two weeks earlier. I joined the unknown mourner, throwing the sash open to let the music in. I wondered if howling back across the courtyard would be inappropriate.

On pay day, Joey drove me over the Brooklyn Bridge to set where the crew filmed a chase scene. This sliver of pavement near the old Williamsburgh Savings Bank divided the artsy Northside from the Hasidic Jewish community to the south. I arrived as lunch was announced and I carved out a makeshift office for myself at a table in the back near the staging of coffee and desserts. Like a moth to flame, the crew knew the money person had landed. I spent the next hour distributing cash and checks, disputing paycheck calculations and meal penalty claims. Two stars of the film, Tupac Shakur and Adrien Brody, ate lunch at a folding table, safe in their movie crew bubble. No one gave them a second look.

Kevin, the location manager, swaggered over and flashed his shit-eating grin. Clearly, Kevin needed something from me. He was the son of a well-known columnist and New York was just one big town of transactions and favors to him. He scribbled out a check request and pushed the sheet of paper towards me, angling for an expedited turnaround on a location site fee.

"Gretchen! We gotta keep things movin'. We're tryin' to make a pic-cha here!" Kevin laughed at his own joke, his version of a Hollywood studio boss. "When the check's ready, you can page me. *Or...*" he paused for effect, "you can call me on my *cellular phone*." He held up a portable phone the size of my shoe with gelled, green buttons. He twisted and collapsed the flimsy antenna, zipping the phone into its case, a tiny black body bag. These phones were only for the VIPs, those conducting important business.

"We won't be able to talk long though." Kevin twirled the case around his fingers. "I have limited minutes—the producers'll put me through the freakin' paddywack machine if I go over...."

I was glad the phone rates were expensive. If they were cheap, we'd all be using mobile phones.

Near a brownstone walk-up under the bridge, the set struggled with the Hasidic community. A swarm of crew in Carhartt jackets worked on one side of the building. On the other side, a group of fifteen men in orthodox garb gathered at the gate. This was an unhappy group—they didn't like the film's depiction of their community and they threatened to protest the shoot. Of course, they were presented script pages in advance, and they had approved them. But it didn't matter. If they protested, we would be shut down. There would be dog whistles and loud crowds keeping us from recording audio. And it was too late to move to a cover set. I calculated the costs of a day of filming and wondered if it could be an insurance claim. I left the set knowing it wasn't my problem today, not on this movie. It was Kevin who needed to hop on his superhero cell phone to save the day.

When I arrived at my apartment, my roommate Tibi crouched on our front stoop. Her long, blonde hair was draped over her knees as she cradled her head. Where she sat was out of character; everyone knew the stoop was for the owners, the super and his nosey mother of this five story-walk up. Tibi huddled into herself, nearly swallowed whole by her blue puffer jacket.

"You're not going to believe it Gretch," Tibi said, somewhere between exhausted and overcaffeinated. Tibi was one of the few people who called me Gretch. "This is much worse for me than it is for you."

"What?" I said. *A fire, a flood? What's worse?* I flicked through a mental filing cabinet of possible tragedies. I sniffed the air for wet smoke, taking instant relief that there were no lingering fire trucks on the scene. I could only spot one police car, double parked, with no flashers. It was the anxiety of the unknown that lurched up my throat.

"The spiderman burglars hit us. Two of them, I think," she pointed to the top of the building and the alley to the right, the side closest to the museum's planetarium. "They came in the windows, down from the roof. They took all my jewelry."

Tibi jutted her chin again toward the window with an exaggerated tick. The superintendent's mother dangled her arms outside: half of her body exposed to West 80th Street. There's no doubt she kept a record of who came and went.

I didn't have any jewelry worth stealing, but my mind blanked on any personal inventory as we huffed up to the fifth floor. Stereo wires rolled around in dust bunnies on our violated apartment floor. I gritted my teeth and rounded the corner to my bedroom. My desktop had been cleared by a stranger and the only thing of value I owned—a Mac computer—was gone.

On that computer were hundreds of documents. Personal writings and research I'd continued to do for the odd documentary. My side hustle. Recreating that work would mean hours of work. My Pentax K1000 camera, along with the rolls of unprocessed Kodak film and its case, a gift from my mother's boyfriend, that was gone too. My red vinyl laundry bag was missing. It had no value, but they used it to carry the loot. I pictured them casually throwing it over their shoulder as they walked out the front door.

They had been clever, and even athletic. They slung themselves on a rope over the edge of the neighbor's roof, easing themselves down and leaping across rooftops. Now we were just another statistic.

The police buzzed up. I hoped they were returning with reinforcement and answers. They dusted for prints from the smudged windows with no recognition of any whorls, loops, or arches. Unable to get a read, they shrugged it off, not even feigning the *Law & Order* zeal we were expecting. An officer asked a round of irritating and repetitive questions we had already answered. Their attitude said, *you'll never see your cute boxy MacIntosh again.* And they were gone.

Tibi and I sunk into the couch for an episode of *NYPD Blue*. Our TV set was a robber's reject; too old to steal. On the screen, Dennis Franz regained consciousness in a hospital bed while his red-headed partner—the one whose name I always forgot—pulled him through.

My mind shifted its grief gears from anger to suspicion, zeroing in on the super's wife, the one who clocked everyone's movements. Then I focused on the super himself; the two of them made a perfect team. Or was it the neighbor's daughter? The one who came by last week to sell cookies wearing a scout pin. I looked at Tibi as she tore old packets of soy sauce into a bowl of steamed vegetables. If I told her the list of suspects I was imagining, she'd think I was nuts.

My panic was driven by guilt. All that lost work that I hadn't backed up to floppy disks. Amateur rule: always end the day as if you're going to be hit by a bus or your computer's going to be stolen. Because it was New York City and both of these things were possible.

Maybe the robbery was a sign to leave New York again. If it felt like I was always chasing work, it's because I was. This time it was back to New England.

DANBURY, CONNECTICUT, 1995

I was in Connecticut on the set of *Reckless*, a surreal neo-noir fantasy starring Mia Farrow and Mary-Louise Parker. It was another accounting job, and another step up in salary.

When movies shot on location, the vices ramped up for everyone. I wasn't producing, so the vices seemed more glaring on this one. With more time to notice and more time to partake.

First virtue under fire: your early morning routine, sacrificed in favor of another hour of sleep. Your workout tapes, the same ones you'd worshipped at home, now piled on top of the hotel room's VHS deck, collecting dust. And evening workouts, well, you never really worked out at night anyway.

Then there was the alcohol. If *never drink alone* was your motto, fear not! On location, you were never alone. And there was always something worth celebrating. Monday: got that out of the way. Tuesday? Why not, because you're here and you made it one day closer to Friday. If you stopped by the bar on the way to your hotel room (you'd have to have blinders on to miss the bar), a quick drink glossed over the nagging discomfort of your cold, stress-soaked socks. A couple pints of beer warmed the extremities and fueled your second wind, the social version of you that racked pool balls like a pro and smoked cigarettes in a chain. There were the rumored one-night stands and there were the confirmed hook-ups. For a while, they cured your loneliness.

And by you, I mean every one of us.

Hard work and long hours were no one's vice on location. At home, workaholism was interpreted as neglect by your family, friends, and pets, but up here it was rewarded. And the beneficiary of all that overtime and exhaustion was the movie itself.

If ever a film set felt like a stage play, it was this one. The former wire mill churned out the pulpy smell of fresh sawdust as I walked through the construction shop. The staccato of nail guns, sanders, and power drills resounded down from the pitched ceilings. The construction team built the sets in this vast stretch between the main stage and the production office.

The completed set pieces were then moved and assembled in the contiguous space, a giant layout free of columns—ideal for shooting multiple sets. Like dollhouses or toy train accessories, each set was designed at three-quarter scale. On camera, this reduced scale left the audience feeling disoriented. Something's off but they couldn't put their finger on it.

Other People's Money was filmed in this giant space and in its heyday, the mill had been commissioned to weave nickel wire mesh for the Manhattan Project. Maybe that clandestine work was related or unrelated to the existence of an army tank that lay dormant in the sub-basement, hiding in plain sight for the idly curious crew to discover. But the mill was so drafty, any remaining chemical contamination had likely seeped outside to Connecticut's frigid air or into its water table.

I looked for every opportunity to visit the art department quarters. They were set up on the second-floor loft in a separate building on the rambling brick complex.

Our own underground production space felt more like a police station suited for interrogations, but the light in the art space was natural and warm. It was lined with drafting boards where the sets were originated and drawn with precise measurements. Above the boards, a long line of foam core with images were tacked on as the references for what was coming to life on the big stage. Color swatches, blueprints, tear sheets from magazines, and oversized art books all told the story of the film and its characters.

At lunch, we worked our way through two mirroring lines. "What's for chicken?" became the refrain for catered lunch. It was usually chicken in some shape or form, smiling up from heated chafing dishes. But it was free, warm chicken cooked just for us and I wasn't complaining.

A production assistant carried cans of footage through the dining hall and disappeared up the staircase. He was back from the city with dailies, just in time to project them in the makeshift theater above our catering space. Dailies were projected silently with no sync sound. It was fun to see the sets and the scenes play out on film, take after take, slate after slate. The director made a performance note, the hairstylist caught the glimpse of wig tape creeping out of an actor's temple. We watched in perfect silence with church-like reverence.

I'd taken the job in Connecticut on one condition: I'd need to be off for a long weekend toward the end of the show for the premiere of *Heavy* at the Sundance Film Festival in Utah. Circling the city's massive lake before landing was like staring into the abyss. The Great Salt Lake reflected a pre-snow overcast sky, but it appeared as though you could fall through to the opposite side of the earth if the plane's engines gave out.

I met the rest of my group up the mountain in Park City: my brother-in-law Andy, my brother-in-law-in-law-from-another-sister, Chris, and seven of their acting friends who alternated shifts at the Hamburger Hamlet in Brentwood. They were here as film fans, as moral support for the opening of *Heavy*. But mostly they were here because they were actors. And since Sundance was within driving distance of Los Angeles, it was possible their chances of finding their next acting gig were better in the Utah mountains than they were back home.

The ten of us had booked a second story motel room on the outskirts of town. We dropped our backpacks in the room and then the gang got into Chris's bald-tired car; a car that worked fine for LA, but didn't translate to this mountain terrain. Snow fell in thick, wet clumps, and we tailgated the sander/salter through a white-out storm.

In a bar at mid-day, the twack of a cue ball cut through all the chatter. Over by a gas-fueled fireplace, the juke box grinded out Oasis' long vowels in praise of cigarettes and alcohol. It was too early in the day for this, but here we were, our sneakers glued to the floorboards of last night's residual beer.

"You've got to be members of this club to buy a drink," the bartender nodded towards four guys in yoked ski sweaters at the pool table. "But don't worry, those guys are members. And they'll vouch for you if you join them in a game of pool." A pact was made with a burly man clearing the eight ball, and pints of local Wasatch beer were raised in celebration of *Heavy*.

"Half the people will shower!" Chris announced. These were potentially the first words spoken in Park City that morning, and they were a resolute command. Chris was not in the military, but he got this from his brother, my other brother-in-law who didn't make the trip. "While half the people shower, the other half the people will pack up the room and bathe *after* the screening." We didn't have time to argue. The group followed his directions and set off for the theater.

Heavy screened at a multiplex outside town, just down the road from the Library Theater where we had premiered a documentary a year ago. During my previous trip to Sundance, I had spent most of my time inside the director's condo, pulling together contracts and music clearances in a completely sober state. We worked all night to complete a sale to Sony Pictures for a film we barely finished in time for the screening. But this screening was at 8 a.m. After the pints from the previous night, our heads suffered a collective oxygen-deprived hangover.

In the final scene of the *Heavy* screening, during that silent beat before the credit roller, I had the urge to sob. I bit my tongue to hold back an embarrassing emotional surge. *My god, no one else is sobbing, keep it together.* The film was good, but the overwhelming sense of the work that went into it, the years of the writer and director's time, the crew's unrelenting commitment, and my own commitment, that's what tugged at me. For a few months, I lived this movie and it had been everything. Now my part was over and it was out there for an audience, projected through light and dust onto a modest multiplex screen.

I tucked my pride into my throat and flew back to Connecticut where my boss no longer smiled or greeted me with any feigned enthusiasm. Under the buzz and blink of the wire factory fluorescents, I stayed late to catch up. And I did the work, tapping through it all, migrating the pile on the left over to the pile on the right. My eyeballs pulsated and I squeezed my lids tight in search of a second wind.

The next morning, I expected a pat on the back or some form of gratitude. Maybe she was saving her praise for the end of the day, but her internal five o'clock bell must have sounded, and she grabbed her things to go. She stood above me, broadcasting a story about her old assistant, the hilarious, dedicated one who wasn't available for this job.

"You're different somehow. Since your Sundance thing," she said, flipping a pashmina scarf over her back, and dumping a stack of purchase orders onto my *to-do* pile.

"I am?" I said. "Well, it was good to see the film. To celebrate a little. But I'm here now." Inside, I knew I had enough of the wire factory and the bottomless *IN* box. I'd stay to the end, but it was time to stop hiding behind triplicate timecards.

| Chapter 5 |

THE NEO-NOIR

NEW YORK CITY, 1995

Over a beer at McGee's Pub, Ted posed a hypothetical on-set crisis: "Let's say crafty announces she's quitting in the middle of your first day of filming. What do you do?"

Crafty was set lingo for the craft services production assistant. I inhaled and held the air, preparing to answer, but he held up his palm.

"Wait there's more," Ted continued the scenario. Thank the interview gods, I thought, this is only his fantasy of production hell. None of this is real, it's just chaos porn. Things to keep you up late on a Sunday before day one of principal. "Then your location manager comes up to you at lunch; you're getting thrown out of next week's location. What do you tackle first?"

New York independent film producing icon, Ted Hope, sat across from me in a corner booth sipping a Black and Tan beer. Ted was Good Machine's head production executive and the gatekeeper of the key roles. He was the arbiter of who was worth working with in the independent film world. And there was a list.

For all of its liberal messaging and championing of outsiders, the kingdom of indie films more closely resembled the hierarchy of the navy than a left-leaning democracy. If I got this production managing job, it would be a step down from line producing, but that was okay with me because a job with Good Machine could make all the difference. I considered it a career side-step, a reshuffle for my greater good.

Good Machine's Ted Hope and Killer Films' Christine Vachon were the unspoken leads of the New York's film world; the cognoscenti of all things indie. If you couldn't *be* them, you wanted to be working with them, or at least for them. At the very least, you needed to be on their list. Together and separately, Christine and Ted had produced the most provocative and daring films in the past few years. Todd Haynes would *only* make his films with Christine. Todd Solondz would only have Ted produce his films. Directors stuck to producers who protected their vision. Their loyalty was ironbound.

If you were a director and you found a producer like this to embrace you, you were as good as gold. These producers forged an unrelenting path for their directors. They found financing in the nooks and crannies where others had looked, pleaded, and failed. Then they did the impossible; they produced films valued at millions of dollars at bargain basement bottom lines. They called in all their favors to get the film in the can. Most of all, the films they produced were seen. Christine and Ted took their finished films to prestigious festivals and sold them to distributors with solid track records. Their films weren't just cordoned off into tiny arthouse theaters, they were showing at multiplexes across America. In malls and city marquees with the rest of Hollywood's wares.

An interview over a beer with Ted Hope implied informality, not interrogation. I expected a laid back "who we know in common" conversation and casual references to the films we loved, or at least the films we were supposed to love. Boy, was I wrong.

Since I wasn't on his coveted list of known New York production managers, I had to be vetted. My career had veered off course from indie film line producing. Lately, I straddled the line between studios and the indies, working in accounting with the mini-majors: the Miramaxes and the New Lines. In this world, the studios usually left filmmakers alone as long as they stayed on budget and screened their dailies and cuts on time. And with the experience I got on these films, I knew exactly what went into a film. I knew how many rolls of gel and diffusion the lighting team would tear through. I knew what the real cost of location filming in New York would be. The real costs after tips, parking, and the unglamourous expenses that kept the film locomotive moving. But the detour I had taken didn't show up on Ted's radar because I wasn't playing in his sandbox.

I looked around as if further clues to Ted's question were somewhere in this room, maybe carved into the well-worn oak bar top that stretched the length of a bowling alley. We were across from DuArt Film Labs on West 55th Street where I had spent plenty of time waiting for film to be processed. A pint would be shared with the cinematographer or another production cohort while you stood by for the lab's news. If a roll of film had been fogged by light exposure, you'd have a big problem on your hands. But you could commiserate with other filmmakers who sat at the bar until their own results landed from the night's film bath.

I conjured up an answer for Ted's question. "I'd hit the crocodile closest to the boat."

Ted raised an eyebrow, cueing me to go on.

"First I'd find someone to relieve the craft services table for a half hour while I talked her down at a coffee shop. Getting away from set, neutral territory." When a crew member threatens to quit in the first week, it's usually a culmination of feeling unheard, lack of sleep, and overwhelm. "I'd let her know how I can help, how we can pull in support from the other PAs."

"Sure. That's a start, anyway. You can't have a hungry crew. And your locations problem?"

"I'd need a bit more time to solve that—I'd want to learn more before approaching the owners of the location. I mean, what happened there? Is it still salvageable?"

"You don't have much time though. No location, no movie, right?" Ted said, shifting in his seat, not revealing whether I'd correctly prioritized. "Tell me...how do you run a meeting? Your heads of department are busy. They don't have time for production meetings. So, let's say you've lured them there with a meal. How do you make sure you're running things efficiently?"

"That's a great question." Did I just say that? If I had a dime for every time I heard *that's a great question* on a festival panel or in a radio interview—well, you know the rest—I'd be rich. Now I know why people said it: to borrow time. In the five syllables it took to say *that's a great question,* a better answer, or an original thought might surface.

I responded with some sort of canned answer, but Ted had already moved on. His was not so much a question as a directive. Don't waste your crew's time. Don't stand in the doorways and block up the halls because the grips are trying to get through with a hamper of heavy equipment. Carry a notebook. Pay attention. Stay on budget. Listen.

"Anything else I should know about? Maybe something I'm not seeing here?" He flipped the resume over and spread his hands across the blank canvas. Number ten card stock, two dollars a sheet.

A cloud of unfiltered cigarette smoke drifted over the booth behind Ted's head. It was the smell of the Starrett-Lehigh Building. The smell of retired police officers in white sneakers grabbing one last smoke before hitting Canal Street. "Let's see.... I worked as an assistant editor for a few years, so I understand post. On one of those jobs, I preserved old film footage for Alan Lomax." Ted knew all about Alan Lomax and his Global Jukebox. I was beginning to wonder what Ted didn't know. "Oh, and there was the spy gig. I was a spy for a while."

Ted leaned in a bit. He didn't hear this at McGee's Pub every night.

"A counterfeit spy," I explained further. "Meaning the goods, they were counterfeit. It was all around Canal Street. An ad I circled in the back of the Voice."

"So, this spy job, what did you glean from that? Did it make you a better production manager, a better line producer?"

Sticky fingers, that's what I'd learned about. That was useful. "I can spot someone who's dishonest. And I learned how to work with retired police officers. I think I understand how they operate, what motivates them." I know this didn't answer his question. What the hell did retired police officers have to do with the price of salt on film productions? But now the wave landed again, and I couldn't kick the mild panic I'd felt on those cold winter Saturdays on Canal Street. The shapely mustaches and the cool reception they gave to the one woman in the room, me. It had fueled my imposter syndrome.

It was probably the Alan Lomax gig that got me the job with Ted. *For* Ted. It turns out that the hot glue splicing that would probably clog up my gallbladder in middle age paid off earlier than expected.

Good Machine had a load of unit supplies, and our cash-strapped production could not say no to free things no matter how much mold was stuck to them. These were necessary but inconspicuous items we needed to keep the set running: coffee urns, tables, folding chairs, and craft paper. A savings on one budget line item meant I could move that money to another, more needy department. Good Machine's office manager led me outside and around the back of the office, spinning a heavy ring of keys on his finger. He identified the padlock key and he asked me to stand clear. Which was good advice because when he rolled up the metal gate, an avalanche of orange traffic cones and coolers flew toward us. This was like winning the lottery. I tugged at two wood-framed director's chairs at the bottom of the heap. These same chairs had graced the sets of Ted's indie legacy, early productions like *The Wedding Banquet, Safe* and maybe Nicole Holofcener's *Walking and Talking*.

Real estate had been slow for Wall Street and our location team found production office space at 75 Wall Street on a top floor. Our outcast contingent wore ripped jeans and t-shirts, so it was easy to spot another member of the crew in the lobby. Slumming it in the financial district, we got sideways glances and weird smiles on the elevator. Some of these Wall Street types were curious about an independent film that made its temporary nest in their tower, but most were not. Most dismissed us and snapped out of the elevators with their shiny shoes clicking down the hallway. They wore suits and pencil skirts, and were all business and all money. Our currency was our novelty, giving the appearance of being free. But we were a fly-by-night operation, and ours was not the currency that could influence the market.

On a suburban street along a mile of hurricane fence, just before the last turn into our principal location opposite the Rahway State Prison, I arrived on day one of filming.

The call sheet said WEAR SENSIBLE SHOES in bold block letters. We climbed up a water tower where our main character had built a nest of sleeping bags and bongs. It was the dangerous kind of hangout that tweens love. A place to elude parents. Our key locations seemed to be carved out of the armpit of New Jersey. Suburbia's children had grown up and graduated from film school, and now the coming-of-age movies of this generation reverse-migrated to their childhood neighborhoods. Ours was not the greatest generation, mired in stories of WWII. It was not the generation that showed us what it was like to endure the Vietnam War. These were today's independent directors, and the emotional hits were in the high school hallways. They were outwitting the bullies and triumphing with the outsiders' clique.

A PA grabbed a director's chair, *Hope,* spray painted through stencil across its cloth back and placed it with a clique of other chairs. Ted took his assigned seat next to the director and settled in for a night shoot. And like clockwork, the garbage barge over the hill purged a fresh load of Jersey trash. This set came with an extrasensory bonus.

I started to get into the swing of things, feeling one step ahead, until I made a huge rookie mistake. I crossed our teamster, Harry.

"What's this, Gretchen?" Harry pointed to my office wall. Usually, his demeanor was so calm that you might forget he was in the room. Harry got things done, and choreographed the movement of our vehicles effortlessly.

"That's my special equipment flow chart." I said, oblivious, proud even. "You like it?" I'd created a giant calendar on the wall, color-coded with Post-its to remind me when to book the expensive bells and whistles: the lifts ($), long lenses ($$), and camera cars ($$$).

"And on this day? This extra genny van?" He pointed to the generator on the next day's preliminary call sheet. Then he turned to me. "Come on Gretchen, you know the rules."

I didn't know. When we arranged to pre-light a scene under the Manhattan Bridge, I put a van with a generator on hold knowing that we couldn't drive into the narrow space with our normal generator. But a van with a generator had to be cleared with Harry, and he had to be the one to book it. I had either deliberately undermined him, or exposed my inexperience, which was worse.

"Harry, I didn't know!" I moved back from his wagging finger, which looked disproportionally larger than the rest of him.

"Come on, we gotta get down to set, right?" Harry led me out the door. I trailed him with my tail between my legs towards the 75 Wall Street elevator. Our finance neighbors didn't fight about generators and extra vans. Their elevator lingo was the stuff of commodities and leverages. It was all market dialogue; the passion of the bulls and the bears. This was the way other people argue, I thought as I looked at Harry. His eyes dug daggers into the descending floor buttons: 21, 20, 19… They duke it out verbally, and then they laugh it off. They share a sandwich or a beer, and it's never mentioned again. For me, an argument or an accusation felt like a fissure in the relationship. If it was unaddressed, the crack would grow into a cleave. If the cleave didn't stop, all would be lost. 10, 9, 8, 7 floors to go and Harry's eyes seemed to lighten. The daggers were gone and…was that the beginning of a smile?

Outside, on the sidewalk, I tried to apologize, but tears flew out of my face like some childish stunt. I apologized for the tears, blaming too little sleep and too much stress. Harry took a beat to cool off, giving me a pass on the generator day-play rig. This time, because it was too late for the right solution. But I second guessed every next move and I was terrified of Harry for the rest of the show.

Back to the suburban set, I arrived just in time for the clouds to break open. The cast and crew ran for cover, and I rode out the thunderstorm in Gayle's passenger seat. Like my old roommates Tibi and Diane, Gayle oversaw all the filming locations on this film. I felt like I had the inside look at this role, having heard the gripes each night before. But Gayle seemed to be made of Teflon. Her hair was perfection. Even in this storm where most had resorted to ponytails or crew cuts, Gayle's warm blonde hair waved in all the right directions. And her attitude was a match. She never panicked on the outside. Inside, she was about to quit this film for the second time.

We watched the Sycamore trees sweat off their bark in big, grey sheets peeling onto the ground in scrolls, like they were giving up. I had spent a few afternoons in this same passenger seat convincing Gayle to stay. So far she had agreed not to quit, but the threat of her leaving always felt imminent. I walked through the scenarios of what would happen if she abandoned me. I had no ace up my sleeve, and no solution I could offer Ted Hope.

The end was in sight, just two more weeks. Why risk your reputation when you're so close? The shoot was tough for some of us—long hours, a young cast, and a salary so low, you hid your paycheck from your roommates.

"What we need," I said to Gayle, "is something to look forward to. Something beyond this film."

Gayle's eyes grew big, all loss of sleep temporarily forgotten. "How about Paris?" she asked.

"Paris?" I was living hand-to-mouth, and I had no idea where my next job would be. I had no business going to Paris. But I did have a credit card. "Yes, sold."

We plotted a two-week trip. We would spend our down time strategizing the itinerary, highlighting museums and celebrity cemeteries in our Fodor's paperback. I thought, what better person to travel to Europe with than a location manager?

First, we needed to get through the last two weeks of filming. When our schedule shifted to a Tuesday through Saturday, it meant we had Monday for banking, laundry, and errands with the rest of the city's civilians. The Upper West Side exploded with teenagers from their school doors. It was a time of day I usually tried to avoid. I dodged groups of four or five, and gave myself permission to walk to Central Park's horse path before kicking into a jog on the reservoir loop. Away from the orange buses and parental pick-ups, the sun finally hid for good. The only sound I could hear now was the crumble of coarse gravel shifting under my sneakers.

When I turned north to push up the eastern stretch where I usually gained some speed, a wild cackling made me jump. I shook out my hands and relaxed, back on track. It was just a pack of prepubescent prep school kids. They sprinted towards me, but I was sure they were looking for someone behind me. I ignored them. Maybe it was a junior high white boys' rivalry. I figured it was best not to get involved.

Until they were on me. Tugging me down the hill and onto the horse path. Tearing at my clothes. The same stand-up kids at their Upper East Side dinner tables and prep school classrooms were unleashed, feral and possessed. They reached toward my pants to cop a feel, pinning my arms down and taking turns. I spit, swore, and scratched, but they were persistent.

The whole episode lasted less than sixty seconds, but it seemed like a tortuous ten minutes in slow motion. Something made them run away, maybe an oncoming runner. I heard their nasty laughs retreating. The same laughs that I had brushed off before now sounded adult and menacing. A male runner duded up in elite-class gear rounded the reservoir path and glanced down at me, blithely jogging by. I was splayed across the horse path, covered in dirt as he continued around the chain link fence and kicked up his pace to get another lap in.

Right then, I wished I had the perfect line of dialogue. That searing comment to hurl at him to help him remember the moment when he could have helped. But it was too late to blame this runner. The moment had passed, the kids had scattered, and he rounded the next turn. I cleared my throat, raw from screaming, and plucked the pine needles out of my palms.

That's when I decided to leave the Upper West Side.

Bad behavior wouldn't be confined to Central Park. I wondered if the film industry itself was perpetuating bad behavior like this by putting it on the screen as entertainment. When Marlon Brando seduced a young girl in a sprawling Parisian apartment, the audience bowed and gave it artistic license. We compartmentalized it and put it in a box called *art house*. We set the inconvenience of statutory rape aside and told ourselves we needed to look at the film in context. Did we need to? Now we were getting wiser and calling it for what it was. But just like those tweens in Central Park, entitlement continued to grab at what it wanted.

New York City real estate's equivalent of the holy grail was a floor-through apartment in Williamsburg. Fortunately, Rachel moved in with her boyfriend making her old apartment available. Rent would be twenty dollars a month less than my portion of the Upper West Side with Tibi. And it was all mine, all seven hundred square feet of it.

I looked out the window and hovered over Bedford Avenue's busyness. There were just a few bars and restaurants like Mugs Ale House, Teddy's Bar & Grill, and Turkey's Nest. There was also The Ship's Mast, a buzzy bar where Nick Gomez had filmed a scrappy black and white masterpiece with a handheld camera called *Laws of Gravity*. Fifteen blocks down under the Williamsburg Bridge there was an abrupt shift into the Hasidic population where we filmed *Bullet*. But like two positive protons, these worlds rarely collided.

I took the steps two at a time and burst through the rooftop door, peering over to the edge. A wave of thick, tinny fumes caught in my throat, probably from the nickel-plating factory across the street that was still rotating shifts. Tilting up from the factory, the World Trade Center's towers owned lower Manhattan. But due west in my direct line of vision was the Empire State Building. This building, strong and centered, would be a touchstone when the rest of the skyline made a dramatic shape-shift over the next ten years.

There wasn't much to unpack and the walls gave a hollow echo when I muttered aloud to myself about plans for the space. I removed a closet door and propped it up with a fish tank base to improvise a kitchen island. Any real decorating—and any adoption of kittens—would have to wait. I had to find the next job before the credit card hit its limit.

With each new pint, the Good Machine wrap party at an East 5th Street bar took on a new layer and the laughter ramped up. All conflicts were resolved, and all grudges were forgotten or reduced to a blur. Gayle finished the film, and she even managed to pull off a few more location miracles by the time we wrapped. Now she joined our group as we danced into an impromptu circle, throwing our bags in the center like an urban tribal fire pit.

Harry, the teamster, pulled me aside and handed me a package as his way of apologizing for something I had done. Inside a cotton-lined box I found a keychain, a handsome gold token decorated with the teamster's logo: the faces of two strong horses, side-by-side between a wagon wheel.

A beat too long to react or I would have caught them. Two strangers reached into our ceremonial pit, grabbed my bag, and ran out the front door. Three of us gave chase. East on 5th Street, up Avenue B and then gone, no sign of them. On the walk back to the bar, I patted down my pockets taking stock of what I'd lost. Harry's key chain was still in its box. A key chain but no apartment keys. They took my wallet, my camera, and my identity.

| Chapter 6 |

THE PORTAL FANTASY

VIETNAM, 1996

The tarmac seemed to undulate in thick hot waves. *Welcome to Saigon,* the sign across the small airport's entryway read. Behind the baggage claim area, separated by a long plexiglass wall, a crowd of spectators waved at me. I raised my hand and wiggled my fingers a bit, unsure whether their enthusiasm was for me. The conveyer belt gave a hiss-boom warning that *your worldly goods will be now vomited up from below.* Tony and his brother rapped their knuckles on the other side of the plexiglass partition, and it rippled back at them. Relieved to see their faces, I knew I wouldn't be unmoored for long.

I came to Vietnam to line produce TonyBui's debut feature film, *Three Seasons*. Open City Films would be the first American company to produce an entire film here. Tony and his brother, Tim, were born in Vietnam. When they were just two and four years old, Saigon fell. The rug was pulled out from under their lives and they fled for California.

Now, a cadre of thin young security guards took measured paces with their bulky automatic weapons outweighing their own heft. I wasn't used to seeing this in the United States. The guards circled the baggage carousel with a serious demeanor, even though the shoulder creases of their ill-fitted shirts slipped too far down their arms. Then my travel trunk made an unceremonious entrance as it rolled down the chute and lunged onto the rotating belt. The cellophane I had wrapped around it no longer mummified the case. Everything flew out onto the linoleum floor.

It was an apropos ending to a twenty-four-hour trip from New York to Saigon. The Cathay Pacific leg from JFK to Vancouver had been seamless. The plane was so empty that they upgraded our tickets to business class. I pulled on my gratis slippers and eye mask, tucked the seatbelts behind the cushions, and stretched out across five middle seats. I rested until we reached Vancouver. A group of loud, gesticulating—presumably Canadians—boarded for Hong Kong and packed the plane. With no available armrests, I cocooned myself in a blanket and sunk my neck into a deflating pillow. Sleep was never intended to be like this.

As we descended into Hong Kong, my seatmate pushed up his glasses and squished his forehead against the oval window. It seemed as if the plane couldn't get him home fast enough. But then a building flew by us, and we were on eye level with the city. Flashing Fuji and Coke billboards were so close, I could see people inside these buildings. I could pick out the colors of their skirts and blouses. People held casual conversations, not at all alarmed that a plane had just whizzed by merely two hundred feet from their window.

Night closed in and for the next eight hours I sprawled onto a row of orange plastic chairs waiting for the Vietnam Air flight from Hong Kong to Ho Chi Minh City. The color scheme and the textures made it feel like I was trying to sleep at a McDonald's. I dozed off between departure announcements with my passport, my vaccine booklet, and my Lariam prescription against my chest with my legs propped up on a duffel. I was content knowing that my cellophaned case had been checked through, but now it was on its own freewheeling journey.

Somewhere along the way to Saigon, the case's hinges were compromised, and the clasps had busted loose. My traveling office was exposed. I put the contents back in, taped it up, and made my way through customs. I prayed my computer would still start up when I plugged it in.

The crowd wasn't at the arrival curb to meet anyone specific. Greeting the international flights was more of a hobby. I thought it spoke well for a city where people took the time to welcome its visitors; even its random travelers.

Tony and Tim waved me through, hailed me a cab, and gave the cabbie directions in Vietnamese. They were giddy with a surprise. Sting was performing a landmark rock concert in Vietnam, and they bought tickets for all of us. After they told me they would meet me at the Phan Dinh Phung Center at 8 p.m., they sent me off in my cab.

Now I was on my own in a strange country. Phan Dinh Phung, Phan Dinh Phung, Phan Dinh Phung. I repeated the destination as a survival mantra.

The road exploded with Vespas wreaking havoc with their devil-may-care moves. They puffed out a serpentine trail of toxic fumes from roaring single-cycle engines. One hand turned the gear shift, while the other clutched a cigarette. With its cobbled together buildings and vertical foreign signs, the city was unlike any I'd known. Louder than the steady buzz of Rome and more otherworldly than southern Spain, it reminded me most of that truncated family trip across the border into Tijuana. And here I was in the back seat again, except this time I would be the one calling the shots.

My home for now was a family-owned, four-story building tucked into a quiet side street in District 5. The family's son hauled my case up three flights to the top floor. When I handed him a few coins, he gave me a confused look. Too much? Or too little? Tim and Tony would have to teach me about customary tipping. Customary everything for that matter.

"Xin Chào," I said, hello. No, that was wrong. "Or, I mean, thank you, *gam un*." My head swirled back into the room, longing for the bed. I had two hours to take a jet-lagged disco nap and then there would be Sting.

The Sting show was the first rock concert in Vietnam, the first Western rock performance since the war. And because it was held in a basketball stadium with the audience in bleachers, it felt more intimate than a high school pep rally.

"ROXXXXXANNNE!" I was so close to Sting I could see the spit fly when he broke the silence and hurled out the words. The audience shrieked and when the drums kicked in, they bopped their heads along, sure of the tune but not necessarily the lyric. I was somewhere between a dream and a sleepwalk, taking in every moment. If Sting could pull off a rock concert in Saigon, we could beat the

odds and make a film happen here. Maybe I could borrow the band's confidence, have it rub off on me across the lip of the stage, and all would be fine. I was heady with undeserved confidence.

There was a weight to being an American in Vietnam in 1996. It had been twenty-five years since the Vietnam War, but the hideous pockmarks of its damage were still raw. For so many Americans, the war and Vietnam were still synonymous, as if the country had been stripped of its sovereignty. Even then, I knew the war's most searing and present ghosts would show themselves. I wanted to be prepared for that moment, ready to say and do the right thing. But for this moment, I let the music and the crowd wash over me. I swarmed in the center of this country's welcome.

I travelled on the back of Vespas, a ride hailed on any corner for about sixty cents, less than a New York City subway token. I memorized the pronunciations of the hotel address and the Gai Phong Studio. The studio took up a square city block, with a breezy courtyard in its center. It was designed to allow air through its unscreened windows in the center of the cement structure. The rooms were stark and bare and matched the raw exterior. In lieu of air conditioning, oversized ceiling fans swept above each production office. A nice *Casablanca* touch, you might be thinking. But this was stark, like a Kafkaesque interrogation room.

The studio's unisex bathroom was off a concrete side hall on the mezzanine level. It was just a large windowless box with a hole in the ground. The hole was the toilet. A heavy metal door swung permanently outward, jammed into the concrete floor, and unable to close.

My sister had warned me about this from her time in Thailand. "Just pretend you're in one of those campground bathrooms: push your tongue up to the roof of your mouth to block out the smell, close your eyes, and squat," she said. I considered the large bottle of boiled and cooled water I carried. Could I survive if I drank no water, and held out until I was back at the hotel?

Tony introduced me to Vu, who would be my translator and assistant. Vu shook my hand and pulled me in for a hug, which surprised me and warmed me to her immediately. She parked her scooter to the back of the studio, and switched her sneakers to a pair of less-sensible, inside shoes. In a quick flash she was transformed, and ready for work. Together, we set up in our office and unloaded the trunk of coveted American office supplies. The Post-it notes, index cards, staplers, and manila folders now felt ridiculous coming out of the case. It had all seemed like such a good idea in New York, but now I considered it halfway around the globe: *This was my special cache?*

I was anxious to get my laptop set up—so much of my prep work in Word, Excel, and Movie Magic documents would get us organized over the next few weeks. I crawled under the table and grabbed for the right adaptor. But when I was wedged under there wrangling cords, a tiny spark shot from the wall. A gasp came out of me and then a trail of smoke came out of my laptop. I had fried my computer.

I entered the first few stages of grief: denial followed by refusal to accept responsibility, one of the lesser-known stages.

Vu forced me to rebound, and she hired two energetic production assistants. In one afternoon, they were able to source a laptop for me. The new PC computer didn't have any Movie Magic programs, so I would have to be creative with my budget and my shooting schedule. For two full days our production assistants motored around the city on twin Vespas in a futile search for a filing cabinet. We gave up. We re-shaped oblong boxes into our make-shift cabinet. We created files, hand folding them from manila rectangles. If this country has an alternate organizational system, I needed to learn how it was done.

It was dark when I returned to the hotel in defeat, with the city's recklessness reverberating in my head. Ma, the daughter of the hotel managers, greeted me in the lobby with a tall plastic bottle of treated tap water. This had become a habit. I recognized this one as the first of three bottles in circuit, its paper label now washed away. Ma poured a glass for me and patted the spot next to her on the couch at the foot of the stairs. She was determined to teach me the intricacies of her language.

I was happy to absorb just a few basics. I pulled out my orange phrase book, but she grabbed it and set it to the side. *Look at me, listen to me,* she seemed to say, *instead of that useless book. Gam on* had been the first phrase I used to thank the cabdriver, being careful to make a hard G. A hard C means *shut your mouth up,* so it's a subtle, tricky language. Easy (for me) to trip over. I teetered on the edge of a great offense every time I opened my mouth.

Ma repeated the basics with patience: food, eat, stop, thank you.

I was falling for Saigon. I loved Ma and the family who ran my hotel. I became attached to Vu who was loyal and resourceful, even with her two-hour lunches which she took at home. I couldn't blame her, because she probably enjoyed modern plumbing there.

I admired the women who seemed to carry the city's heaviest loads. These women were in perpetual motion, propping the city up. The men worked hard too, but they found respite. They would crouch together for long breaks, shirtless and chain-smoking curbside. They managed to carve out privacy in the most public of spaces. The busyness of the city was dizzying. And it was growing, as its Western tourism industry was just beginning to boom. Blocks upon blocks of scaffolding, like vertical pick-up sticks, were rigged against its rising hotels. The boutique hotels like mine would be sitting in the shadows of these monsters before long.

For the next few weeks, I fed my stress with street cart food; something I had been told to avoid. At an outdoor noodle shop two blocks from the studio, I treated myself to a pile of delicious, seasoned vermicelli. I began to gloat that I had an iron stomach. Knock-on-wood, I experienced no upset digestive system yet. But my nervous energy was burning off calories so fast, I couldn't seem to fill up. I was struggling to pull the film together.

We visited the equipment house to take stock in the state of the grip stands and lamps. I was assured everything would be in tip-top shape because the equipment was all used on *The Lover,* a beautiful French film that had filmed in Vietnam only four years earlier. The TV studio owner across town greeted me with a firm handshake.

When he flicked on the lights to a dank low-ceilinged dungeon, lamps and stands toppled over each other. I loosened the gobo arm from a C-stand, but the handle deteriorated into orange rust in my palm. The only dolly was a doorway dolly; a model I didn't recognize. It was going to be a large list of casualties. I kept it to myself, but I knew we'd now have to ship equipment by boat or air from Hanoi or Hong Kong.

At a standstill in traffic on the way back to the studio, Tony announced he was going to buy a Vespa so he could get around faster.

"No way..." My answer was unequivocal. I laughed and gestured out the window. "Besides, our insurance would never let you do it." I knew they wouldn't allow it, not if they did their research into Saigon's daily road carnage.

The Gai Phong Studio was delighted to show me the rain bars which had also been featured in the steamy scenes of *The Lover*. We would need this set up for several scenes of consistent rain, and we couldn't count on Mother Nature for continuity. The studio's technicians rigged the system into the courtyard and fired it up. A series of pumps and pipes with holes were in place, and we prepared for a deluge. Instead, we got a trickle.

Then the elephant doors were pushed back to reveal the studio's sound stage, a giant space that dwarfed the four of us. I stood in awe for a moment. We could build several of our sets here and keep them standing for the run of show. Just then the roof erupted in what sounded like a team of horses roaring overhead. As if Apollo himself cracked the whip and drove his chariot in circles. We all looked up, but the studio manager seemed unfazed.

"It's the roof. It does that when it rains." Tony pointed to the ceiling and shouted something else, but I shook my head, unable to hear him over the hammering. "It's not insulated—it's made of tin!" Tony shouted.

Tin, an excellent conductor of noise. In Vietnam, there was no need for a real sound stage: the audio was recorded as a guide track. They dubbed over all the actors' dialogue in post. As long as the roof didn't leak, the Vietnamese productions continued shooting throughout the rainy season.

If I were a smoker, this was when I'd take out a pack of cigarettes, walk out the studio gates, and light up. Instead, I thanked them for the tour and left through the stage door. I stumbled onto the studio's sidewalk and tried to remember how to breathe.

The sky was thick and angry, dumping water in thick sheets, but I'd already learned it would only last twenty or thirty minutes. In this rainy season, there were usually several downpours each day. A heavy buzz of motor bikes sprayed past on the wet pavement, Saigon's unrelenting soundtrack. The drivers threw colorful rain ponchos over their headlamps for full coverage, creating an array of bright lights; like a street of vibrating Christmas bulbs. Then just as soon as the deluge landed, the sky became a clean slate.

A woman down the street in an apron gave a wild wave of her arms. I looked behind me for her target, but it was me she wanted. She called me into her shop, a simple cozy spot carved out under the studio's concrete corner. A respite.

"You. You need food," she said in English. There was no disobeying this woman's clear direction. She sat me down and placed a napkin in my lap.

How did she know? Did she also know that I needed to be knocked out and taken back to New York? That I had been thinking about jumping into the street in front of a beer truck? That her city was driving me mad, and that New York City was a lazy seaside resort by comparison?

She cooked me a plate of baked chicken nuggets and French fries. Well, salty baked potato medallions anyway which was close enough and tasted like the glimmer of heaven and home.

When I returned to the hotel, Ma was waiting for me with a notepad and another bottle of lukewarm distilled water. No matter how late, no matter how tired; she was there for another lesson. I tried again to pronounce the hotel's street, and she corrected my intonation. Every up or down tone could change the substance of a sentence. Even Ma and her brother Bien's names could have different meanings if they were mispronounced. She drew each of them out in her notebook: wavy lines representing the sea, jagged lines for something chaotic. Bien could also mean change.

On the weekend, I visited a sprawling outdoor food market and walked through my neighborhood of craftspeople and tailors. I packed only two pairs of pants, and they were quickly wearing out. I presented one to the seamstresses as a pattern and selected a few swatches of material. For ten dollars and a hefty tip, I would have two new pairs of pants in a week.

And since the only bra I traveled with was hooked to a netted laundry bag and snarled into a ball in the hotel's rinse cycle, I hitched a Vespa ride to the city's only mall to buy a new one. Like the airport, the mall was an entertainment destination. It had the city's first escalator and families lined up for the ride. Grown adults giggled like children, holding hands and taking polite turns up this magical ascending staircase. Then they shot down the steps and lined up again. They came to the mall for the ride; any shopping was incidental.

I slurped down another bowl of vermicelli noodles in the studio while I typed an update for the financiers. I planned to print it and fax it down in the Gai Phong production office. I was warned there would be a delay in the receipt of every international fax because the government censors first captured the letter's image and recorded it, maybe even in real time. I doubted that technology was possible, but I still scanned my words and stories with my censor hat on. I reviewed a final draft before marching down to the front office to push it through.

This time I used the seldom-used staircase behind our production office. I thought I was alone in the empty hallway until I heard a door creak open, revealing a secret room I hadn't noticed before. A construction worker saw me and pulled the door back, obscuring my view. On my way back, I was more curious. Another worker came out and left the secret door open for a glimpse inside. They had created a pedestal in the back of the space. *What's he building in there?* Tom Waits's gravelly voice played in my head, obsessed with his neighbor's sawing, grinding, and drilling. The unknown on the other side of a door could drive a person to madness.

I made an excuse for yet another trip past the construction. This time, there was plumbing at the base of the pedestal. The jig was up. They were installing an aboveground toilet for the arrival of royalty. Royalty in the form of a James Bond movie coming to Saigon for a two-week scout. Over the next two weeks, the studio's team of workers power washed every corner of the building, except ours.

After a day of our own movie's location scouting, Tony's uncle Don Duong, the actor who would star as the cyclo driver in the film, took us out for a beer. If you chose to drink beer in Saigon, it was served warm. I felt that warm beer defeated its purpose. Beer existed to celebrate a mid-summers lawnmowing, or a late-day five-mile run. But cold beer in Saigon required ice cubes.

When Don Duong carried three half-pints back to the table and planted one in front of me, I stared down the melting ice cube like it was a horror film villain. I had seen blocks of ice the size of bread boxes strapped to the back wheel of bicycles and delivered to restaurants. I imagined the mother ice block from which these blocks are spawned. Somewhere in a freezer, in a cave beneath the city. But chivalry trumped ice cubes. And showing grace towards the lead actor in your film required sacrifice. I threw back the beer, double-timing it in a race against the melting ice.

I woke up with *I-told-you-so* stomach cramps, curled into a ball to keep my organs from exploding, knowing I'd lost my high-ranking iron stomach status. Just one ice cube left me flat out. But I managed to drag myself to the studio because there was too much to do. It had been several weeks of slow progress, and we were still wading through it all. The money was still not landing, and my nerves were pitched high. I had to reach Jason Kliot, the owner of Open City Films and the head producer with his partner Joana Vicente. I phoned Jason at midnight, timing my call for when the crew broke for lunch on the set of his other movie.

"Gretch, I'm sorry," he said. "Hang in there, the money's coming." Jason was another one of the few people who abbreviated my name. I wasn't sure when I became one syllable for him, but it was too late to tell him I didn't like it. And right now, I found my nickname comforting.

"Can we secure a bridge loan? Something..." I said, aiming for desperate, but not too desperate. They might be testing my resolve. "The thing is...I'm tapping my own bank account and trust me, that well's almost dry."

"Look, I'm heading to the bank after we're back in from lunch," he said. "But here's the great news: Sharon's flying to Saigon this week, so this is happening!" Sharon was the film's production designer. I wanted to be enthusiastic, but I didn't yet have the money to pay a crew to greet her or the hardware and lumber to build her sets.

Vu noticed the twitch in my clenched jaw when I hung up. She crouched down and rested her palms on my knees, looking me in the eye.

"You need to breathe. You're not breathing," she said. "Not just short survival sips, real breathing." We practiced long, deep, lung-gorging breaths. Then Vu patted the back of her scooter and threw me her spare helmet.

A morning squall had left puddles of mud in the zoo park. We hopped off the Vespa and skirted around them, but Vu moved straight forward, her eyes fixed on a specific cage. She put her hand through the bars where a group of monkeys squawked back at her. They looked happy to be together, but hungry and confused about their captivity. Vu called to one monkey, and he leapt over to her. He knew her. This was a reunion. And then they were blowing kisses at each other.

"He was mine, he lived with me," she said. "But I had to give him up."

"Why?"

"Because...my boyfriend wouldn't allow him," now she turned away from the cage, like it was too much to bear. I wanted to say, what kind of jerk makes his girlfriend give up her pet for him? On the other hand, I wasn't willing to take the monkey to safe harbor myself. "He's a doctor, a Western doctor, my boyfriend. He could probably help you."

Vu's German boyfriend poked inside my ears and measured the size of my pupils. I held a paper apron around my waist and dangled my legs over the doctor's table, keeping my socks on for dignity. He nodded his head and adjusted the stethoscope around his neck like a TV doctor. There was no comforting bedside manner, just a few *hmmms* and a dismissive shrug.

"Yes, typical," he said. He'd already concluded my mainstream malaise. "This is a Westerner's condition. One gets it merely by living and working in Saigon." The German doctor gestured towards the window. Did he mean the cause was out there, and not inside me? "I too had it when I moved here," he revealed. The tumultuous pace of the city was unrivaled, but the pace didn't seem to match the progress. So, Westerners internalized their stress, causing it to eke out in twitchy ways.

He scribbled something, ripped a prescription from his pad, and extended it to me, just out of reach. I thought of Vu and her monkey; this guy liked to be the one with the power. Finally, I clutched my paper gown and took a step towards him to take the scrip.

I lay on the edge of my hotel bed, split a pill in half along the indentation, and swallowed the smaller half with a gulp of Ma's water. They were as big as horse pills, designed to relax my jaw and charm me to sleep. For every cause, every ailment, a Western solution in a pill bottle.

I dreamt of the Police. First in a half-conscious state, I remembered the real story: In high school, my friend Mara showed up at my house in her Volkswagen Beetle with the new Police album tucked under her arm. We sat on the floor cross-legged by the record player, lifting the needle and dropping it in the groove. *Don't Stand So Close To Me* over and over again. The Police album travelled with us like a vinyl bible until summer came and we left it in the back windshield of Mara's Beetle. The vinyl melted, its grooves blurring in the summer sun. We tried baking it in the oven, warming and reshaping it. But the album cracked and was pronounced DOA.

Now the night disappeared, and I woke up on the floor in a pool of sweat. My body was rubbery cool and my cheek was indented with a cross. It wasn't a sign from above, just the cross-section of the four ceramic floor tiles under me. A gecko slithered across the ceiling; the only movement in an otherwise lifeless room. He rolled out his tongue and snapped at a clueless mosquito. Then the Police dream wormed its way back. I bent the album to make it fit, pushing the soft vinyl into place and trying to make it spin. But it collapsed when I pressed too hard. It shattered in my hands leaving just shards of vinyl and blood.

I flushed the rest of the pills away, and watched them circle the toilet's black hole, fearing for the fish who might eat them and float down the river in a catatonic state. Apparently, all the Westerners knew about my doctor and his penchant for prescribing pills like candy.

I left the episode behind and decided to embrace the frenzy of Saigon.

Sharon would arrive in a day, and we'd set her up at the Sunny Hotel where we'd booked a rooftop room. At the Sunny, we'd struck a deal to house the bulk of the crew traveling from New York, Hong Kong, and Europe. Eventually, I'd have to leave Ma and her family at the boutique hotel and join the rest of the crew here.

But the next day, the bad news hit. The dreaded call came in and the film's financier pulled out of the deal.

Tony took the news badly. The film he had been directing in his head for years—the story he had been scouting and shot listing on his annual trips back to Vietnam—was cancelled, or at least postponed. He expected to shoot his first feature before he turned thirty. He counted on a hero's homecoming to Saigon, acting roles for friends and family, and an award-winning blast toward a Hollywood career. Now that was all on hold. The film was put into "research mode," meaning we'd stay for another month to collect a plan; a roadmap on how to get it done.

But we had to postpone our grief for now; Sharon's plane had landed, and she'd be in the city within the hour. Tony and I met her by a cluster of palms at the Sunny Hotel. We loaded her bags into a cart and escorted her to her room. We were like an overzealous concierge team, and I suspected she suspected something. I threw open the doors to her balcony, and a sticky breeze set the scene. Our bad news had transpired while Sharon was on layover in Hong Kong, possibly drooling on the same row of orange plastic chairs where I'd tried to sleep four weeks ago.

Sharon surprised me as she gave a loud laugh and shrugged it off. She had a round-trip ticket home, and she would enjoy her time in Vietnam without the pressure of designing a movie. And as a seasoned traveler, she transcended jet lag. Moments after ducking into the bathroom, she transpired in a flowing white linen suit. She leaned onto the balcony rail and craned her head towards the river, like she already owned Saigon.

"What the hell," she said. "Let's get some food. Show me this city!"

Tony and I shot each other a look, shrugging it all off with a smile. He led us to the seafood district where barkers waved tourists into a long row of prawn houses. Six of us took a seat around a picnic table covered in a red-checkered tablecloth, straight out of suburban New Jersey. In this back yard the city quieted to a lull, and the pace slowed. The waiter dumped a bucket of crabs in the center of the table. And then the sauce: a salty lime concoction good enough to make use forget that the film had been abandoned.

The rest of the group had had enough, but Sharon and I peeled off to a second-story bar. Two beers later, we hatched a plan to travel north towards the beaches of Hue. When we looked up, a small crowd of young women surrounded us; their ears and necks weighted in costume jewels. It was Sharon who engaged and drew out the history of the place. We learned that we were in a former American GI hangout. It was the early hour, before the men showed up and the women were activated for their service. Working girls. For now, they wanted to hear about us.

"Tell me your story," a young woman asked. She couldn't have been older than eighteen, hiding under the veneer of foundation and lip gloss, bangs cut straight across. "How did you come to be here?"

"I want to hear your story," I said instead. She laughed and grabbed my hand, pulling me to the dance floor. Within minutes, our group formed a chain around the floor while Mick Jagger panted out *Start Me Up*.

The men trickled in while Sharon and I made our exit, but we left with a solid itinerary in mind. We would take the train north in the morning. It felt like a gasket had been tapped and I was cut loose. I barely knew Sharon, but I wanted to tell her all my Saigon stories. My aching loneliness, the half-pill melt-down, and the monkey-in-a-cage saga. Her mouth curled up on the edges when she shook her head laughing. Now I could laugh at myself too. The hard stuff seemed to roll off Sharon, off her gauzy linens, and out of her thick curly hair. Dignity intact.

If this were a movie, I was Ethel to Sharon's Lucy (in a film that old Hollywood never dared make, but television mastered). Sharon charted the map, uninhibited by the sharks that lay ahead, or oblivious to them. I was willing to go along for the ride, because I was there, I was penniless, and I had my own round trip ticket home. Yes, we were going a little rogue, leaving the city before our research was completed. But what were they going to do, fire us?

| Chapter 7 |

THE PERIOD PIECE

MASSACHUSETTS, 1996

November in New York competed with Saigon's rainy season. I leaned against a payphone and watched water ooze through the cinderblock walls of Port Authority's upper concourse. I folded my ticket and prepared to board a Peter Pan bus to my mother's house in Western Massachusetts—a place where I could lick my wounds. I was ashamed about landing back in my mother's house. Successful thirty-year-olds do not retreat home, only the ones who have lost the plot do.

My subletter, Noah, was on the other end of the line. He was less grateful than I hoped he would be that I wasn't busting in on him. I had to honor his sublet window, and I had options. I could crash at Rachel's apartment, but two months was a long time to squat with a friend; especially in a tiny Brooklyn apartment. The other option was to go home.

"There's a boatload of mail here for you," Noah's tone was panicked.

I told him I would deal with the mail after Christmas, after he moved out. Noah paid all the rent and utilities.

My student loan payments were up to date. What else could there possibly be?

Time was still my Achilles heel. Like a blindsided horse, I could only see twenty yards ahead. I moved forward competently within any current scenario, but I feared what lay beyond. At the same time, I was like a generous clairvoyant. I could see other people's futures, and I could tell when a crew member was going to have trouble. But I excelled at shoving my own problems to the side. It was probably the fear of dealing with those problems that kept me from making bigger leaps in my career—and in my life—earlier.

"There's like a ton piling up on the kitchen table. I don't even eat on the table anymore, because there's no room." I pictured him shoveling in Cheerios in the galley kitchen, backing far away from the growing pile of mail. "And it's not all junk mail. I mean I'm seeing red block letters on the envelopes. That can't be good."

OK. It was just mail. I took further stock: apparently the cats were alive (he barely mentioned them), there was no cockroach infestation.

"I'll tackle it when I'm back," I said. "And thanks for taking care of the cats." Words, I hoped, to remind him to feed and water them.

The cats would no longer be talking to me. I'd abandoned them in their first year of their sweet furry lives. It was easier to refer to them as generic *cats*; saying their names aloud would cause my throat to clench up. Instead, my stomach took a guilt lap beneath my ribs.

I arrived at my mother's house, ready to be able-bodied and useful. That was my currency. I would stack cords of wood. I could stare down piles of unwieldy logs with a problem on my mind and come out of it with a solution.

By nightfall, the logs were piled into neat stacks even the Norwegians would admire. I took off my gloves and sat on my mother's cold fieldstone steps. In this hill town there were no busy lights to obscure the night sky. There were more stars visible now than I had seen in months. Leaning against the front door, I watched a plane slice through Orion's belt, and my mind drifted back to Vietnam.

I didn't tell my mother the whole story of my futile attempt to make a film in Vietnam. I told her just enough to make her sympathetic.

"I'm sure Tony will get to make his movie," she said in an effort to comfort me. "And if it isn't with you, at least all your research will go to good use."

Could a comment feel like a hug and a slap at the same time?

I wanted to say, "You don't get it; how hard all that work was. How I'll never get credit for it even if it does happen someday." But if she didn't understand, it was because I never took the time to explain. In the past, I started to describe my work to her, but I sensed her attention drifting. I would stop, mid-story, passive aggressively testing the waters. Did she care?

"Come on Larry. He's open!" After dinner, my mother shouted at Larry Bird as he grabbed a rebound on our tiny tv—the same 8" black and white one I grew up with. "Get it to Robert!" Larry took her direction and tossed the ball downcourt to Robert Parish for two easy points.

I popped us a bowl of popcorn for the show and took a seat next to her, but when the game's tension grew, we were on our feet. A Celtics vs Bulls game in this era was like no other theater: beginning, middle, and end. It was beautifully choreographed, but surprisingly spontaneous. Nothing was written, and no one knew the ending.

My mother liked movies, she went to the cinema, and she took time to watch all the ones I worked on, but if the Celtics were in the playoffs, the game would be on. If she were a character in a film, you would say there were inconsistencies. We were surrounded by a house of carefully curated antiques, but the final minutes of play were all that mattered right now. We pulled our chairs closer and watched the spectacle escalate on Boston's parquet floors.

When I woke up, an orange cat pawed at my face. We called him Tri-puss, because he had two back legs and one front leg. As an adolescent he stepped into a bear trap in the woods and managed to chew his own front leg off to escape. He stood back, mission accomplished now that I was awake. I looked around me at this fierce cat, this survivor, and this space over the garage surrounded by paneled windows. I let the cast iron stove's coals cool to ash and each panel was iced over. Lazy flies still littered the space between the interior and storm windows.

I drove my mother's jeep to drop her at work in Deerfield, down a sequence of winding hills along the river and into the valley. After a few minutes, I worked the rust out of my stick-shift skills and skipped into fourth. The valley would be ten degrees warmer than the hill towns, a steady rise of the mercury every two minutes, just as it had always been.

I could sense my mother was at least pretending to enjoy the road as a passenger, but I caught her toes arching forward, hitting her imaginary brake on the jagged turns. I worried about her on these snowy hills by herself, but she'd been doing it by rote for over twenty years. This was her turf, and I was the interloper.

We were eleven, thirteen, fifteen, and seventeen when she was left to raise us on her own. But after we'd left home, she thrived. She got a graduate degree in history; she published books about pewter, family, and landscape. She presented lectures, projecting carousels of slides for a rapt audience. Then she conceived of a stage performance, role playing as the wife of a blacksmith; a fully imagined life she derived from the chicken scratch of an artisan's ledger book. She worked the show in demand, on rotation, like a modern Jane Austen heroine complete with a romantic denouement.

Then it hit me. My mother operated in the tangible. Without a film to show her, the thing might not have happened. If I needed to show her what Vietnam was to me, she would need my photos as evidence.

I planned to set the scene and cook a risotto with a nice bottle of wine. No basketball on TV; just my images, my cast of characters, and the stories that went with them. I drove the jeep at high speed along the river route from the valley into the hill towns of the Berkshires. Just drive.

When Sharon had come to Saigon, she empowered me to make things work on my own terms. We stayed in Vietnam for the month, scouting locations, assembling photos, making lists of local contacts and talent, and building a plan for the team who would eventually come in to make Tony's film. Maybe the two of us would be back for the shoot, but there was no guarantee when the money would land. We needed to present a road map for any producer or production designer. *Act as if you could be hit by a bus* became the motto, which didn't feel like an impossibility.

Sharon and I had taken the train to Hue to scout for temples in the north, but mostly we boarded for our own adventure. We tossed our overnight bags into a sleeper car—a cave of four metal beds. It was as if someone had taken a subway train, painted it shotgun metal, and pushed two sets of bunk beds on either wall. Like a jail cell on rails equipped with just the essentials.

As we switch-backed up a mountain and down the other side, we were stunned by the countryside. This wealth of landscape was never advertised in any Vietnam war movie we had seen. At least not without fiery explosions and a high body count. My stomach lurched to think about the scorched earth we left behind.

Couples of sisters, mothers, and children joined our sleeper car for shorter stretches of the trip. The train's cook lugged a ten-gallon vat of soup into our vestibule and set the steaming pot on the ground. After the ice cube incident, I was cautious, and I waved off the soup. Sharon finished a bowl and held it out to the cook for a second helping.

Hue was home to a new cache of temples, tombs, and pagodas, nothing like what we'd seen in the south. We continued to take photos with a great deal of enthusiasm.

But by the second afternoon, we began a half-hearted search for a joint. Pot would be just the thing to help us relax and get past the Saigon jitters. Through a combination of rudimentary Vietnamese and broken sign language, we finally found the place. It turned out 4:20 was the international symbol for weed and our cyclo driver was the linchpin in the transaction. He pedaled on to a village by the sea, assuring us that every grain of sand on the beaches of Hue had been combed and cleared of land mines. All was peaceful when we walked through the village alongside a group of uniformed school children. They posed for our cameras with shy smiles.

But when we lay down our towels on Hue's sparsely populated beach to enjoy the warm salty spray, two young women approached to sell us bottled water. Each woman was missing an arm. Then others on the beach approached us, asking us for anything we could spare. We were finally faced with the victims of the land mines, explosives that had been buried and left behind.

On the hearth of the fireplace in Massachusetts, I swished my hand around the wooden bowl of Christmas cards and separated the photos of the kids and families. I pulled a tin photo box from the bookshelf and captioned the new pictures and dropped them in with the growing collection; a celebration of other peoples' children. Annually, we retrieved this tin to settle arguments about who married whom, who divorced whom, and what they named their kids.

Mixed in with the friends' photos, a cache of our old family pictures had found their way into the tins. I pulled one close to focus on our tiny faces that were squinty in a mid-day sun. It was my sisters and me, lined up by age and by height in our Danskin. We looked scrappy; our leaky blue tent propped up behind us. My father stood to the right with his pipe, but the top of his head was cut out of the frame. He was six-foot-two and it was impossible to get all of us into the same frame without a sacrifice. But I noticed something else; we were all shoved far to the left side of the frame, leaving plenty of empty space on the right side. I flipped through the series of photos and realized they were all off balance, all in the same way. Was it the Kodak instamatic viewfinder that was out of whack or was it my mother's aim?

By the time my subletter gave me the all-clear to move back home, it was New Year's Eve. I grabbed the bus back to Port Authority and crashed into my stripped bed (sheets still in the dryer, too tired to walk down to the laundromat again). The cats assumed their pre-Vietnam positions at my feet and head. But I kept one eye on the dining room table.

My subletter had been right about the boatload of mail. Thick envelopes with warnings in red print and all capital letters threatened an escalation of urgency. The return addresses were from stores I recognized: Circuit City, Macy's, and Radio Shack. I ripped open the first several envelopes and like the impending doom of a horror film, the plot became clear. Someone had opened an account in my name in each of these stores. Then came the bills. Thousands of dollars in television sets, high end stereos, and microwaves. Overdue, past due and finally, referred to collections.

Identity theft was rare in the '90s. It was years before someone's virtual profile could be plucked from the internet and exploited, but this analog attack was just as deep-seated and harder to fight. A person out there—a ring of them I was told—was pretending to be me. They waved forged plastic cards around in my name on wild shopping sprees. Over and over, I called the stores directly, appealing to them with my story. But the resolution was out of their hands. Too much time had passed, and the damage was now a scar on my credit rating.

I had to remediate this the same way I would produce a film. The mission: to erase the amounts owed and boost my credit rating up from zero. If I was ever going to get another credit card or buy a car, I needed to make this right. I found my copy of the police report I had filed the night of the wrap party and created a folder for each store.

In the movie trailer of this nightmare, our heroine hits rock bottom and the audience is okay with that. Our heroine trips over a curb, laughing and tossing her hat in the air: "Now…this Summer…a clean slate, a chance to reinvent herself. To…atone. She'll pull herself up by her bootstraps…" and every other cliché about falling up from poverty. She will triumph, but only because it's a freaking movie.

In real life, it sucks.

I prepared a script for the call to my sister and rehearsed the bullet points from underneath my down comforter. I underlined the key arguments. With interest accruing, I needed to suck up my pride and borrow money.

"Vietnam didn't work out," I said, as if it could have happened to anyone, not just me. The one who's great with other people's money, but a train wreck with her own. "The movie lost its financing."

"Yeesh, that's too bad. I mean, that sucks," she said, LA traffic rumbling behind her car phone. But what I didn't hear was the judgement I anticipated. Instead I heard, "What's next? What are you gonna do now?"

"I'm looking. I've got some options. Nothing great." Deep breath. "But that's not all." Now it all came flying out. "I had my identity stolen while I was away, and someone charged tons of electronics in my name. It's a shit show. My mailbox blew up. I'm faxing like a mad woman to clear my name."

"Do you need a loan?"

Right there. The sweetest words I could imagine. Two thousand dollars. The amount I calculated for one month's rent and utilities, a payment to my credit card, and a small living allowance for food and movies. It was so easy. Should I have asked for more?

After the Vietnam experience, I was unsure if I wanted to stay in the film business. It all felt like diminishing returns; too much pain with too little sleep. And even after the company reimbursed me for my out-of-pocket expenses, I had nothing to show for it except an anemic bank statement.

I answered every call that came in, grabbing at the receiver like a teenager waiting for a date. The next incoming call was not Circuit City, it was from Jason at Open City. I heard myself say yes before I knew what the job was.

| Chapter 8 |

THE ROAD MOVIE

SOMEWHERE IN THE SOUTHWEST, 1998

Amir threw together a salad on the tailgate of our rental car outside the Santa Monica IGA. He would be the director on this film we scouted, but for now he played a more utilitarian role. He slashed a bag of ice with a matte knife and dumped it into the Styrofoam cooler. I snapped a photo of him as he prepped the food from our shopping spree, and he flashed a grin.

Amir didn't drink, and he didn't smoke. He didn't eat meat, so the golden arches were out of the question. Amir had a mission to rid me of my evil habits and convince me to eat healthy. It began with this parking lot salad, and a cooler of prescribed ingredients.

Oh, and he didn't drive either, so that was on me.

We'd landed into the tall palms and blue skies of LAX that afternoon. In winter, it was hard to believe the Northeast shared the same approximate angle on the sun as the Southwest. The desert's forced vegetation rolled out on LAX's lush welcome mat. And outside the airport came the signage: neon fixtures in chunky letters advertising bowling alleys, cafés, and motels. The West Coast's fast-food options were unparalleled in the East. Sexy LA names like *Johnny Rocket, In & Out Burger,* and *Sonic.*

In New York I'd contacted two Austin, Texas-based casting directors. I gave them the thumbnail sketch of Amir's screenplay, *Sound Barrier,* and the cast of characters. Amir wanted to cast local talent, but we weren't yet sure where filming would be. My production brain wanted to make it work near Austin or Los Angles. But, even if that was possible, Amir would first need to be inspired by the fifteen hundred miles of back roads between these two cities.

The story of *Sound Barrier* itself was a road trip: two young kids, one was a deaf-mute boy, the other one was a salty, teen-aged girl. The girl latches onto an audio cassette tape, with a recording that could unlock the secrets of a lost parent. With a pet monkey added in, this unlikely trio had a mission. But there would be unforeseen and unwelcome obstacles. At its climax, the story was a mother-son reunion that no one saw coming. Not even Amir, because it was all still a work-in-progress. Our road trip scout would determine each character's fate.

We researched dry dusty airports and abandoned Western towns. The map was Amir's treasure hunt; highlighted and dog-eared with Post-it notes. Road signs warned *tangents ahead.* For a filmmaker like Amir, every dot on the map was like a shiny new penny winking at him.

The tangents I could manage, it was the fact that we were working in reverse that I needed to get used to. Scouting for me had always been about looking for clues from the screenplay—discovering locations aimed to thrill the director. It could take weeks of back and forth: close, closer, no-no, cold, wrong, cool, hot, hotter. *That's* the one. Sometimes the director was also the writer, but usually the location was the place to leave the writer persona behind and inhabit the story solely as the director. Not for Amir. The practical location was the muse; it held the puzzle pieces to complete the story. From these practical locations, the characters emerged. They would come out of cellar doors and airport hangars, taking on heft and auditioning for him.

I sliced cherry tomatoes in the back seat and tossed them in with the rest. I needed to prod Amir along from the salad parking lot party. The sun was going down and we had to find a hotel before dark. He drizzled olive oil over the mixed greens, juiced a fresh lemon, and added a dramatic toss of chunky kosher salt. Then we ate on the tailgate while confused Los Angelenos watched our sunset picnic. Beat this, Johnny Rocket.

In the roles we played on this trip, Amir and I could have been polar opposites. He was an expelled Iranian, transformed into a naturalized United States citizen, and a renaissance man full of fire and drive. I was the listener, weighing all the options before making a decision, until I cleared a path to let the talent through like a personal bodyguard. Amir peppered his sentences with barking passion. "Gretchen! We embrace the day! The beautiful road ahead!" Amir charmed everyone he met, and I sat back to watch passion play itself out.

Three months earlier, I had been on the periphery of his circle, impervious to his girlish giggle and his stories of a New York in the '80s. I had first met Amir at his birthday dinner, when he was surrounded by a lair of mostly female admirers in an East Village restaurant. Three steps down into a private back room, I took a half-step backwards, but it was too late. I was spotted, and my friend Lisa whispered my name in Amir's ear.

"Gretchen—you must join us!" Amir waved me in as if we were old friends. "You've come!" Too late, I had to commit.

Off the bat, his gregarious energy reminded me of my college playwrighting professor Alonso Alegria. All the hot shot drama professors had been on sabbatical the year I declared my major. Alonso had taken me under his wing, encouraging me to write, to workshop my plays, and to submit into competitions. For a while I felt important, and it was Alonso who helped me find a place behind the scenes. I had to be careful not to assign Alonso's personality onto Amir, the way you might spot a TV star in the grocery store and mistake them for an old friend—one who used to hang out in your living room every Thursday night at 8 p.m.

Before this trip West, I popped one of Amir's films after the next into my VHS deck—an indie film binge in the name of research. Like anyone who watched these movies, I ached for this cinematic 1980s New York; a city full of movie theaters and gritty rooftop romances. But I had no idea I was signing up for a road trip film school when I accepted the job.

Now Amir leaned forward in the passenger seat, meditating on every barnyard animal and shifting cloudscape. Even the mile markers fascinated him. He snapped photos in rapid sequence like a paparazzi for the dusty terrain.

"Junkyard!" Amir shouted. "Gretchen, this is the place!" Amir pointed to one of the Post-its on his California map and I veered off the highway as I followed signs for a silver mine.

Two brothers in their eighties greeted Amir with hugs and tears. There were snapshots, and a tour of their Disneyland-like wonder—acres of collectible junk. I wandered off on my own, exploring old tractor wheels and pyramids of stacked stovepipes. Then I saw Amir behind a sculpture as the wind caught the flaps of a metal wheel, and it spun in a circle causing a metal frog to leap. Amir was jotting down notes. I could tell his mind was racing with a new scene; his childlike curiosity at home amongst the whimsy.

Where did his ideas come from? Did he just pick them out of thin air? How does anyone creative generate original thoughts? I had been told that Michael Jackson was inspired to write the opening to *Billie Jean* when he coasted down a hill on his ten-speed bicycle. Was it just the right clue at the right time? Or was there a method to it; a ritual to coax more lyrics or more story? I thought it must be like any other muscle that you exercised. It's just that not everyone has the luxury of time and circumstance to flex it.

I sympathized with Amir, but I couldn't empathize. If I ever did direct a film, I wouldn't direct my own material. I would need distance, with the knowledge that someone smarter than me was behind the bones of the story. Over the years, I watched writers direct their own scripts. These were brilliant artists who memorized the landscape, knew actors' craft, and mastered storytelling. They marinated in their stories for years, sometimes decades. But it wasn't a perfect formula and it often failed. Where were the checks and balances when the writer was also the director, the producer, and sometimes the source of the financing? Who was going to say *no* or *let's try something else*? If power means no obstacles, then this was indeed power, but at what cost? No one will be sober enough to drive the movie home if everyone gets drunk at the party.

After a full day of driving and junkyard surveillance, we stopped at a hotel just off the highway. The nonchalant desk clerk checked us in in that mundane way they do, but behind him a set of twenty-foot-high drapes were tied back like proscenium curtains, and a gigantic exotic terrarium loomed. Two sides of the hotel were connected by a theatrical glass greenhouse. The center featured an amoeba-shaped swimming pool and a circle of palm trees bowing down to the lobby.

In my room, a sliding door faced the terrarium. I wrestled it open to let the steamy jungle air in. Were those birds in there? An entire ecosystem existed here. I wondered if they had counted on the birds in the original plan. I pulled the sliding door shut and clicked on a blast of air conditioning, with filtered relief coming in from what I hoped was outside air.

In the beginning, every hotel room is perfection. A blank slate with no flaws. It's an invitation to start again, and to reinvent yourself. A gravity-defying, pillow-topped mattress pulls you into the embrace of deep sleep. A coffee pot with a modest selection of single serving ground beans and a mini fridge with just the things you need (and maybe a few of the things you don't in the minibar). All your requirements reduced to three hundred square feet. For one night, life is sublime.

But in the morning light, the flaws of the room begin to creep out. The threadbare curtains and coffee stains on the carpet. The mold where the shower walls meet the floor. The coffee pot churning out muck and the creamer pods whose contents have never seen the inside of a cow.

A tweak of anxiety jolted me awake in the hotel, reminding me that my big ordeal—my identity theft—was still real. I had no doubt that a new batch of collection letters were being sorted at the Brooklyn post office and thrown in a bag for my address. But I couldn't do anything about it from here. For now, my Williamsburg cat sitter took care of all that by tossing the mail onto the growing mound on the kitchen table.

I dialed the cat sitter to check in. No answer, but his machine launched into a detailed message in a heavy New York accent: "I do dogs and birds, whatever you've got. Dogs are five bucks a day. Cats are extra. Cats are extra on a *per cat* basis." There was more. "So, let's say you got one cat: that's ten bucks a day. Two cats: that's twenty bucks a day. Let's say you've got three..." And so on with higher denominations of cat calculations and instructions on how to page him for pet emergencies. I hung up before the beep. He had my number if there was a cat problem.

Las Vegas wasn't on Amir's original itinerary because we followed the detours in his imagination. And when I learned that a new scene was being conceived in Las Vegas, we set out to find it.

I rewound my working roll of color negative and replaced it with black and white stock. Even in a still photograph in the daylight, Vegas pulsated with lights too bright for Kodak color film. One direction of the Vegas strip was shut down for the afternoon while a crane erected a two-thirds scale replica of the Eiffel Tower. I snapped a shot of the process and the replica's tilted spire.

It was all money, show business and glamour but at the end of the Vegas drag, we turned a corner and landed in a part of town that you don't see in the tourist books. Liquor stores were busy at noon, and prostitutes marched around in broad daylight. There were no marquee lights and Trump hotels here. This was the seedier side; rife for the next scheduled knock-down to clear the way for more casinos and designer hotels. Amir hopped out to take a 360 degree photo panorama and I imagined the real estate moguls salivating for these lots. We turned back in the direction of the Eiffel Tower and settled into a motel off the strip. It was within walking distance to the casinos for the few that did walk.

I snuck out at night for a fix of fries, a Big Mac, and a chocolate shake, slurping them down in the parking lot. Halfway through my Big Mac, I stopped, dropped it back into its cardboard carton, and tossed it in the garbage. Grease and guilt would permeate the car until the next day, and I committed myself to parking lot salads from this night forward. Amir-style.

I brushed the residue off my lap and pulled down the mirror to check my lipstick before heading over to the Bellagio. This would be the Vegas I knew from films like *Bugsy* and *Rain Man* with the likes of Dustin Hoffman and Warren Beatty drinking martinis and sharing a craps table next to me.

That's not the Bellagio I found. I entered through an automated door into a haze of cigarette smoke and an infinite line-up of slot machines. Hard-boiled women—and some men—with mason jars of quarters were parked on stools. They loaded coins in and pulled levers holding out for the moment of *ca-ching*. From the size of the ash on the end of their cigarettes, it didn't look like anyone had scored lately.

Twenty-four hours was enough time for Amir to get what he needed from Vegas. By sunrise, we were already thirty miles east of the city and approaching the Hoover Dam. We emerged from the back roads and grabbed a few photos before we drove across the dam and took in this ominous structure.

Pushing on through Sedona, a retirement oasis dropped into an awesome landscape of glacial red rock that was decorated with nature's striations of pink and red. I lifted my camera to try to grab a shot, but it was impossible to do it justice with my lens. There were forces at play here; rumors of a vortex phenomenon or cosmic energy that inspired great healing and self-exploration.

It was jarring to see new condos going up here, all within striking distance of these geological icons: Bell Rock, Cathedral Rock, and Coffee Pot Rock. Spanish-tiled rooftops formed a systematic staircase of homes and shopping centers that attempted to fit in with the rock formations. Here, developers staked a permanent claim. It was a rare moment for Amir when he showed no signs of inspiration, so we moved on. The sun hit the horizon behind us taking its sweet time on the way down.

The further east we traveled, the more remote and run down the Western towns became. We pulled up behind the town saloon for an appointment with the manager of Old Tucson City. The floating heads of Kiefer Sutherland and Emilio Estevez were high up on a billboard, showing off a recent Hollywood Western shot here. In an earlier era, Gene Wilder and Harrison Ford had swaggered through these same saloon doors when they filmed *The Frisco Kid*.

We walked through the schoolhouse where Melissa Gilbert and Michael Landon shot during *Little House on the Prairie*. Now, the town was an active tourist destination. There was still the occasional week or two of filming exteriors for a movie, but filmmaking and TV had slowed down here. Creatively, a set-up like this could be a dream for a director's vision, but there was no financial incentive to film here now. All the crews, stunt people, and horses had plenty of work at home in Los Angeles.

We headed north again, and Amir popped a Santana cassette into the deck. Along these infinite stretches of highway, I propped my eyelids open and my right foot weighed onto the gas pedal. Amir gave me a look—if I drove over sixty-five, he would miss what he came here for. A single tumbleweed rolled in front of the car, and I eased up on the brakes.

Up a mountain, the speed limit increased to 85 mph but even the motorcycles around us weren't afraid to hit 90, or even 95. After we passed through Truth or Consequences in New Mexico, we flipped over the top and began to descend the mountain. Everyone flew down the hill faster, even with the road sign warnings: twisted lines and arrows, threats about low gear, jake-brakes, and emergency off-ramps.

Two hours into Texas, we were the only car in a long stretch of the Chihuahuan Desert heading towards Marfa, the fictional home of Amir's heroine. We were already two dry dusty airports and one Western town into the day when a giant white balloon took over the horizon. What the hell was that? Amir was sleeping and I cleared my throat. If I was going to be abducted by aliens, I would need Amir to bear witness. He came to, mumbling something about weather balloons. But this white mass seemed more clandestine, like a spy operative. I hadn't seen another car for miles, and I wondered if we had lost our way. I checked the gas needle and the position of the sun. A clearing the size of four football fields lay ahead. Four, maybe five balloons were tethered to the ground by massive concrete cylinders.

Maybe this is what the Marfans are spotting at night, I thought.

"This isn't it," said Amir. "The Mystery Lights? They're east of Marfa." He was reading my mind now. We were that old married couple; the ones finishing each other's sentences.

The Mystery Marfa Lights were legend. For every citizen, there was a different story behind their origin. Pragmatists dismissed them as campfires or flickering headlights, reflected in the sky. But we settled on the story we read in the guidebook; they were the wandering spirit of an Apache chief executed by Mexican Rurales.

We made a loop around Marfa and its neighborhoods of one-story adobe homes. Amir shook his head; his characters weren't showing up here either. The Marfa in Amir's story was an innocent landscape; a modest town with working class homes and family farms. A town that was home to Elizabeth Taylor and James Dean during the making of *Giant*. But the new Marfa was a hip escape for celebrities like Kim Basinger—writers and artists who parachuted in and out on a whim. We continued east in search of the next airport, leaving Marfa before the Mystery Lights had a chance to dance in the sky.

Over a broad plate of huevos rancheros and coffee, we met our first casting director candidate in Austin. She hawked a pile of headshots representing the local talent. If we could manage to find all our locations within striking distance of the city, we could cast most of the roles here. Amir presented her with a collage of images pasted into a wire bound notebook—an homage to each of his characters. She took the notebook and flipped through it further, beyond the character portraits and into swatches of dusty colors and desert textures. Then she flipped through the section on the airports, Western towns, and the images of his characters inhabiting them. Here, something clicked for her, something that hadn't registered when she only had the script as her guide. She had seen it all, read it all, but this was something new. To be fair, what layperson ever got excited about the blueprints for a house? The thing that could make this film exceptional lay between the lines of Amir's writing.

Amir retired to his hotel room early, and I sat in the lobby flipping through an Austin Chronicle—the go-to paper for local music. "Screw it," I said, out loud. It was my first time in this city, and I was going to find some of that live music.

In a club downtown, I focused on the band and drew slow sips of a warming beer, trying to feel unselfconscious about being alone. I would never see these people again. Why did it matter that I was by myself at a bar? With this simple thought, my jaw released its clutch, and I took on the role of Bar Patron #6.

There was one last Western town on our list before catching a plane to LaGuardia. We rolled through stone gates in the town of Luck, just west of Austin. This was Willie Nelson's sprawling ranch, Willieville, built for the filming of *Red Headed Stranger*. Imagine, building a town on your estate so you can make a movie in your own back yard? We took a self-guided tour around the grounds. Amir identified spots where Carson McCullers's *Ballad of a Sad Café* was filmed, and I added it to my long list of unwatched films. Then he pulled out his spiral notebook to sketch the details of the smaller buildings and the ranch's layout.

In Willieville, all signs pointed to the ubiquitous Western town center: the swinging door saloon. We hung back when we saw a few figures in conversation at the far end of the room, but the bartender waved us in and poured a generous round of ice water.

"Darn, you just missed Willie," he said, jutting his chin up the hill. "Mr. Nelson was sitting on that very stool not ten minutes ago." I expected the bartender played this line on all the visitors, but I still got a shivery sense that greatness had just left the building.

And it was just the right note to hit as we wrapped up Amir's trip.

I took a plastic baggie of film rolls from the Southwest scout to be processed at Spectra Labs in the East Village. A liquid chemical smell came from the machine churning out wet prints behind the countertop. A glorious, toxic smell—the smell of photochemistry. I put a separate batch on my personal account for the shots I'd taken with my Pentax K-1000, some photos for my own collection. These would be printed with a matte finish (never glossy) with white borders.

Then I headed toward the West Village, stopping at Dojo Restaurant for a less than satisfying bowl of brown rice and vegetables. It stared up at me, lifeless and sad. In Texas, there would have been something fried and filling on top, accompanied by a selection of a dozen hot-sauce brands. I shook a bottle of salty soy sauce over the rice to drown out the dullness. Unemployed again, I was free to make my own mistakes. Maybe I'd take up cooking again because it would have to be better than this.

Heading up Eighth Avenue, there she was with those eyes and those cheekbones, it could only be her; Debbie Harry was walking towards me.

"Debbie, hi!" I smiled and pointed to myself, an awkward habit I still had, sparing the person who might not remember my face. "It's Gretchen, from *Heavy*. Upstate?"

"Oh yeah!!" She at least pretended to remember me. "Jim's film, how's Jim?" she asked. It was just a nicety;

she likely had more contact with Jim than I had since the film wrapped. "Hey, you should come by the Knitting Factory later. I'm playing there with some friends."

I hopped on the L train feeling giddy, like I'd been asked to the dance by a big shot. I hadn't been to the Knitting Factory since it had moved from Houston Street, a claustrophobic lower level with a ceiling of stitched together sweaters hovering overhead. No one dared lift a lighter or the place would have spontaneously combusted. But now it had shifted to a Tribeca home.

I had helped make *Heavy,* but the film would never be mine the way it was Jim's, Liv's or Debbie's. My job had been to help get the structure up, but I wasn't the rebar, bricks, and mortar of it. When the film was complete, the actors were still in it, the director's house was built. But the scaffolding was pulled down, loaded onto the flatbed, and moved to the next job. Transient and expendable.

I entered Columbia University's gates for Amir's gallery-opening six months later, on a night where cold rain slapped the campus pathway. Over twenty-five large images filled the walls to the vaulted ceilings. The room was packed with Amir's friends, fans, and colleagues. Amir, of course, held center court in the gallery. He hadn't been able to make his film yet, but he had made a room full of beautiful portraits and he was already planning a new film.

In the gallery, I took a step toward a shattered black and white photograph of a woman's face; her image broken into a thousand pieces. It was like a mosaic but made from a true human image. Amir stood beside me and told me how he created it: photographed, left out to dry on his back steps, smashed, and rephotographed repeatedly to a haunting effect. He tagged it with a green dot for me.

Amir did finally make *Sound Barrier,* and I expect he made exactly the film he set out to make. And the portrait he set aside for me now hangs in my home office, on the wall above my writing desk.

| Chapter 9 |

THE JUST-RELEASED-FROM-JAIL-AND-NOW-WHAT ADVENTURE

BUFFALO, NEW YORK 1997

Buffalo '66

Producers make lists; it's what we do. We make lists of cast hopefuls, lists of editors we'd like to hire, lists of pros, and lists of cons. We make lists for the lists we need to make.

The self-help gurus tell you to figuratively drop your list of worries into a shoebox, put a lid on it, slide it under your bed, and forget about it until the morning. But this one kept creeping out of its box, tugging at my throat, and haunting me. I was flying solo without the help of a production manager, and my entire coordinating team was threatening to quit.

Sleep was still nonexistent, so I finally gave in at 3 a.m. and wrote down a new *to do* list.

1. *Deal with the Mickey Rourke thing*
2. *Snow guys re: testing foam with firefighters*
3. *Wig$$ for Angelica*

4. *Angelica Huston lighting clause*
5. *Bond company—new budget*
6. *Beatrix glitter shoes*
7. *Bowling Alley scout for fake snow*
8. *Christina Ricci mother call (or agent? Manager?)*
9. *Reversal film lab test results—projection? (the Bono turnaround time)*

There was another list; the list of reasons for not taking the job in Buffalo.

Reason one: I had seen the Tylenol commercials—the ones where the snow blew sideways. Pedestrians held umbrellas like futile shields that were sucked up and churned out in a mangled mess. People lost their footing in six-foot snowdrifts, and the wind howled on a punishing soundtrack. It was the lake effect rolling off Lake Erie that would pummel anyone choosing to live in Buffalo after watching that commercial. Even though we were approaching March, winter was the longest season in Western New York. I was not good at driving in snow and ice—no one really is. I envisioned an impending principal photography crisis: our camera truck slammed into a snowbank, our cast at a standstill as the tires spun out under their minivan seats.

Reason two: We had just four weeks to prep the film before shooting, otherwise we would lose vital cast members to another movie. *Buffalo '66* was not a complicated film, but we needed at least six weeks of prep to do it right.

Reason three: This was supposed to be my *Year of No*. Or at least my *Year of Not Saying Yes to Everything*. I was saying *yes* all year and working non-stop. I was leapfrogging from the Good Machine feature to Vietnam, across a long swath of Southwest territory and back to New York.

And after that Southwest scout, I was escorted out of my league and up to The Carlyle Hotel penthouse for an interview with Ed Pressman. This was *The* Ed Pressman: producer of *Wall Street, City Hall,* and *The* (infamous) *Crow*. His suite of gold-trimmed doorways and velvet-upholstered chairs made me wonder if I should back out of the room bowing.

The meeting landed me on *Two Girls and A Guy,* a quick-but-intense film that James Toback directed. During lunch breaks I would head to the production office to make calls, leaving Toback and his star, Robert Downey Jr., the run of the set. They would write new scenes together in the set's bathroom. Robert would shout out new lines of dialogue from the dry bathtub, fully clothed. It was Robert's first film after his final stint in rehab and Pressman was willing to pay the price to insure him. Robert was followed around by an escort each morning, to ensure the production (or more importantly the production's insurance) that his urine was clean. Clean urine, we shot. Dirty urine and the plug would be pulled.

From the production office, I lined up my calls and a film technician sidled up next to me, waiting to use the phone. He lay out his Zig-Zags and a stash from a plastic baggie and proceeded to roll a joint.

"Really?" The audacity, I thought. "Here? One floor above a drug addict?"

He stopped mid-roll and glared at me, probably more annoyed that I screwed up what looked to be the creation of an award-winning spliff. I was sure that any proximity to drugs was going to ruin the shoot, that even a waft of second-hand smoke could show up on Robert's urine test and we'd all blow the most expensive insurance policy I had ever bound.

We made it through wrap. There were just a few bruised egos and no urine incidents. But I had enough. I was exhausted, and I didn't need a fourth reason to avoid Buffalo.

I took the *Buffalo '66* meeting because I remembered that an unemployment check would barely cover my Williamsburg rent. And it was never a good idea to pass up a meeting. The New York film industry is as huge as it is tiny; every mistake could be one degree of separation from success.

Over sparkling water at the Soho Grand Hotel's mezzanine, Chris Hanley, the producer of *Two Girls*, introduced me to the *Buffalo '66* director, Vincent Gallo. I knew all about Vincent from his downtown chic reputation. As a Basquiat sidekick and a permanent CBGB's fixture, his cronies considered him the uncrowned prince of New York's underground scene. He had a wiry presence, skin-tight jeans, and unruly curls of brown hair. His eyes popped so fiercely blue that it was hard to look anywhere else.

Vincent's script painted a beautiful picture. It was a story of lost souls, unlikely bonds, and distracted parents, culminating in revenge for an icon's failure. He had another film after this one and it would be even better, he said. I was thinking Vincent missed his calling; he should have been an auctioneer or a carnival barker. I could barely get a word in edgewise.

"You say you're not sure, but you'll wanna do it once you've read it." Vincent held out the script with its oversized brass fasteners folded back on themselves. "I'm not gonna work with anyone else but you. They keep trying to set me up with creepy people." By creepy, he probably meant people who would say *no* to him when he wanted more of something. I looked like a *yes* person.

Buffalo '66 was centered across the script's front page. Once I held it, it felt like mine. But I heard my jaw clicking inside my head when I tried to speak. Was it telegraphing an SOS from the future? I took the script home but made no commitments.

Over the phone with me, Vincent told me about his disturbed state. His head hung over a bowl of soup in the corner booth at Kasia's Restaurant, a Polish diner on Bedford Avenue, twirling noodles around his spoon. His hair was unwashed, and he hadn't slept in days; but this was normal for Vincent. He did some of his best thinking when he was sleep deprived. He stared down the cooling soup, but dropped his spoon into bowl and walked to the phone bank on the street corner. It would be his fourth call to me inside of an hour.

"Why do you have to be so cruel?" he said while etching his name into the pay phone's metal coin box. He used the diner's dull knife to complete the "*ent*" of Vincent where he'd left off on the last call. "Why won't you come to Buffalo to make his movie? Don't you know if you pass this up, your career will wither? It will be a slow, low-budget, indie movie fade-out." He dragged out every word, every vowel, prolonging the agony. "You have to say yes. Until then, I'm on a hunger strike. I'll camp out at this diner. I'll survive on chicken noodle soup. OK, maybe some Matzo ball soup, but with noodles."

If I wanted to, I could hang my head out my window and catch a glimpse of him at the phonebooth. He might have been telling the truth, but I shrugged it off. I had my three reasons. I had to remind myself that Vincent was only fixated on me because he thought I was a pushover.

I told Vincent *no*. The phone cord twisted around my fingers, its snags and coils memorizing our dialogue. Once I said no to him and offered a final goodbye, I felt the clench in my jaw begin to surrender. An exorcism of the built-up stress from the past year. No longer a victim of the eighteen-hour day, and free from the 4:30 a.m. alarm bell.

I popped a Tae Bo VHS into the deck to work up a sweat with its guru, Billy Blanks. Resolved for my new mission: getting into the best shape of my life.

Then I heard a buzz at the door; a production assistant coming up the stairs to pick up the script for another producer. Was there only one copy of this script? I wiped the coffee mug stains off the cover, handed it over with a smile that probably looked maniacal—a warning of sorts—and shut the door. The exorcism was complete. In the freeze frame on TV, the guru threw me an upper cut.

But I was too restless to enjoy unemployment. By the end of the week, I'd convinced myself I'd never work again if I didn't take the job. I said *yes* to Vincent, abandoned the cats again, and moved to Buffalo for fifty-six days.

When Vincent and I showed up at Buffalo City Hall, we were escorted into Mayor Masiello's corner office. As I reached forward to shake the mayor's hand, I noticed a protective plate of glass covering his oversized desk. Team photos and family mementos were encased in it, trapped behind a glass veneer. Masiello towered over both of us with his former basketball-player's frame, but he gave us a warm reception. When Vincent launched into the story of the film, Masiello threw his head back and let out a booming laugh.

"A classic Buffalo ending," he said, one of two Buffalo natives in on the joke. I hoped that he thought the film could take Buffalo's image up a notch, transcending those Tylenol commercials. He scribbled down some names, providing a list of contacts for our production offices, and he promised to get the word out to business owners.

That's when I felt the moment; that beat when the meeting had reached its natural end. It was the gut feeling you get when you meet with a busy person and it's time to make your exit. Movies are fun but they're our priority, not theirs. But Vincent wound up for his big whammy. *This is not the time Vincent, not the time to bring up your politics*. He proceeded to blurt out his own Republican-leaning voting record, looking to spark something. The mayor nodded, but the conversation ended there. On cue, a red button lit up on his phone. He stood, graced us with another disarming, *that's enough now* chuckle, and shook our hands.

Outside, the cold Lake Erie air slammed us and I couldn't help but think we'd missed an opportunity with the mayor by overstaying our welcome. We might need to call in a Hail Mary in a couple weeks. What was the point of coming all the way here, flying cast and crew across New York, if we couldn't capture all that was quintessentially Buffalo?

Before I could unpack in my hotel room, we had to move into our production office just three blocks east. The building was a former stretch of connecting storefronts, faded wall-to-wall carpeting degraded to threads where office chairs used to roll. It was cheap, so it was perfect.

Our office storefront shared a wall with a coffee shop with an unsettling jazz soundtrack. Its floors were lined in overlapping area rugs and flea market couches, complete with fleas. And the coffee beans were bitter. But with enough milk, it was a luxurious brew. We held most of our meetings here, fueling the long days.

Buffalo was having a love affair with Styrofoam. Containers full of take-out meals were stacked beside my desk. I couldn't eat until at least 5 p.m. when the phone stopped ringing on the East Coast and when Los Angeles took its lunch hour. If too much time passed, the meals would join the leaning tower of Styrofoam boxes in the refrigerator. Most of it would go straight to the trash.

The wastebasket wasn't emptied every day, so the food piled up. I gagged, catching a glimpse of the overflowing trash. My ear cradled the receiver in an awkward tilt with my shoulder hunched up to lock it in. I convinced yet another crew member to abandon New York and join us. I was on a mission to finalize four more heads of department before I could leave my desk. Looking toward Vincent's office door, it occurred to me that I was using the same tactics Vincent had used on me.

I stood up to stretch and continued my Buffalo pitch, (the culture, the food, you will be surprised!) when my Lee corduroys slid down my hips a few inches. I tugged them up and pulled two loops together with a piece of string, making a mental note to borrow a belt from the wardrobe stock that accumulated in racks in another corner. Even if Buffalo lacked other cities' redeeming qualities in 1997, this was only a fifty-four-day commitment. I wasn't scratching tally marks into my hotel wall, but anyone could make it through fifty days, anywhere.

Except, apparently, me.

I'm jealous of smokers. Smokers have an internal ticking time bomb, rousing them from their desks every hour. They step outside into the sunshine and breathe deeply. Sure, it's a fiery stick of ground up fiberglass and arsenic. But it's like a meditation because when you smoke; you need to inhale. In lieu of a cigarette break, I walked to the bank to deposit my paycheck. And there on the screen was a glimmer of hope. My bank balance was finally healthy enough to pay back my sister's loan.

At 9 p.m., I finished a long call with the bond company, offering assurances we were on track and able to pull this off. I pushed back my chair, salivating over the thought of our crew grabbing spicy chicken wings at the local tavern. My appetite was making a comeback.

A crackerjack group of creatives from Los Angeles and New York rounded out the crew of local talent. We worked with a local scout who had connections all over town. He opened doors to bowling alleys, the jail, and a handful of other key locations. But it was another skill to lock locations and manage our accelerated schedule. What we needed was a closer. We needed Tibi.

I don't know why I didn't think to ask Tibi to come earlier. Maybe I thought she'd balk like everyone else. Or

I thought I could get it done without her. I made the call and thankfully she was able to come up the following day. The local scout and I settled into the coffee shop with Tibi and Vincent for a debrief. Every idiosyncrasy about the script and this town was summed up in one long, caffeinated session.

And a match was made. Vincent and Tibi laughed with the same staccato, like a weird little a cappella duet. Maybe it was my sleep deprivation or the fact that I subsisted on leftover chicken wings, but I was not feeling in on the jokes. *Look at me,* I thought, *taking a step back, becoming the observer of this new bond.* It didn't matter if I was the odd man out; the movie would be the beneficiary, and that's what mattered. Wasn't it?

En route to scout a bowling alley, we passed a movie theater with a grand facade, *Closed for Good,* disintegrating on its marquee. The city seemed to have a rash of defunct cinemas, as did the rest of the country.

Just the week before, my mother had clipped an article for me about the demolition of the Showplace Theater back home. They were clearing out debris in the building and discovered a decomposed male corpse slumped in the balcony seats. Twenty years earlier, that same movie theater had saved me. During the summer after my father died, my uncle showed up with a fistful of eight tickets for each cousin to see *Star Wars*. It was that summer, the one transporting me to a galaxy far, far away, that I began to heal. It had all started at the Showplace. Now there was only one option for movies near my hometown, the Garden Theater. It had spooky vaulted ceilings where you had to duck to avoid swooping bats at the midnight shows.

Back in New York, the movie houses had always been a respite from sweaty summers and icy winters. And a good place to bide your time between jobs. I checked myself into a double feature at Theater 80 on St. Mark's, where the seats were raked at such a high angle that you could almost touch the screen. I frequented the elegant red velour seats of The Biograph on West 57th (where you might need to grab your popcorn and move down a few rows when the daytime perverts inched closer). Or down the hidden escalator to the Sony Theaters across from Lincoln Center, where I could get lost in any French film. If a movie was good enough, I would see it alone during the day and then again with a group of friends that same night. Before starting a new job, I would stockpile movies like a squirrel, not knowing when I'd be back.

Angelica Huston, Christina Ricci and Mickey Rourke were cast on *Buffalo '66*, their contracts and travel plans finalized. I recognized the excitement Vincent had about Christina accepting the role. It was the same thrill Jim Mangold had when Liv Tyler agreed to play the lead in *Heavy*. It brought a full dimension to a character who had only existed on the page before. Vincent worked with the costume designer on Christina's shoes and dress, sketching out every detail of her costume like a paper-doll collection.

Our cinematographer arrived one week after Tibi landed. This stretch of time felt like an on-location time warp. We hit the road to show him the film's locations. We considered film stock, cameras, and crews. As a UK-based cinematographer, he was open to the crew and houses we recommended. Our biggest challenge was the film stock.

Eastman Kodak, located one hour from us in Rochester, no longer created reversal stock in anything longer than a one-hundred-foot rolls. That was just over a minute of footage per roll, too short for dialogue scenes and long takes. And Vincent wanted to shoot every scripted, daytime exterior scene with reversal stock.

I reached out to our Kodak representative to request a specially produced batch of one-thousand-foot reversal stock rolls. I worked with our rep, Bob Mastronardi, for years and this was a big ask. On *Two Girls*, I had sent Bob a Tiffany's silver rattle when his first child was born. Maybe that good-will gesture would come around now.

The reversal stock colors are beautiful with washed out blues and bleeding reds, but it's an unstable stock until it's processed in a chemical bath. Unprocessed, the ink might squish around. This can be a cool effect, but you still want to get material to the lab as quickly as possible.

The only lab that would work with the stock and treat it the way we wanted was in Washington D.C.; the lab that serviced the National Archives. It was a big risk for an unstable stock and a bonded film that needed its dailies processed and screened quickly. When Spike Lee shot with reversal on his films, he struck a stable print from it, treating it like a negative, or *cross-processing*. We were going to treat our shot-stock like the print itself, so we'd need to strike a negative from our prints. It was a costly, time-consuming process. On top of that, given the transport to the DC lab and the less-than-urgent approach there, we would not see our dailies in the editing room for a week or more.

Vincent and the cinematographer got into a groove with locations, working with the storyboard artist and sketching their own scenarios. They built a shot list; a descriptive breakdown of all the angles and sizes they'd want to cover within each scene. Shot listing this early in pre-production meant there would be seamless communication with the crew. With so little prep time, it was a huge leg-up.

But then came the giant disconnect. You know that moment in your college movie theater when the projector seizes up and the bulb's heat burns through the frame? A burnt hole bleeds into the screen and the audience gives a collective groan. A flustered student in the projection booth scrambles to fix it. You've seen this movie at least six times (was it *The Wall* or *The Big Chill*?), the school owns a print (probably why the abused celluloid jams in the projector). You could just go back to your dorm and eat pizza with your hallmates for the third time this week. Or you could stick around to see how quickly the splice can be made. How quickly the reels could be mounted, threaded, and spinning again.

We hit that kind of moment, the moment where the hole burned through the print. And we screeched to a halt.

It wasn't the film projection test that caused the disconnect here; that was successful—maybe too successful. In a reversal of, well, reversal, Vincent decided he wanted to shoot the entire film with reversal stock. With this one decision, the perfect shot list, the perfect schedule, and the technical crew we had lined up began to disintegrate. Eastman Kodak would need to work nights and weekends to create enough stock for our film. Our budget would have to absorb the blow of Kodak's overtime. I ran the calculation and swallowed hard.

One thing I've learned about revealing bad news to directors and bond companies was to always have solutions ready in your next breath. Bowling alley location fell through? We have two great options, and here's why they're even better. Lost your best costume designer prospect? That's OK, we found someone local, so we'll save travel costs which means more money for shipping costumes from New York.

Here was today's bad news: The cinematographer left us a handwritten resignation note, ripped from a yellow legal pad. He was already on a plane back to London. We were just two weeks away from our first day of filming, and I had no solutions for this one. With no brilliant stand-in waiting in the wings, I lay in bed wrestling with the drama. Like a child's doll, my eyes clicked open when I sat up. There would be no sleep.

Vincent took the news well. In fact, it seemed to inject him with energy. He was the one to call the bond company because he knew what to do. He would have his friend Lance Acord drop out of the sky to shoot the film. Lance was known for innovative Spike Jonze music videos and sexy Nike commercials, but he had never shot a feature film. He didn't work in the world where nearly four pages of dialogue and action were filmed each day. He didn't know the secret language of character arcs and through lines. He wasn't on The List.

The bond company took the news in stride too. Chris, the producer, just shrugged it off.

"Well, we'll have to make it work, I guess," he said. "These things happen!" Then, as if he were Robert Evans, he spun some yarn about a larger fiasco on another project, which I think was an effort to make me feel better. I was wondering if trouble had followed Chris to Buffalo. Or if trouble had followed me from Vietnam.

Was I the only one who saw principal photography surging toward us like a ten-foot wave off Lake Erie? We could not push our start date under any circumstances. We would lose our actors, which was a worse scenario than losing our cinematographer. Lance flew from LA to Buffalo via Logan (the fastest route, because apparently Buffalo is not the center of the universe and therefore not an airport hub). We scrapped the old equipment plan and put together an order with Clairmont, Lance's camera house in Los Angeles. This left us less time to negotiate, but also less time wasted with the back and forth. My mind snagged on all the overages I would have to absorb: the flights, new crew from LA, and the cross-country, expedited equipment shipments.

But with a few minor replacements, Lance was happy with the same camera crew we had already hired. He began shot listing with Vincent. We shot a test, and the lab turned it around in time for us to screen it and make adjustments.

Deb the local teamster made an Olympic-worthy parallel parking maneuver in a twenty-four-foot truck. She unloaded the first batch of Kodak reversal stock, waving off the production assistants who hovered over the cargo. Glorious cardboard boxes glided onto the office floor from her hand-truck, a yellow and red "K" embossed on each box of film cans. It was pure gold.

Day One: We were, only by coincidence, shooting the first scene of the script. It's a luxury to film a movie in-sequence, but the luxury ended there. Everything else would have to be grouped together by location, by cast availability, or by weather. In this scene, Vincent's character, Billy, was leaving the jail on a quintessential only-in-Buffalo cold, snowy day. But in real life, there was no snow in Buffalo. In any other year, it would still be smushed high against the jail's walls.

A special effects team from Minneapolis drove to Buffalo through the night; the same team responsible for the iconic snow in *Fargo*. They showed off the formula in a vessel affixed to the snout of a fire hose, an environmentally sensitive option we chose in a test. On the other side of the hose, foam snow flew out and dissolved into the parking lot within a few hours. We were framed near a few hydrants and two local engines loaded with firefighters stood by, eager to help spread this fake winter wonderland. There was another contraption rigged from three cherry pickers to spout snow from above. Mole fans, with giant, metallic rotary blades, were added for wind. What we had created was the Tylenol commercial—my first reason for not coming to Buffalo.

Ben Gazzara made me late for call. He arrived at the more upscale cast hotel, housing that was a step above the utilitarian bones of the crew's Hilton digs. I admit that I was a little starstruck. His performances in the Cassavetes films were one of the reasons I was here in Buffalo. But

Ben scared me a little, in a way that I knew would be great for his character and for the film. He maintained that same look I recognized from those films, that knowing smile and winking eyes that said, *you should know better*. There was a great Cassavetes line: *the greatest location in the world is the human face*, and Cassavetes absolutely found it in Ben's.

Ben clung to three cassette tapes and begged me to find him a portable deck. I drove with him to the production office and sat him next to the coordinators who chatted with him for ten precious minutes that they could not spare. This freed me up to accept the final red-line comments on the final cast contracts. It had been weeks of negotiating, and we'd landed on the final deal point demands like wig approvals and key lights. These were the agent's additions, clauses I had deleted, but they kept creeping back into the document. It was a war of attrition—and time, because I needed the actors to get their asses in seats on a plane to Buffalo—and the agent had won. I faxed my signatures out to the agency myself.

Rolling in on the fax machine was a letter with a booming IATSE letterhead. This was the union that would represent most of our crew if they were members, but most of them were still getting their footing in the industry or busy in the non-union commercial or music video world. I didn't have the stomach to read the letter yet, so I folded it up and put it in my back pocket. Then I grabbed our office cassette player, placed it below Ben's feet in the passenger seat, and drove him to his wardrobe fitting. The tapes might have been the way Ben learned his lines; they could have been music, meditation tutorials, or pre-recorded satanic rituals. I didn't ask.

Finally, I made it to set. The masterful work of the production designer and his crew had transformed the bowling alley. Christina's shoes sparkled against the red linoleum floor like Dorothy's had on those yellow bricks, showing off the talents of the costume designer. Vincent had drawn inspiration for the film's costumes from an Elmer Batters's photography book. Batters's images were saturated in deep oranges and browns. His models were stitched up in fishnet stockings, and casually draped across mid-century couches. A Batters book was an elegant addition to anyone's Taschen collection, but it was just as at home on a garage mechanic's wall.

Vincent looked through the camera's eyepiece, nodded his approval on the set up, flew in front of the camera, and hit his mark next to Christina.

"Action," he yelled, making the transition from director to actor. Then, it was like a spell was cast. The crew and equipment in the foreground became frozen, grey silhouettes against the actors' spotlight. No one dared to move until Vincent gave the signal to cut.

A production assistant tapped on my shoulder, which snapped me out of the reverie. "You're wanted in wardrobe. It's Ben."

Ben burst out of his fitting with the wardrobe assistant trailing behind him, still removing pins from his shirt. "I had an idea," Ben said. "I think we could make things a whole lot simpler if you were the only person I had to deal with. Like my go-to." He signaled with his hands, a narrow corridor we could walk down together. Good for him, not so good for me.

There's a reason for the structure and the hierarchy in filmmaking. It keeps the grey areas out of communication. You know who's above you and you take direction. You know who's under you, you manage them and make sure they have a plan for every moment of the day. Ben knew I was a producer, but so far he had only seen me stealing a cassette deck and chauffeuring him around downtown Buffalo. So, it was possible he assumed I didn't have much else to do. It was the assistant directing team—the ADs—who needed to manage Ben's daily dance. If I stepped in, I would blow the choreography. Costumes would make him look sharp, along with the make-up team applying all the right touches, just enough for his character. These were experts with carefully-honed skills. The thing I did was hire the right people and help them prioritize.

At our original introduction for *Buffalo '66,* Vincent had sketched out a car rig on the hotel's cocktail napkin. On the roof of the car was a giant hole, as if it had been peeled back by a can opener. This was an innovative approach to capturing a high angle inside the car. We would see the top of our actors' heads, and a specific dynamic when they turned toward or away from each other. We would have a double—a second, identical car on the side—allowing us to rig one car with a hostess tray attached to the side of the car, and a front hood mount for a variety of angles. The other car would drive around unencumbered with rigs, free to film from the street from a tripod, or "on sticks." If we scheduled it smartly, this method would help us cut back on a third of our rigging day. Now, on the second day of filming, the back of the napkin came to life as we filmed Vincent and Christina driving down the street in the can-opener car.

I dug my hands into the pockets of my pants, the same tan corduroys I'd been wearing all week, and felt the letter from IATSE. The pervasive tightness in my jaw now took up residence in my throat like a sore lump. As I read the letter, I pressed my fingers to my throat with just the right amount of pressure to alleviate the pain. IATSE was planning a set visit in a week and asked me to call them.

Before I could plan a response, Vincent hopped up and down and pulled me to the monitor. "I know, we're behind schedule, but look at this," he said, now pointing to the scene on the call sheet. "I'm hacking off this shot and combining these two scenes. It's gonna save the day. It's *genius*." This is what he does, he thrives when the pressure is on.

I slipped away from set and hunkered down with the accountant in his tiny back office to run the numbers; the cost of the union organizing us. There was no insurance to cover this kind of intervention, no risk management aside from a contingency on top of the budget. The accountant's calculator buzzed out a long roll of tape and he ripped it off with uncalled-for zeal. I pressed my fingers to my throat again but this time the trick no longer worked. It pounded in full force, with a life of its own. We ran a tape on several scenarios. We punched the worst-case scenario into our Movie Magic program to be sure, but the figure was higher than our remaining contingency. The union organization would shut us down.

I called the bond company and offered to quit. I saw my own mistakes—ones of omission—and I prepared to walk away and allow the film to go on without me. I respected the unions and the crews right to organize, but we were entering a new era and most films of this size would be flipped.

There were other reasons. Things I saw that pushed my buttons and caused me to think about whether I wanted to stay in this business. For these same reasons, several of my production office team had left. I had felt the weight of their absence, their unhappiness. The gnawing sound I heard was the clenching of my own teeth, but now I'd managed to bite the inside of my mouth. I dragged my finger along the inside of my cheek and felt a protruding raw line of flesh. When I looked at my finger, it was covered in blood.

The bond company asked me to reconsider. They said that the hard work was done, and now it was just a matter of completing principal photography. I had set up this production and laid the groundwork for its success. But my mind was made up and I felt morally obligated to leave. I would stay until I could get my replacement up to speed.

By the time I walked my replacement through the graveyard (it was an apropos set for my last day), we were three weeks into filming, a week from completing the shoot.

The things I'd feared about Buffalo never came to fruition. Lance came through as the hero cinematographer. He and Vincent inspired one another. The brutal weather never came. The abbreviated prep time was tricky, but we managed. And the money was miraculously found to cover the overages.

It's the other surprises that brought me to my knees.

By the time I headed home in a cargo van, ten pounds of me had evaporated in stress. Ten pounds I had no intention of losing.

I made a perfunctory detour to Niagara Falls, wondering why anyone would want to get married here. Maybe it was its skewed association to Love Canal, the disastrous neighbor to the west.

For a moment, the Falls' beauty swallowed me and let me forget everything toxic. The cold spray baptized me, in the same way it cleansed every tourist or newlywed crossing its planked bridges. I leaned over the bridge toward the cascading two-hundred-foot plunge. This was the place where brave, stupid men stuffed themselves into barrels and let the current carry them over the falls. I wondered about what I had just done in Buffalo. Had I contorted my own self and my own career into a barrel, and gone overboard?

If it's true that we are the sum total of our experiences—the books we read, the people we meet, and the jobs we take—this film might be a big factor in my equation. A scar, yes, but also a reminder to trust my instincts. The word *no* has entered my vocabulary.

In this beat up can of a van, I drove back to New York City. I obeyed the highway restrictions on commercial vehicles and stuck to the main arteries. I was sad to miss out on the winding, meditative back routes. Instead, I pressed into the pedal and crept up beyond the limit, allowing each stretch of asphalt to expand the distance between Buffalo and me.

| Chapter 10 |

THE REVIVAL

"Any chance that's available?" I asked the car rental attendant when I returned Buffalo's production van to its city lot. A relatively sporty looking blue sedan showed off its best angle. It was trapped by the chain link fence along the roar of the West Side Highway and I sensed it needed some country air.

"Sure. But it's running on fumes—you'll need to fill it up on 10th Avenue." A low, New Jersey sun set off a twinkle in his sunglasses, "Is that gonna be your getaway car?"

I smiled as he tossed the keys to me. What I really wanted to do was unzip my skull, lift out my brain, and run it through the carwash across 11th Avenue. But the ocean and a bottle of wine seemed like a more sensible option.

I headed due east to Montauk. In town, I bought a bottle of Sancerre and a few books. I enjoyed the crunch under my wheels when I rolled across the Surf Lodge's gravel parking lot. Mid-April meant it was still the off-season, so a modest amount of cash from my stockpiled Buffalo per diem covered a few nights. My duplex was so close to the ocean, I could feel the sea spray from my deck.

The first sip of wine was a cool drop of relief in the back of my throat. A minerally taste mingled with the salty air and dripped into my empty stomach. If innocence was a bottle of wine poured down just to the top of its label—the rest saved for another day—this was not that innocent day.

A few pages into the hardcover of *Angela's Ashes,* it occurred to me that Frank McCourt's memoir wasn't a good pairing to a generous pour of Sancerre, or any other form of alcohol. But if I could fill my head and heart with the details of someone else's saga from another era, there wouldn't be any space for me to wallow in my own.

My own saga was that I might never work in the feature film industry again. I had bowed out on *Buffalo '66* when the challenges got too steep. Maybe that was OK. Maybe I was ready to break up with the whole thing. I wasn't afraid of hard work, and obviously, I wasn't even afraid of failure. I had New York grit and a good amount of experience to fall back on.

Was I on the right track, really? Or is it always going to be a struggle? I wasn't sure, but I knew that in this odd industry you were only as good as your last job.

Montauk juts out into ocean, earning its nickname, *The End*. Here there was the guarantee of anonymity. No one knew me, and no one cared if I dined alone. While making a film on location, there are an unrelenting barrage of humans surrounding you. Humans that are lined up to take a swing at you with questions requiring quick, resolute decisions. And even when those decisions didn't make them happy, at least they were resolute.

The condo's drapes couldn't block the blast of morning sun, so I gave in and took a run high along the bluffs.

Just a few surfers braved the cold waves of Ditch Plains, the best swells in New York State. I watched the surfers' trials and errors from my bird's eye view. Like any other day, thousands of waves would crash into that beach. But if a surfer caught a few good ones, it was an awesome day for them.

Back in my hotel room, I dialed in remotely to cue my message machine—*tell me something new, something good.* The first voice was Jason's. Jason, together with his partner Joana owned Open City Films, and had been the producers on the film in Vietnam. I had no doubt they would find the financing; it was just a matter of time. Maybe this would be that call—I could return to Vietnam and redeem myself. I pushed hard on the series of buttons of the phone's keypad, cueing the machine to rewind so I could hear Jason's message clearly. My instincts were wrong, but not too far off. It wouldn't be Vietnam yet; it was a new Miramax movie. And could I dig in quickly and begin prep next week?

The Miramax film was *Down to You,* Kris Isacsson's debut feature set to star Joaquin Phoenix and Liv Tyler. I carried a dented banker's box of binders and supplies down the familiar steps into Open City's SoHo office. Entering these offices was like boarding a submarine designed by an 18th century architect; its steam pipes and snaking white halls formed a series of small, oddly-shaped and low-ceilinged offices off a center hall. But the lungs of the place, an open courtyard in the center, would be used for meetings when the weather was good and when the upstairs neighbors didn't complain about the voices that ricocheted around the brick walls. Open City was a welcome home for filmmakers and Jason and Joana collected them. Everything about the space was an homage to film. Even the bathroom walls were plastered with *Film Forum* movie schedules.

A new film with enough time and enough money is like a clean slate—an opportunity to get everything right. On its surface, Kris's story seemed simple, a small indie film dressed up with a studio cast and a cool visual effects sequence. But like that hotel room after the first night, the veneer wears off.

Even though I had read the script a couple times, it wasn't until I spent the night breaking it down into scenes that I recognized its complexities. The ensemble cast, the whole group playing together in every scene, would have no down time. That was a lot of choreography in small city spaces and a big expense for the production to carry. New York locations would be a high cost too. We weren't just slumming it with a small footprint and a non-union crew in New Jersey or Buffalo this time. Location owners would have dollar signs in their eyes when they heard the magic word: Miramax.

I hired Gayle to begin location scouting. A few years after working together on the Good Machine film, Gayle was a seasoned pro at the top of every producer's hire list. Then Open City brought Randy Balsmeyer on to help us design a visual effects plan for the flying sequences. Our main character would fly—like a stoned superman—but without a cape and enhancement of a Hollywood visual effects budget.

Fine tuning the budget is a lot like icing a triple-layer cake that just came out of the oven. You drop a blob of frosting on the top and spread it out over the sides (the basics) before using the reserve frosting for the troubled spots that need more attention (enhancements). It is a delicate dance and you've got to avoid tearing the cake apart with an uneven spread. You must include enough days to match the shooting schedule, enough crew for rigging and set dressing, and enough cash for construction and materials. The frosting left in the bowl is your contingency. To get the budget approved by the financiers, you'll be required to reserve 10 percent of the budget for anything that could go wrong.

Often, the first pass of any budget feels like even-handed perfection—every creative dream achieved on screen. But that was where the frosting metaphor ended, because without the money there was no film. No cake, no frosting, no movie.

Invariably, the bottom line on the first pass is too high. It takes some careful excavating to cut a chunk out of it and keep all things even.

I printed out my one-hundred-and-fifty-page opus. Kris's film boiled down to zeros and ones. Then, I headed for the Miramax offices to meet with the one person who could shut it all down.

Kevin's office was a pack rat's den. Piles of scripts, budgets, and cost reports grew like moss over every surface; their titles were marked in all caps with red sharpie on their rippled-edge bindings. Piles on top of piles. He searched through a stack on his desk and miraculously pulled up what he was hunting for. Then he adjusted his glasses and cleared his throat. He was ready to address the red marks he had made.

"There's a lot right with it," he explained in a measured voice that didn't match the chaos of the room. "But there's a heck of a lot wrong with it." Miramax wanted assurances that the costs would show up on screen. They wanted to see more of a robust costume line and support for the cast.

"I'm still proving I can pull things off on a shoestring," I said. Low-budget was my specialty, but it had become my Achilles heel.

"Well, you've got more than a shoestring here, but there's above-the-line that you'll need to support and you've got to work on that." Right, he meant that certain cast were going to need attention—the kind of attention that cost money. Their contracts might require dedicated make-up artists, wigs, and drivers. "Transpo seems light too."

I hung on Kevin's every word—even the words I didn't like. And I dug back in for another round.

If you've projected your own household budget, you can fantasize all you want about how little you'll spend each month on restaurants, alcohol, and clothing. But the proof is in the past; it's the forensics. You've got to go back to your credit card expenses and look at what you *actually* spent. It's more than you want to admit.

At Open City, Jason's work environment was one hundred and eighty degrees from Kevin's paper stacks. Jason dreamt of a paper-free world.

"This is the future, you'll see," he proselytized his vision to us. "We'll scan all the old paperwork and file it away. We don't need to print out messages or memos, we will just email them to each other." Emailing Jason when I could throw a paper airplane over his head from my desk seemed ridiculous. And promises about the future were fleeting, even suspect. I remembered that guy outside the United Nations hawking umbrellas attached to his head. His dream was not yet realized. But I adapted to Jason's philosophy, and then we all did. We embraced the Instant Message feature and group emails. But we started to spend more time staring into our computer screens and less time sorting things out face-to-face.

Each time we hopped into Gayle's car for a scout, it was more like a treasure hunt in our favorite city, and not like work. We zeroed in on college dorms at Fordham University, and a summer shoot ensured we would have great access there. Gayle discovered Block Hall, a Tudor style building hiding around a corner in the Wall Street district, surrounded by office towers. We walked through it with our jaws on the floor; reimagining it and mentally redressing it for Kris's film. We could put our production offices here, build our dorm rooms and at least three other sets. But another production filmed there now, its producers and shooting crew unamused by our tour. I expected the building was their unicorn; a secret they wanted to keep for themselves.

If it all seemed too good to be true, it's because it was. Mid-scout, Kris got the call from Miramax—the film wouldn't be going forward. Something about cast availability. Once again, we had to figure out how to pull the plug with some dignity and keep the door open. *Down to You* would be made some day, but for now we had to walk away from the blueprint we created.

Without tax credits or other financial incentives in the region, film work in New York was slow. *Must find work, must find work* was my internal mantra that accelerated each day, but I wasn't seeing much filming on the horizon. This couldn't be sustained much longer. I had to pull my parachute cord.

My parachute was the lucrative sell-my-soul work at Mediaworks. On the high end, it produced beautiful videos of conceptual artist's projections for the Whitney Museum's concrete walls. But the company's bread and butter came from pharmaceutical industrials.

"Something soon," my inside contact at Mediaworks said. He took a beat and lowered his voice, "You know, if you find yourself in LA next week, you'll be in a good spot to start prepping on an HIV drug spot. You didn't hear it from me but...BOLO swimming pools with a view." By which he meant *be on the lookout* (I had to ask).

After clawing my way back from the financial ruin of identity theft, my funds were running low again. I was burning through my credit card limit. But if work was imminent, it was a good bet to catch a flight to Los Angeles. I tapped a favor owed to me and stayed at a Venice bungalow. It was a sweet cottage behind Pico Boulevard with a loft layout, less than a mile from the ocean.

By six in the morning, I sat down with a highlighter and my Thomas Guide. The Thomas Guide was a Los Angeles area road map, a thick-ringed book with a diagram of every neighborhood street broken down into digestible quadrants. A bright green garbage truck rolled through the back alley as it threw the dumpster over its head. By the time the truck groaned away, I had circled three swimming pools and planned the day's scout. The HIV drug promotional gig, the Mediaworks industrial, was greenlit.

The morning fog burned off in Industry Hills and Greg Louganis was pitched on the end of the diving board in his Speedo. He bounced high, squared his shoulders back, kicked one knee up, and dared to dive. The stylist nodded after touching up Greg's salt and pepper hair. He would have to resist the leap into the pool until we wrapped. On cue, he walked the plank with confidence, hit his mark, and delivered the lines in favor of the HIV treatment.

I clocked the Mediaworks set; a spotless, chlorine, blue swimming pool that overlooked the San Gabriel mountain range at an aquatic club due east of Los Angeles. It was a small crew, including a few LA-based friends who had worked with me at paltry indie rates back in New York. But they made a decent wage here today, my attempt to atone. Following a trend, these crew members had abandoned New York and made the trek west.

The director called cut and gave thumbs up on the recorded playback. The happy client did the same, and Greg got the nod to take his dive. The diving board stuttered into a blur when he leapt and folded his fingers to his toes in mid-air. There was barely a splash, and the show was over.

Since it was an industrial shoot, we wrapped neatly in time for dinner. We took the crew to a beach-themed Thai restaurant in Los Feliz. Crowded across a table filled with shared dishes, we joked about the museum names in LA. Why did they all sound like designer coffee drinks:

the LACMA, the MOCA, and even the La Brea Tar Pits could be an extra-dark, triple espresso. And our hotel, the minimalist Mondrian, had the cool whitewash of a museum; a flat-white made to order.

It was all so comfortable. The warm holiday lights draped above our picnic table. The evening air was warm enough for a T-shirt and jeans. This was my life sponsored by the pharmaceutical industry. The cushy salary with the crisp white bedding in the designer hotel. I was on location where I liked to be, but why did I have the nagging feeling I was only doing it right if I balanced on the razor's edge?

| Chapter 11 |

THE CHICK-FLICK ADVENTURE FILM

COSTA RICA, 1999

The first panic attack hit me at the airport departures in paradise.

Two weeks before filming *The Citizen* in Costa Rica, the axe fell hard when the director fired our lead actor. It threw unsettling waves into every corner of production. Firing your number one cast member is not something you'll find in the "how to make movies" books. Not ever, and definitely not without the staging of another, more talented actor waiting in the wings.

We broke the news to the actor (we'll call him TT) in an unceremonious ambush under the buzz of the production office's fluorescent bulbs, because doing this under the shade of palm trees in the warm Costa Rican sun just didn't seem fair. Then I whisked TT to the airport, six weeks sooner than he expected to walk that tarmac again. TT buckled up next to me in the back of the van, silent and stone faced. Letting him go was a giant mistake, I thought, but I kept it to myself because it was already done. I had to follow the fold of the cult; if the director had moved on, I needed to move on too.

I love my job; I tweaked my mantra even if it was a lie that day. *I love my job.*

"It's just chemistry," I said, struggling for the right words. "Sometimes it just comes down to chemistry."

TT shot me an incredulous glare and snorted a laugh. The vibrant humor and inimitable charm that had glowed through the lens during his camera test was now siphoned out of him.

Of course, it was more than just chemistry. It was a tug-of-war between the way TT and the director interpreted his character, and the director won. Independent filmmaking is not a democracy; it's a hierarchy with one clear leader and one vision. Before filming, each director must pass a physical exam. A tap of the kneecaps, ten seconds of a stethoscope's bell against the breast. But there's no peering inside the brain's grey matter, no one to say *nope, this one's not ready for prime time!* Instead, we all say to ourselves, *he's directed movies before and nobody died on those sets, so we'll survive this one, right?*

At this time, I resented the hierarchy and the distinction between above-the-line and below-the-line. On paper, it was a physical line in the budget, putting producers, writer, director, and actors above; cordoning off these costs attributed to talent. Without most of these people and their talent, the movie wouldn't exist. Everything else: production manager, cinematographer, production designer, and the rest of the crew, they fell below the line. And this was talent too, but each one was a gun for hire. They were replaceable. And this time, even the cast was replaceable.

Strapped into the back seat, TT and I stared ahead as if our laser focus on the road could avoid a crash. Now

I understood why straight men sat at bars without turning their stools towards one another. They'd go to the movies together, but keep one seat between them as they clutched separate buckets of popcorn. The side-by-side was so effortless, so much more nonconfrontational than the face-to-face. Every few minutes I glanced over to TT to see if the color had come back into his face.

He would rebound, and he would have a kick-ass career. He would have his Julia Roberts moment, strutting back to us while waving those Rodeo Drive shopping bags. And he did. TT would go on to star in an HBO series; the equivalent of box office gold. That series would be followed by another hit, and he'd become a giant star of the small screen.

I waved goodbye from the curb, and then my limbs went numb. I was sure it was that tingling sensation in the left arm that they describe when you research *heart attack symptoms*. I got my shit together enough to fall into the back seat for a semi-private panic attack. I reached deep into my lungs to fish out the air that had been stuck.

TT's replacement would be picked up at the same airport curb tomorrow and I'd greet him with a smile. *Buenos dias, welcome to our chaos*.

When Deirdre and I had first landed in San José, the tarmac walk melted the soles of my sneakers. I thought of that egg-frying cliché and my stomach gave a fierce growl, angry with me for passing on the plane's cheese omelet. But the air was a sweet shock to the system, a welcome respite from the chilly Northeast.

We hailed a cab next to a vendor at the arrivals pull-in; her stand was piled with green sliced fruit that marinated in plastic baggies. She caught me looking, and I gave in.

"It's an addiction, you know," the cabbie said. "Green mango with salt and lime. The locals add hot sauce." And did I know it wasn't even high mango season yet? And did I know there were twenty-five types of mangoes in Costa Rica?

"There goes another one," Deirdre said and nodded toward a white guy in khaki pants and a pressed powder blue shirt. If she was right, the San José Hilton's lobby swarmed with CIA agents. He looked like any other fraternity guy on his way to a macroeconomics class. "C-I-A," she winked at me, and said, each letter drawn out.

"Really? He looks like…a *New York Times* reporter, not a spy," I said, as if my counterfeit spy career gave me an advantage, as if I could single out military intelligence.

"No, no, no. 100 percent spook. That's their uniform."

I followed her down to our production offices—a cave buried under the lobby, deprived of windows, and bathed in the soul-sucking wash of fluorescent overheads. The lights zapped and blinked, as they threatened to leave us in the dark. Not even the CIA spooks wandered down here for fear of being strapped to a chair and forced to give up state secrets. I sat at a makeshift desk on a folding chair in front of a card table. From this light, it was hard to imagine the thick vegetation of rain forest fifteen-minutes north of us.

I developed a routine caffeine trek up a steep hill to a shop scattered with dozens of burlap bags full of local beans. The shop was easy to find if you followed the burnt odor churning out of the back roasting room. The owner told me her best coffee beans shipped up to the United States where the sale price was higher. But the beans left behind still brewed a mean jolt.

At lunch we grabbed a quick order of arroz con pollo. We tried to be civil like our Costa Rican crew and eat our lunch away from the office, sitting down and leaving as much of our per diem on the ground with the local businesses. But too often lunch was thrown into a carton and eaten in a fifteen-passenger van on a scout or en route to a meeting.

Rebecca Grynspyn interlaced her fingers into a neat tent on her desk while I pled my case. I inhaled for a conscious beat, trying to slow down my rapid speech and heartrate. I was nervous—I'd never met with a head of state before. Costa Rica covered a relatively small amount of ground, but this tiny country had rounded up enough soccer players to punish the US team in a recent World Cup match. A head of state here could wield plenty of power.

Costa Rica could be busy with high-end commercials and small chunks of Hollywood features, but independent films were a rarity. And when local equipment was off limits to us (we couldn't afford those commercial rates), we sourced it from an equipment house in Miami (we could barely afford theirs). They shipped our grip and electric packages on pallets by sea. And as the crow flies, it looked like a direct route. Until those pallets were apparently bobbing around on a ship in the Caribbean, taking a dog's age to dock. I wondered if our ship had been highjacked in Cuba, or rerouted to someone else's production in the Bahamas. If it didn't arrive by Friday, we would have to push our filming dates. It was beyond our control, but the thing we could control was the customs process. So we begged, and were granted a meeting with Costa Rica's vice president, Rebeca Grynspan.

I needed to strike a balance with her. Could I communicate frantic and polite at the same time? I shifted my pose, hooking my fingers against each other in my lap. *Stop talking,* my knuckles begged me. *Breathe. Listen.* Then I endured what felt like three long minutes before she responded (the production manager told me later it was only ten seconds). The *pregnant pause.* It was enough time for the air to rush out of my ears, like the vacuuming sensation you get when your train rushes through a tunnel. It was my one shot.

Diplomats like the vice president have learned how to negotiate using this pregnant pause. It can be a powerful stunt leaving the other person floundering and waiting for this interminable pause to end. She jotted down a few notes and picked up her phone's handset to page an associate. This was the diplomatic process of the wheels churning towards a solution. No frills. In a matter of minutes, she expedited the Miami equipment through customs. She also offered access to a few government-owned locations.

I left the building shouting *thank you* up to the city's tall palms. We had taken the production two steps forward. But for every two steps forward, we managed to take another one backwards.

I didn't see the disconnect with continuity coming. Two weeks before filming, the costumes department held a *show and tell*—a fashion exhibit of their selected wardrobe. And it was a gorgeous display. Much of it was original pieces sewn by the department head himself. The two celebrated costume and set designers of San José theater fame had ticked all the director's boxes, and exceeded his expectations. But the look and the durability of these costumes was just half the battle. Performances were always in sequential order in the theater, and continuity was getting lost in translation here. They had no system for tracking the filming of scenes out of order. Their scribbles in the margins of their script were their master guide, and their system would not hold.

"How do you feel about the jungle?" I called Tibi, as if she were standing by in New York, waiting to be activated by me. She had a full life, restaurant and club dates scribbled into every available white space of her diary. I took a chance that she was overwhelmed, willing to put it all on hold and escape to Costa Rica.

"I'm not a wardrobe supervisor," she said. "I've just done styling on commercials." I heard chewing and the click of chopsticks; she was probably probing into a bowl of steamed vegetables. I loved that she was comfortable enough with me to chew in my ear.

"But you understand continuity. And you're so patient," I said, with the not-so-subtle subtext *come and save me again*. "You can do this with your hands tied behind your back. You're the fixer." I said with flattery while referencing Harvey Keitel's horrific role in *Pulp Fiction,* a movie we saw together. I pictured her now grabbing the elusive snow peas from the bottom of her bowl. She would be seated under that *Pulp Fiction* poster taped up next to Wim Wenders's *Wings of Desire,* that singular shot of a lost angel looming over Berlin. I knew just where that poster curled up on the bottom.

"This isn't Buffalo. It's a hundred and eighty degrees from there." I wouldn't do that to her again. *Buffalo '66* had been five years earlier. Costa Rica was more like the Club Med ad in the subway trains—the warm palmy heaven you dreamt about when your fingers clung to the overhead bar under someone else's armpit. "What's it going to take, Tibi?" Then, the Hail Mary: "Would it help if I cried?"

We loaded up a people mover van for the tech scout. Just one week before filming, this scout was an opportunity for the department heads to walk through all our filming locations. It was one last chance to shout out their concerns, to point out where they were expected to make the impossible happen. One last chance for Adam, the first assistant director, to vet these concerns and try to work out the solutions.

At the coffee plantation above the jungle, Adam twirled the shot list above his head and walked us through each shooting day's theoretical rundown. The prop master leaned back and shoved his hands into his pockets; worn marks were visible in his jeans where the knuckles had rested for years. PJ, the assistant camera technician, crouched and kicked one foot forward to tie his shoe. He jumped up and switched feet, lacing the other one like a dance from *Fiddler on the Roof*. I wondered if he would still have the energy of a Broadway performer when we were into week four. Adam led us into the jungle as he pushed vines back along the river path. We followed him in single file.

"*Peligro*!" our transportation coordinator stood near a cave entrance, pointing above his head "Oh shit! Colmena!"

"Where?" I asked, not entirely sure what *colmena* meant, but paired with *peligro* and the tone of his voice, it had to be urgent.

"Wasps. Or beehive," he crouched down with him for an angle on the cave entrance. And there it was; a humming nest of frantic insects right alongside our only path to set. An angry swarm like that could mean the end to this idyllic setting. I expected spiders and snakes, but not an active beehive. We couldn't forge a new path because the rain forest was sacred.

Perennially, we debated our footprint in the film business. How much space would the production take up? Would adding too much crew and too many vehicles increase our footprint, slow us down, and add to our bottom line? To maintain a small footprint is to move stealthily, swiftly, and independently. Here, treading lightly took on a new urgency. We risked pulverizing the rain forest—the lungs of the earth—or what was left of those lungs.

We did not have an *Apocalypse Now* or a *Romancing the Stone* level of impact. No cadre of helicopters would circle over our film set and land in a sliver of jungle opening. No stuntpeople would freefall down a two-hundred-yard mudslide. But the same mud that caked those production's cables would suck ours into the earth. And moving through this obstacle course was going to be the same challenge that those bigger productions endured. There were just fewer of us to get it done.

We made a note to avoid swinging our C-stands and ladders around the cave entrance. And we planned to lay a series of wooden planks, encouraging the cast and crew to stick to the path. I tucked my pants into my socks, pulled my sleeves down to my wrists, and forged further alongside the river towards set.

The crew sat down on the perimeter of the jungle in a catering tent, a Bedouin-style canvas structure fit for a wedding. We devoured scrambled eggs, sweet plantains—the works—also fit for a wedding celebration. Here, it would be a crime to deprive a crew of a full sit-down breakfast. In the States, you just grabbed a burrito wrapped in foil. You might see a partially-eaten breakfast roll sticking out of a grip's pocket or abandoned in the windowsill. In some instances, you would be instructed by the call sheet to arrive "having had" breakfast. No sit-down breakfast was served on those sets.

"Lizano, pour favor?" I asked, ready to cover my rice and beans in hot sauce.

"Don't get addicted," the grip passed the bottle to me and warned me. "Americans, they love this stuff. They pack a case of it on the way home."

Like a crack addict, I casually searched the label for the ingredients. There had to be sugar in there, but what else? I was growing accustomed to the civil ritual of enjoying the first meal of the day in a chair, and it was not just the hot sauce converting me.

In the jungle, I clipped a chunky pager to my belt for easy access to see updates from the production office. On this little device, I could also retrieve news headlines, sports, and weather. It also showed me my daily horoscope which was an amusing distraction when ducking under wet branches of the rain forest. *Moon child: If you have a choice between fight or flight today, choose fight.* It was just an incoming device, as good as a printed magazine.

For any real emergency like snake and spider bites, we hired a set medic—a sage soul who stood by knitting baby booties in a folding chair.

Amid the jungle's sumptuous beauty and rain, mud bubbled up along our now well-worn pathway. The wood planks began to sink, and with every step and every drop of jungle rain, miles of electric cables were slurped up. I doubted that we would be able to extract all the cables, let alone clean them for their return trip to Florida.

Exhausted from wading through muck, the crew retired to the hotel bar, somehow reserving enough energy for a nightcap. Here we unwound the ball of nerves we had rolled up during the day. I saw PJ take a disco nap at lunch, as he folded his arms and tilted back on two apple boxes. Now at the bar in a freestanding stool, he leaned forward and found a comfortable balance. It was hard to tell what was going on under his straw hat, but a quiet snore made things clear. We sat on either side of him telling stories, swapping crew gossip. Once in a while, he would wake up and join the conversation. Changing out lenses, racking focus with a quick measurement on the fly, these were all part of PJ's craft. But the art of sleeping anywhere would be his enduring talent.

Our crew wasn't accustomed to the long haul, to the consecutive weeks of work. Each day was pushed further into the night until Friday became a full night of shooting. In the feature industry, Friday had invaded Saturday so often, it had earned its portmanteau: *Fraterday*.

Enrique, the costume designer, redirected a stray bird back into the sanctuary behind his kitchen. We were one week into filming, and like all responsible film crews, we didn't let the moment pass without patting ourselves on the back with a celebration. Enrique and the production designer, Luis Carlos, had invited us to their home for a feast. Just like any other room in the house, the sanctuary was populated with singing technicolor birds. But the sanctuary had grown like bamboo, invading the other rooms of the house as its leafy green extensions reached the kitchen and living room. Like everything else in Costa Rica, the line between sanctuary and living room—between work and play—was hazy.

After this film, Luis Carlos would return to the theater, directing and designing. He didn't need to spend long hours in the jungle. Instead, he would have reasonable days of rehearsals on the stage, and then he would retreat to the privacy of his own home to enjoy nature. Or he would celebrate another performance with his cast and theater crew. But now, we toasted *pura vida* and gave thanks to Costa Rica and to our crew. Glasses were raised, shots of *guaro* were drunk, and then the singing began.

Why would anyone want to get used to the lifestyle of filmmaking with the long hours, the high anxiety, and the crowded sets? A life that tears away at routine and challenges the core of families? It's not the life humans were meant to endure, especially in a city whose backyard is a lush hammock of rain forest.

One location still eluded us: a New York City apartment. Sleep will elude any producer who doesn't have all the key locations contracted in time. But Tibi, who had flown down to solve the wardrobe department's continuity concerns, now shapeshifted into the locations team to find a viable option.

We needed to "cheat" our New York apartment here. The budget wouldn't allow us to travel our cast another leg to the States to get the location in its native environment: The Upper West Side. Every apartment option in Costa Rica had been eliminated because of its unavoidable angles on the tropical flourishes. Like Enrique and Luis Carlos' home, the walls between interior and exterior were often blurred. The intellectual's self-consciously decorated brownstone didn't exist in San José for a reason. We had one more week to find it and dress it, but I needed to step away for a beat and get out of the city.

Deirdre and I soaked in Arenal's volcano-generated hot springs, two hours north of San José. I stared at my hiking boots on the side of the springs.

"It could blow at any moment, you know," Deirdre said, always the optimist.

"Well that's the chance we take," I said, wondering whether we all had a little Icarus in us, the need to stare over the lip of the volcano. To plant a stake and say *yup, I was there*. "Anyway, Arenal doesn't care. If she blows, she blows."

"So, a volcano is a *she*?"

Maybe it's the same inner Icarus drawing us to a city like New York. Living in an apartment in the city carries its own risks, but any bet that molten rock would land on the tar paper of my Brooklyn rooftop would come in at high odds. Just the past spring, Arenal had erupted and covered miles of surrounding towns. The resort had tiny, wooden arrows tacked to its trees, like elfin signs in a

Christmas Village mapping the path to Santa's workshop. But these weren't directions, they were warnings: *If you see hot lava, RUN!*

On the way back into San José from Arenal, a good chunk of the road had washed away, barely allowing one car through at a time. The roads were lined with cardboard boxes placed side by side, and gave shelter to families who had lost their homes, or left their homes in Nicaragua. These were mile-long stretches of shantytowns. Just when you thought there could be no more boxes, another stretch began, more and more dense until finally the city loomed over the next hill.

Eureka, Tibi found it. The New York apartment. It wasn't ideal, but with a little well-positioned East Coast greenery, we could avoid the lusher angles and pull it off.

After blocking out the scene, our lead actress met me at the craft service table and poured herself a cup of coffee. She eyed me in a strange way. She cleared her throat which usually meant she needed something from me. Had she measured her trailer and it was one foot shorter than her co-star's? Sometimes, everything seems great on set with actors. You'll be greeted with air kisses and overflowing joy in the make-up chair. But then the agent calls to express where we've fallen short. A visceral wash of doom lands on me in these moments. What did I miss? How had I failed this somewhat reasonable cast member? This is the moment when you wished you worked in animated films where there are no actors, no talent to play games with. Why was she not telling me how she felt when we conducted small talk over rice, beans, and Lizano?

But she didn't look me in the eye. She pinched the sleeve of my knit cardigan and rolled it between her fingers. Then she gripped Enrique's shoulder as he shadowed her.

"Look at this, it's navy. Light-knit—she'd wear this," the actress said, referring to her character in the third person. She tugged my sleeve towards her as if to remove it from my body. My armor, my most beloved piece of clothing. But I exaggerate here a bit for your sympathy.

"Are you sure?" I protested, "I mean, I've been wearing this for the last five days." I lifted my elbow and sniffed my pit. *Subtle*. "I can't remember the last time I washed it."

"Here, let me take it," she said, before I could list the sweater's other negative qualities. I stripped down to my camisole and handed it to her.

"You're a star," she said over her shoulder as she walked away with the prize. Pat, pat, pat, little one. That's what it feels like when an actual star says *you're a star*.

But I could not be the one to slow down progress. I was meant to spark it, to keep momentum going. Enrique took my hand and walked me towards the wardrobe trailer. He picked through the stock bin, the one they used to dress the extras players who came to set with the wrong outfits. I took my consolation prize—an oversized Yankees sweatshirt.

"Well, we're looking at a lot of mud here," the owner of the Florida equipment house was on the line. I was back in New York, trying to wrap up the jungle from the producer's Soho offices.

The equipment had been sunbathing on the Miami lot, hosed off several times to attack the caked-on chunks of rain forest. The cargo had weighed in at over 120 pounds heavier than the original delivery. Could that be right? I had worked with crew members who weighed less than that. I hung up after the mud negotiations and noticed a small crowd in the bullpen. Tibi held up a sleek box no bigger than her hand. We had seen the advertisements and we knew it was coming, but to behold it in person was like watching the velvet curtains swing back to reveal that new car. She unwrapped it slowly to reveal her shiny red Nokia cell phone.

Its technology and design was nothing like the phones we had used on set before, with their dull, green, clunky plastic digits, and thin ineffective antennas that twisted and snapped off. This was one neat, adorable unit, a candy-colored coating that a child could gnaw on. Tibi signed up for a package deal and a three-year commitment.

"Hallelujah. Now I can throw away my crusty, old pager," she said.

"Yeah, but that phone won't clip to your belt" someone said. A twinge of jealousy coming through. "You'll need a fanny pack to carry it around."

"I guess I'll put it in my pocket?" Tibi said, modeling the options. "Or in a holster, like a gun?"

The phone passed around the room and landed with me. I cradled it for a moment, admiring its simplicity. This, I could carry with me everywhere. For better or worse, now we would never be lost.

What I didn't know then, in the year 2000, was that we'd all be so emotionally invested these plastic portals of information that we couldn't remember our lives before them.

| Chapter 12 |

THE ELEVATED HORROR

NEW YORK CITY, 1999

I said *yes* when the producer of *Buffalo '66* called for help on a portion of Mary Harron's *American Psycho*. I said *yes* because I thought Bret Easton Ellis's book was brilliant and because I wanted to work with Mary.

I sat against Mary's apartment wall taking notes while her editor scrolled through the editorial system's placeholders, highlighting the shots and inserts they needed. The *save-the-day* producer— the one brought in to collect the missing pieces—was a new role for me. With some luck, some time, and enough money, I had an opportunity to make something good even better. Mary and her crew had done the hard work already.

I converted my chicken-scratch notes from the edit review into a shot list, then into a schedule, then into a budget, and then it was ready for the studio's eyes.

It took a few simple scenes to add more New York texture to a film that had cheated much of New York in Toronto. Canada was luring the studios over the border with a hefty tax credit and an exchange rate that financiers salivated over. At sixty cents to the US dollar, the exchange rate meant you would receive an instant 40 percent discount before even factoring in a tax credit. New York still had no financial incentives, and it was only getting more expensive to shoot here.

But we weren't making North American Psycho; he was *our* American Psycho. A New Yorker who could be your upstairs neighbor in 5A or seated at the table next to you ordering sushi. A serial-slasher hiding in plain sight, but with Christian Bale's handsome stature and a wicked sense of humor. If the audience recognized exteriors and lobbies—the quintessentially Manhattan exits and entrances—it would keep them invested in the story. And just a few days of filming in New York for Mary's film could remedy this. We would place these new shots throughout the film and heighten the film's New York texture.

The studio looked over my presentation and numbers (their eyes flew past the details and landed on the bottom line). They chopped back the schedule and budget, leaving us just enough to shoot only the title sequence. Following suit, I cut back on our ambitions and put together a Plan B.

We all have our magic bullets. In any business, there's that person who can save your day. Tibi was mine. Mary's might have been Toshiaki Ozawa, the gaffer and cinematographer. Toshi had a scientific knowledge of photochemistry and the skill of shaping light. On *Buffalo '66*, Toshi had estimated the time for set ups within minutes. He nailed down the right equipment package, kept it to a minimum during check out, and didn't overcompensate in volume. Anyone could pack the kitchen sink that allowed for every option; we nicknamed shooters like that *flame-*

throwers. But Toshi could work small, tell the director's story, and still craft a great looking scene.

Blood dripped on purpose. It trickled out at a painstakingly slow speed. The *American Psycho* credit sequence began with what appeared to be blood, but when the cameras pulled back, there was no body, no murder, and no weapon. The bright red streaks had transformed; they were now a reduction sauce drizzling over a minimalist entrée at a Michelin-rated restaurant.

Or was it? Here, we were cheating the audience again. It was a clue into the real Patrick Bateman—the sick character Ellis had dreamed up. Reading the book on the subway years ago, I remembered how clever the writing was, and how Ellis's humor cut against Bateman's gruesome killings. This created even more discomfort and embarrassment for the reader.

"I need to return some videotapes," Patrick Bateman would say, like a broken record. Anyone alive in the 1990s understood the stress of the late videotape return. Two ridiculous bucks for each day-late tape, that was money down the drain. But for Patrick, it was the line he employed to get away from a situation, to exit stage left when he needed to feed his murderous desires.

We had loaded into the Greenwich Stages, a studio with a surprising amount of elbow room for the West Village. Before this, on any tabletop shoot, we had been shoehorned into a tiny stage-like stable; an actual former horse stable. But on this day, we needed space for a massive Phantom camera and the rig and sets that accompanied it.

The Phantom camera was designed to shoot through two piggy-backed, one-thousand-foot rolls of film stock in two minutes. At its normal twenty-four frames per second speed, one-thousand-foot roll of film would last for a twelve-minute take. But at the slow-motion speed we were filming, we would shoot so many frames per second we could liquidate all our film stock in just two hours.

Lions Gate hovered over me about the budget, and I wanted to avoid a restocking charge from Kodak. So, my stomach swirled in a nauseating dance, *should I or shouldn't I buy more film stock*.

Toshi climbed up the ladder and fired up the Phantom for another take. The food props department stepped into place, on their marks to squirt eye droppers of red, sticky goo against a pristine white muslin cyclorama. The Phantom chewed through about a hundred feet before it roared up to speed, allowing my stomach to slip a double knot around itself. And Mary called *action*.

Over the summer, by the time I was prepping the pilot for Amy Sedaris's *Strangers with Candy*, Kodak and Fuji film stock had begun to fade out in favor of high-definition video. We shot side-by-side tests and the cast and producers leaned in to weigh the better look. Could they tell the difference between film and video?

Film won again. Still, I wondered how long film could keep itself alive. Purists like Jarmusch, Tarantino, and Scorsese held film in high esteem, but spending more money on the photochemical process wasn't sustainable for the low-budget indie.

By now, I thought I had acquired a trained eye for the look of film. Lighting for *Strangers*'s comedic look and transferring to video made the difference difficult to discern. I guessed that 90 percent of home viewers wouldn't appreciate the difference either. And yet there was something there, something that gave the grain and texture of the film transfer an elevated quality over video.

With the decision to shoot with 16 mm film, everything cost more: lighting equipment, stock, lab work, and even editorial. Something had to give, so we consolidated the shoot days and locations. We had to move fast, and we had to do it in New Jersey. But once we were on set, the film stock took on a certain reverence for the cast and crew. We were more careful not to keep rolling like we had grown accustomed to with video. Continuing on take after take would exhaust the talent. More often, we got it right the first or the second time, and we moved on.

Sam, the prop master, loaded his kit into his pick-up truck. With the exactitude and discipline of a lab technician, he kept his kit in good order. No one except his border collie Sally dared to get near it. I joined his dog in the passenger seat, as we shared a ride to the New Jersey suburbs. Sally whimpered down at the terrarium full of turtles that I straddled between my sneakers.

"You know, I could take care of them," I heard myself saying. "I can keep them in my apartment." Who was I? An overzealous kindergarten volunteer? I did a cut-to of myself struggling with the terrarium up my third-floor walk-up, cursing every step.

You don't become intimate with the slime of a turtle until they come to live with you. Some days, we didn't need the turtles on set, so they stayed in the apartment to climb over each other's backs and ooze around their glass domain. On screen, the turtles had their time in the spotlight until they were killed by Amy Sedaris's character (along with a cheerleader in a plot twist the audience never saw coming).

It was fun to watch a troupe of comedic actors play off each other in *Strangers*. Their familiar rapport made the crew forget that this was work. The ensemble had a shorthand with one another. There were no prima donnas. Every player was on equal footing, much like a theater troupe.

Two full passenger vans and seven crew cars snaked along the New Jersey Turnpike and through the Holland tunnel to celebrate the show's wrap at the Old Town Bar. The first floor held the line-up of regulars, but the second floor—with its old mahogany booths and intimate lighting—was all ours. Courtesy of Comedy Central, an icy pitcher of cold beer landed on the table. Sam and I leaned in close to hear Stephen Colbert talk. It was a private moment, a story about how his childhood was thrown off course when his father and two siblings were killed in a plane crash. He was eleven years old at the time; the same age I had been when my father died. But the grief of losing three family members in the same accident was incomparable—it was too much to imagine. Maybe that's when you turn to comedy. You turn to the safety of a troupe that's got your back.

There was another cheat I'd somehow steered clear of so far in the movie world: gunplay. Replica guns, prop weapons, and blood squibs mimicking the violence of gunfire and its excitement eluded me. Until the dead of winter in Brighton Beach. We were enacting the pomp and circumstance of a Russian wedding for a new Open City film, *Taxman*. The budget tipped heavily toward one line item: the careful execution of violence. Safety was key but safety cost money. So heavy gunfire action and its impact on body parts were usually played off-screen on the lower-budgeted films. Here we had a separate budget, with a sacred allowance for firearms, permits, and stunts. And a budget for squibs to mock blood spurting when a character was "hit" by a blank.

With Jason and Joana now in Southeast Asia, finally funded to shoot *Three Seasons*, I was brought in to be their proxy on this show back in New York. They couldn't be in Vietnam and in New York at the same time, so I tried to be a close second. Sure, I could jump into the discomfort of an ice-cold, brutally windy Brighton Beach winter. But because there was already a line producer on set and because I hadn't helped to develop or prepare the film, I had the cool veneer of detachment. I watched this line producer pick up the phone to clear the virtual sticks and stones out of the production's path. For the first time on a film set, I was a gun-for-hire at an arm's length.

I know what it's like to be on the other side of that equation—to feel watched, judged, and second guessed. In this supervisory role, I tried to hang back and help with solutions, solutions that were remarkably easy to see from my uncluttered perspective. What I didn't know at the time was that this would be the end of my freelance career. *Strangers* had been my last real freelance show and *Taxman* was the beginning of my crossing over to the other side.

| Chapter 13 |

THE COMING-OF-AGE FILM

PARK CITY, UTAH, 2000

I hopped a crowded festival shuttle van from the Salt Lake City airport. As the air thinned, my brain throbbed against my skull begging for oxygen. Then I remembered that the headaches showed up every time I climbed this mountain. I pushed my forefingers against my temples and prayed for relief.

"Here, take a couple of these," a veteran Sundance festivalgoer in the passenger seat shook out a couple aspirin and extended his palm, recognizing the international symbol for migraine. "Give it twenty minutes."

The aspirin's chalky residue tickled the back of my throat and threatened to make me cough. I closed my eyes and took a gulp of local plastic spring water. Fresh rivers and streams crossed just beneath this Rocky Mountain pass, but I sucked on a plastic bottle of water sourced in Maine. In exactly nineteen minutes, I'd be transformed back into human form again without a pounding headache.

I listened to the stories around the van and took mental notes. Which films to see, what the hot ticket was, and whether Paris Hilton was going to be there. But I felt I had no currency to trade in this conversation. For the first time, I hadn't come to Sundance with a film I helped make. A pile of scripts had replaced books in my carry-on luggage. I was now an executive at Open City Films and our new scrappy production initiative, Blow Up Pictures.

"You have a movie here?" the aspirin hawker asked.

"Me?" I said, opening one eye again. "No, not this year." Then I thought better of it. It was part of my new job to help our film find its way, to find its white knight, its distributor. "Not me, but my company has a film here. It's called *Chuck & Buck*." Since I didn't work the long hours to shoot this film, or the weeks of tearing my hair out in the editing room, I couldn't hawk it as my own.

My resort was the shuttle's last drop in a sequence of condos peppering the mountainside. Condos so new, the final nails must have just been pounded in. Maybe in a bid to host the Olympics, the town's real estate stock appeared to have tripled since my last trip here. But the familiar chimney smoke settled into the valley at the base of Park City's ski slopes. It was a strong hickory smell; sweeter than the maple and ash we burned on the East Coast.

Our condo featured a knotty pine theme, with a living room of matching patterned floors, beams, and furniture. This segued into a kitchen with even more knotty pine. The islands, cupboards, countertops, and even the dishwasher was encased in pine swirls. On the kitchen table was an open pad of paper with a floorplan diagram that had arrows directing me to where I would sleep; on the top bunk with more knotty pine. Next to the pad was a plain manila envelope with my screening ticket to the premiere of *Chuck & Buck*.

I hadn't planned on becoming an executive. I was on the freelancing track, and I'd watched others balance their freelancing lives with families and houses. I was thirty-two. I was living job-to-job, insurance-less, and irresponsibly.

Executives were "other" to me. They were the ones standing in the way of progress. When the executive arrived on set and wanted to *get close to camera,* I would redirect them to a designated area near video village for executive-type conversations. I made sure they were kept close to the entertainment, far from me for as long as possible, and far from the business of the set. Chatty executives and grunting grips pushing a Fisher dolly through to set were a bad mix. I would never be *one of them*.

But Joana had called needing help. She seemed to genuinely want me around to help them make movies. With this job, I could have a regular paycheck and health insurance. They would even give me a 401 (k) if I wanted to take a chunk out of my salary. And there was the promise I could keep producing. I would oversee most productions as an executive, but I would produce a few of my own.

What was the catch then? Well, the budgets would be scrappy, some of them lower than my first film *Heavy*. The thirty-year-old version of myself had thought I was on track to produce films with huge budgets, with enough money available to throw at every problem until practically no oversight and no management was necessary. But that's a myth; there's never enough money. As the budgets of films grow, the expectations grow with it.

After Joana and I spoke, and I had thought it through, I showed up. And I left the freelance world behind.

At the Sundance screening, I felt like an imposter when I was ushered to the reserved seats that were cordoned off to the side. It was at the Eccles Theater—the festival's largest screening venue with twelve hundred seats—and it was sold out. Miguel, the director, graciously welcomed the crowd from the lip of the stage.

"My mother, she'll never believe the size of this audience!" He held up a disposable Kodak camera and waved it in the air. "So, this photo I'm taking, it's a gift for her. She couldn't come to Park City so please say hello."

As Miguel flashed a photo, the audience roared in applause and waved their arms for another shot. *Now buckle your seatbelts*, I thought, *here comes Miguel's movie*.

Fifteen minutes into the screening, Chuck stalked Buck at his Los Angeles home and I scrunched down further into my seat with each *oh shit, he did not just say that* gasp from the audience. The nervous laughter and incredulous hisses were palpable. I slunk down further, the way we used to in horror films, as if the back of the seat would protect me. Miguel and his writer and performer, Mike White, were getting precisely the reaction they had hoped for. This was not a *Cape Fear-gonna-bite-your-cheek-off* kind of horror. It was a stalker movie of a different breed: a boyhood obsession trapped in a case of arrested development. It was a 100 percent hormones and knee-jerks.

Chuck & Buck was shot on video, and the feeling the audience got when it was blown up to 35 mm film and projected was like being socked in the face. The electric grain was clear and present; it was a good kind of sock in the face.

The classic films, the ones audiences have always loved were the well-lit historical dramas like *Reds* or *A Room With a View*. Shot in twenty-four frames per second on 35 mm stock. These sumptuous color palettes transported them to another era and suspended their disbelief. But in *Chuck & Buck*, the video's hyper-real frame rate made the audience feel like they were in the same room as these characters, suffering the same consequences as our hero. Film says, *this happened to someone else, sit back and enjoy it*. Video this raw says, *this is happening right now, and it could be you*. I turned back to scan the faces of the crowd, bathed in electric blues and greens. Could this hack that used low-brow tape stock be the future medium—the future of filmmaking?

I arrived at the party earlier than Jason and Joana. It was a company condo event at the foot of Park City's ski run. Ski-in/ski-out they called these high-end condos, but mostly I wanted to ski out and disappear. Now I was truly an outsider, as I circled among other executives. I leaned back against the curtains of a giant picture window and counted night skiers. A father skied behind a toddler with his hands on his shoulders. He steered him around the base in a controlled snowplow. If I couldn't be out there, maybe I could disappear into the fabric of the drapes. My sweaty palms incinerated the ice cubes and diluted my wine to water. I adjusted the cup in my hand, held it up to the light, and give it a ridiculous sommelier's swirl. This gave me something to do, some business, while I waited for Jason and Joana to appear.

There were no familiar crew members here, hopped up and excited to take me to the keg and refill my blue plastic cup. No film technicians nudging me to sneak off to the deck for a hit of weed. It was as if I had been tap-dancing through my career; firmly rooted in the actual filmmaking, becoming a pro at the steps, and now I was handed a pair of ballet slippers and asked to perform on pointe. From my safe distance, I watched the executives and producers work the room. I even knew a few of them: the Ted Hopes, the Christine Vachons, and a few of the agents and the actors. But I couldn't think of how to open a conversation, let alone hold up my end of it. I couldn't seem to move in to dance just yet.

Then Jason and Joana entered the front door of the condo and there was a hush. They didn't so much walk in as they did float. A glass was raised and there was a round of applause, old Hollywood style. Their smiles broad and grateful, they were firmly rooted in this habitat. They were a handsome and photogenic couple; they just fit together. Joana's business acumen and beauty complemented Jason's sense of humor and knack for storytelling. Like most couples, they argued passionately, but it usually was a fight worth fighting; often about the filmmaker or the film they *must* make. And I was used to the arguing; I had been working with married couples in New York for years. But what I truly admired about Jason and Joana is that they had one another's backs. They were a team.

Jason and Joana had taken a risk on this daring script of Miguel's by bringing it to light. They had convinced the investors to take the same risk on Miguel and Mike White's talents to produce the film. Now came the business of selling the film, and at this party there were interested buyers. Like many film sales acquisitions at Sundance, the deal could go down in a producer's condo into the wee hours.

Back in Open City's SoHo submarine-like office, I carved out a desk space for myself in the back room under a skylight. Above me, pigeons bounced around, cooing on top of each other. By 2 p.m. the harsh winter sun hovered overhead, kicking off my computer screen and blinding me. I found some old scraps of Coroplast and built a box around my monitor, the same low-budget hack that they used to shade the camera's monitors on set.

At Sundance, we had hawked Blow Up Pictures' paraphernalia with stickers, post cards, and buttons borrowing Gil Scott-Heron's banner phrase: *The Revolution Will Not Be Televised*. With the first film now out there, filmmakers were paying attention. What we got in return was an armful of new scripts. These were all coming from the time we spent with filmmakers; a good pitch, an inspirational meeting, or just a good spider-sense standing in line next to them at a festival screening. We pushed to close the deals and we pared it down to a reasonable five projects, or what would be our slate.

Blow Up Pictures' mission was to make feature films with a smaller footprint: to keep the cast and crew size small, and to shoot on video with budgets under half a million dollars. We hoped each finished film would premiere at a festival and make a sale to a distributor. But the *big idea* here was to break the mold, to not to make miniature wannabe Hollywood films that were shoehorned into tiny budgets. *Surprise us, shock us, show us something we haven't seen*. We continued to proselytize our mantra in meetings and on panels.

In an upgrade from its former spot, the current Film Forum's flyer was now posted outside the office bathroom door, with a few obscure films circled in yellow highlighter. Jason and Joana instilled creativity and a team mentality in us. They instituted a movie night where we paraded our small group across Spring Street to the cinema. If we finished work on time, we would screen Godard's *Band of Outsiders*, *Z*, or *The Battle of Algiers*. On these nights popcorn was dinner, and we gnawed all the way through the cartons to the un-popped kernels. We were a cheap date.

When I freelanced, it had always seemed that the producers managed most of the work, while they spoon-fed the executives anything they really needed to know. I was terrified I would have nothing to do as an executive, or nothing to contribute. It had been cocky to think that the film set was the center of the filmmaking world. I was only beginning to see how wrong I had been.

I had to truly grasp certain clauses in the contracts that I accepted by rote until now. I was in the practice of copying and pasting from a lawyer's template. A producer that was starting production on Nicole Holofcener's film called from Los Angeles to ask me how net profits would be recouped. I referred them to the clause in our contract. I gave the lazy answer, but the producer needed more. The cut and paste definition from the standard template was not going to suffice. Structuring recoupment deals that weren't derived from a lawyer's template had not been my purview; they were someone else's problem. But now the someone else was me. In the past I had been offered and received back-end participation on films. They were written into my own contracts, but I had been too intimidated to ask how it all worked.

When I worked up the courage to ask, Joana was ready to show me. She tore off the back page of a recycled script from a letter carrier box under the table.

"Have you ever been on a cruise?" She flipped the sheet over and sketched a diagram.

I had not been on a cruise, but I knew that wasn't the point.

"The champagne fountains. When the guy pours a magnum over the stacked-up champagne glasses? It's sort of like that," she said, drawing what looked like the roots of a tree, the liquid champagne now replaced with numbers. "We take the film to Sundance. Let's say we sell it to Artisan for a million dollars."

"Is that enough?" I asked. "I mean, is that enough for everyone to make their money back?"

"Well, we'd have to go through all the contracts to confirm. Then we align it with our clear profit participation definition. But if our theoretical film cost a half million to make, then let's model it." She was patient, drawing more glasses of below. I was learning how waterfall worked through a rudimentary drawing of bubbling alcohol. How did I get this far without knowing this?

"The sales agents and their expenses are on top. The next tier is the recoupment for the guild residuals, WGA, SAG, DGA, because sometimes the distributors won't wear that. That's on us. Then the investors begin to recoup until they get 100 percent of their investment plus an uplift, let's say another 20 percent."

"OK—I've got those figures. I know the guilds hold those residuals in reserve," I finally offered something of substance. But already that big million-dollar check was evaporating quickly.

"Now we split the pour in half after the investors recoup. The investors continue to get one half and the other half is the producer's share; the part that we get to commit in our cast and crew contracts." I had to remember that after the domestic sale, there could be international territories sold and a new magnum would pour through this champagne structure each time we sold to a new foreign distributor.

She continued for a few more tiers. "At the end we've got deferments. Some of the cast has deferred a portion of their salary. The DP, the director, all those glasses are in the same tranche, and they recoup proportionately." What was left over, if anything, after all these payments, was split between the remaining participants, the deferment pool with uplifts.

With this simple image, it all became clear. Now it was obvious how money flowed through to each participant. It was clearly a waterfall. But it's only a waterfall when the film is successful, when it makes a sale, and there's a profit to trickle down to every participant. If it's a huge success, those who put a chunk of their salary aside are rewarded with an uplift, as a good return on their sweat equity investment.

For Blow Up's next film, we ran test after test, working with the lab and with effects houses on grain structure and a "film look" that could be imposed on the image before going through the lab's photochemical process to a 35 mm print. The testing brought new directors and cinematographers who were curious about these options into the mix. The purists turned up their noses and stuck to film. Lots of cinematographers felt this way, but we didn't need them yet. We just needed the willing to be on board.

It wasn't long until much of the independent film community was involved, projecting shared tests in the lab's screening rooms while collaborating about the best practices for cameras, lighting, and workflows. There had always been a shrouded and competitive atmosphere between films, and between production companies. But now we were all suffering the same growing pains and we culled our resources.

Before long, tape stock shifted to a digital file capture. The upgrade away from tape attracted another set of creatives. These filmmakers had been pushing back against this new medium, stuck on the image of a flimsy cassette tape as their medium. Which was fair enough, because surely an expensive day of filming deserves more respect than that.

In our own parallel universe, we continued to make films under the Open City banner the conventional way. Many of these were gun-for-hire jobs, a home for filmmakers from Europe to get their New York-based film in the can on schedule and on budget. We made a fee on these films, enough to fuel our overhead. But these projects didn't just land in our laps—we had to fight for them.

The Villa Urbig's back yard rolled down to a river in the Potsdam section of Berlin. From the back windows of the conference room was just miles and miles of forest, then rolling greens behind either side of the river. Winston Churchill had called this villa *home* when he came to the Potsdam Conference in 1945. What he had seen in post-war Germany had devastated him; flattened buildings, death, and destruction. But now it was the home of the film studio Vif Babelsberg.

The villa was neutral territory for us. Far from our homes across the Atlantic, it was an apropos location to stage a duel. Wolfram Tichy, Potsdam Studio's chief, held court at the head of an oversized antique boardroom table. He squished his meaty palms together and rifled through the shooting schedule's pages. He would produce *Love the Hard Way* starring Adrien Brody in the upcoming winter, and he boiled the location down to either New York or Montreal. The best presentation would be awarded the work.

Squaring off against Montreal, our neighbor to the north, I felt like a contestant on a gameshow. As if I needed to grab a shopping cart and wheel through unfamiliar grocery aisles. Without the boost of a tax credits (there were still no film tax incentives at home) and without any codified low-budget union agreement, the argument in favor of New York was difficult. I had to sharpen my pencil.

What New York had going for it was, well, New York. For a contemporary film written for the city, which *Love the Hard Way* was, the practical locations, extras, and bit players were right there on home turf. In Montreal, we would have to "cheat" all of that and the film's production values would be sacrificed. Montreal's day-to-day costs were exponentially lower than New York's, but cheating would cost money too. Building and flying sets, traveling expensively contracted lead cast and day players, would all be a burden on the budget that wouldn't show up directly on the screen.

Wolfram's team sat around the table surrounding him, and eager to please. If they were going to travel to help make this film in the winter, most of them preferred New York.

"So, what's the plan?" Peter, the director, pulled me aside in the mansion's manicured gardens during a break. "How do we make New York win this contest? Because you know I can't do this in Montreal."

"The numbers don't really lie," I shook my head, not sure if I could deliver the goods. "But the intangibles are harder to prove." I knew that wasn't what Peter wanted to hear. The studio wouldn't speak in intangibles. Even with a careful list of caveats, or what we call *critical assumptions*, accompanying my presentation, Wolfram would rush to the bottom line of the budget.

I spent the next three days in my pajamas, pushing through on a plan from my hotel room. With my nose to the grindstone, I subsisted only on room service's squid ink pasta. Like clockwork, I left the empty plate and cloche outside my door thirty minutes after it had arrived. But in the evenings, I showered and joined the living.

Wolfram's team picked me up for dinner and escorted me to a restaurant on the ground floor of a handsome, wide brownstone. I mock-rehearsed my New York pitch with the group, and the line producer from Montreal did the same pitch for Quebec City; all in good fun. On Saturday, the presentations would be held in the boardroom. Wolfram would make his decision. Win or lose, I would return home.

By Friday, I felt 80 percent ready to prove New York was the right place to shoot the film. And with a few sacrifices, it could be the most economical too. I planned to finalize a few things Saturday morning.

I had no expectations for Friday night—maybe just another date with my pajamas and my laptop—but three female executives in Wolfram's cadre had another idea. After another brownstone dinner, we parted ways with Peter and the male executives, and we took a taxi to the Eastern Bloc.

Now I was eager for entertainment, and excited to see the city through these thirty-something-year-old women's eyes. Since the Berlin Wall had come down only ten years earlier, the West's curiosity with the East (and vice versa) was nascent. We walked down a concrete block of steps behind a surviving section of the Wall and entered a creaky old dance hall. In this room with the climate and the personality of a root cellar, everyone was at least twice our age. A round of a brown liquid was ordered and I obligingly threw back a shot, chasing it with a big glass of lukewarm water, my attempt to neutralize the alcohol's effect. A single disco ball spun in the center of the room, lonesome over the concrete floor. But when the accordion player stepped up to the stage, the spotlight found his face. He squeezed into a peppy tune and activated the audience. Couples rose to populate the dance floor. I wondered if they had been separated by the Wall. Or had they come here every night for years? I could have stayed in this one spot all night, content to have seen all I needed of Berlin. But someone grabbed my hand, and we moved on.

The entrance to our fourth stop of the night was lined with large glass containers, bloated ball mason jelly jars, shelf upon shelf, climbing the walls. Maybe those mysterious brown shots were playing with my head, distorting its contents. Could these hairless creatures be snakes, fetal pigs, or…human? The cool blue eyes of a doll stared out of a jar at me, submerged in water or pickled in vodka. Probably just plastic Mattel toys appropriated for art, I thought. Another shot landed in front of me (it would have been rude to refuse it—I was their guest!) and I was pulled onto the multi-tiered dance floor. We jumped around to an electronic beat across layers of unsteady wooden planks. You could disappear in a place like this, laughing and dancing like you're swirling down a drain. And we did, at least until the ungodly hour of 4 a.m.

I peeled myself up from my hotel bed, ready for the shower's punishment. But I sat down again, hit by a clobbering headache.

The 1945 Potsdam Conference had brought together Stalin, Churchill, and Harry Truman, the vice president who had become president just months before, after the death of Franklin Roosevelt. It was a big deal; the leaders of the "big three" who had defeated the Nazis, now at this summit in Germany. Halfway through the conference, the UK election results came in after the final straggling votes were counted. Churchill was officially and abruptly voted out. Churchill learned his term was extinguished right here in these same halls.

He continued to work hard here, determining the post-World War II balance of power. But at the conference, an ugly tension with Russia started to seep through. The chill of the Cold War was on.

I arrived back at Churchill's mansion, with bags from my hotel in tow. It was a relief knowing I would be on a plane heading home by noon, whether the job was awarded to us or not.

"Let's talk about New York..." I took Wolfram's seat at the head of the table and made my presentation. I pitched with all that was left in me: the projected tangibles and the inevitable intangibles. The end would surely justify my means, because production values would win out.

After all, no one looks at the Brooklyn Bridge, marveling at its feat of engineering, and says "Sure, it's beautiful, but do you know how over budget and over schedule they were?"

| Chapter 14 |

THE MEET CUTE

NEW YORK CITY, NOVEMBER 2000

Al Gore looked calm. The TV network's stock image of Gore was boxed into an electric blue graphic on the left side of the screen. George H.W. Bush's face claimed the right box in red. It had been a tense night as the votes rolled in and ABC News quickly called the East Coast results, stamping a badge of blue or red on each state.

We combined a scout for bars and apartments for a new Blow Up film, *Love in the Time of Money*. At 7 p.m., we landed at a horseshoe-shaped tavern near Tompkins Square Park. We paused the rest of our scout until we could get election results fed to us. With all the cockiness of a rock star (it was his night in the limelight after all), Peter Jennings announced Gore as the projected winner of Florida. There was a roar of relief and a thundering of palms on the bar top. The panhandle had turned decidedly blue. That's it; Al Gore would be our next president.

The apartment owner wouldn't wait for us, so we tore ourselves away from the TV screen's drama and picked up on our scout. We looked at the East Village apartment at night, the same time of day we would eventually be filming it. We tested the light leaking in from the streetlight and the interfering sounds like the barking dogs and the arguing upstairs neighbors. That could be a problem.

During my second summer in the city, I traded apartments for a sixth-floor studio walk-up in the East Village that was just a block from here. It was the summer of the Tompkins Square Park rallies and riots, and the city seethed in a volatile, sweaty protest. I walked past the park each day on my way to work in an act of solidarity; its encampments and signage daring to burst through the borders of the park.

On the most sweltering sequence of days, my mother had come for a visit, and I unfolded my futon couch and flipped the box fan to high. Outside the building the next morning, I produced a carefree and safe East Village scene for her. *Not that street, let's go this way.* We circumvented the park for a white-washed tour of my so-called life. Your audience only sees the angles you've lit for them.

It's the same with bars. When you scout bars in the unforgiving light of day, you get the whole picture; the sticky, worn floors still soaked with beer from the night before. The night patrons don't get this view. The music was loud, the crowd was distracting, and the shoes walked the same floors, but by nighttime it's all a blur. The senses are dulled, or at least unwilling to remember what lies beneath.

Even as I watched Gore's win announced on that tavern TV, I knew we couldn't film there. We were priced out of this location. The bar we could afford to film at was located over the bridge in Williamsburg. There, the rent was cheap because the residential community still mingled with garbage-transfer stations. But not even a slower Monday night would be affordable in Manhattan.

We moved on and scouted an old synagogue, home to a woman who floated around in a velvet cape. The chairs, seats and even the tabletops were upholstered in a similar lush material. We were a small production, a tiny footprint, but we could destroy her velvet paradise and I knew we were wasting our time, and hers.

Even with the synagogue's television muted, Peter Jennings seemed on the edge of frantic. The owner took the remote out of her cape and gave him voice.

"Say it isn't so, Peter," she said to the anchor.

"Hang on, he's backpedaling on Florida," someone said. "This is unreal."

And right there, in the comfort of a velvet synagogue, Florida took a whiplash turn from blue to red, flipping in favor of Bush. We felt deflated, so we called an end to the scout and returned to the bar to figure out what the hell just happened.

Over the next winter months, the Blow Up film and the Open City film from Berlin moved forward on parallel tracks. It was a bipolar prep period, and I was pulled in two directions by two opposite films. One film would shoot 35 mm, and the other one would use video. One film was a union crew, while the other one was so tiny it could get by under the radar. One film had visa issues for the cast and crew from Germany; the other film hired a New York-based cast and created a schedule to work around them. The German film would shoot all over the city at will, the other would stick to a tight grid, mostly within Williamsburg.

The thing these two films had in common was shooting at night on New York's coldest December day on record. It wasn't officially winter on the calendar yet, but in this weather it was a good idea to schedule interior filming; which we did not do.

A row of humming, high-slung sodium vapor lights glowed onto the pavement in the Brooklyn Navy Yard. This section was no man's land, as it jutted out towards the East River. Weeds pushed up from the cracks in the asphalt where the parking lot lines had faded.

The wardrobe supervisor stood by to wrap our actor, Vera Farmiga, in a head-to-toe puffer coat; the bottom of it brushed dangerously close to a portable heater. And it was cold comfort when Vera had to shed the warming jacket and leap back into character in her skimpy costume.

I crossed the 59th Street Bridge, and returned to the German film at a mid-town hotel. They had the smarts to shift to an interior, but the crew still hauled gear and props in from the cold. A helium balloon, the size of an SUV, was tethered to the ceiling, and provided flattering light into each nook of the lobby. The balloon was an expensive rental for the day, but it would save time and money on a pre-light and give us more available angles. It left the floor unobstructed by grip stands and the choreography of the cast was liberated.

Then I saw Bob, the grip.

He was just about six feet tall, and he didn't move quickly, but he crossed the room with efficiency and grace. In a moment, he was on the other side of the set by camera, as if through a time warp. A few seconds later he adjusted a flag, reshaping the light in anticipation of the cinematographer's view through the lens. In the European system, Bob and his team would be under the gaffer's department, answering to the chief lighting technician. But here, he worked directly for the cinematographer and his loyalty lay there. Bob's top-notch work, and his ingenious ways of solving problems, put him high on New York's most-wanted list. In turn, Bob's crew was loyal to him, and that allegiance continued from film to film.

Inside the Tribeca Screening Room, we filmed Adrien Brody while he cradled a bucket of popcorn alone in the theater. He propped his feet on the seatback in front of him and the projector's dusty beam hovered above his head. I stepped outside to take a call from the immigration lawyer as I paced the perimeter of a tiny park; each lap of this triangle marked the progression of the conversation.

"We have a runner standing by," she said, having stationed a proxy to camp near Vermont's visa offices, "but it's just slow going with the work visas. Slow for everyone, not just you."

"OK, so now what can I do? I mean, what else *can* I do?" How could I keep making this movie when the Germans could get deported at any moment? We had jumped through all the right hoops. The letters of recommendation, the proof of their special abilities, and their singular vision. I had collected support from every relationship I had in the business, every union, guild, and every expert. I was prepared to request an endorsement letter from the man in the moon if I thought he could help.

"You've done what you can do. Now just…keep everyone going as if it's all good; the visas should come through in time for Friday's payroll." And in time for Friday's anticipated visit from our Screen Actors Guild representative. The lawyer knew enough to steer clear of the word *relax*. Too much was at stake.

"And if not?" I asked.

"They always come through," now she exhaled, weary of the red tape herself. "And we have documentation that everything's in progress. You've got a movie to make, so go make it. We'll talk tomorrow morning."

I liked this lawyer. She didn't speak in platitudes like *I'll circle back to you* or let's *think outside the box* or even *cut to the chase* (that was the one that I fell prey to, frustrated by long development phases and always ready to shoot). I'll take my bad news straight up, thank you.

With my stress temporarily alleviated, I curled out of my hunched over pose, and raised my head. For the first time, I realized I was standing at the mouth of the Holland Tunnel. A roar of traffic drove past me and across Canal Street.

If you can't be on set all morning, the best short-cut to gauging the set's dynamic is to have a conversation with the first assistant director and the line producer. Seated between them at lunch, you'll get the scoop on the director's relationship with the cast, and the rapport with the crew. You'll learn about the respect given to the director from the cinematographer, and in turn to the cinematographer's crew. A bad attitude could be infectious. If there's a bully or a prima donna at the top, the tone would be gelled. It could shiver its way through the whole set by the end of the first day. A great attitude isn't always as contagious as a bad one, but it helps.

As I sat with Jay, the line producer, and Saskia, his production manager, for the German movie's update, they sorted through schedules and call sheets. We sat in the lounge area of the theater, now repurposed as a catering hall. I felt eyes on my back, and I tried to subtly scan the room to see where they were coming from. There was Bob, the key grip, holding court with his crew at the head of a table.

I thought Bob looked like a stronger version of Sting that could lift his own amps and carry a dolly up the stage steps. I only knew Bob by reputation, and he was his own kind of rock star in the New York film business. He worked on most of Spike Lee's films from *Malcolm X* to *Jungle Fever* and across the iconic ones like *New Jack City*, *Naked in New York*, and *The Cider House Rules*. An Actor like Adrien Brody would walk on set, see Bob and feel reassured. *OK*, they'd think, *there's an adult in the room. A professional.*

Bob stood up to bus his lunch plate and brushed behind me, leaving his team back at his table while they cracked up over some inside joke. My head must have whipped around to watch him go, and I was caught looking.

"Nap time," Jay said, looking at his watch. "Bob naps after lunch in the back of the grip truck. He'll be back on set ready to go though, right on time."

"Bob? Such a sweetheart," now Saskia chimed in. "He just got out of a divorce though. Pretty raw still, so, you know." Saskia grimaced, as if to say, *don't go there*.

"What? No!" I said. "I'm not..." Blood took the express veins to my face, and I heated up with an involuntary blush.

"Everyone loves Bob," Jay said. "He sticks to his guns, protects his crew, and stays on budget. I mean, listen to me, I think *I've* got a crush on him." Jay unleashed his laugh; a high-pitched cackle that made the whole room smile.

The downtown A train rumbled beneath the theater as my cue to get going.

There was a pile of unfinished business, but there was an important lunch meeting that couldn't wait. Jason, Joana, and I took Tom O'Donnell, the head of the theatrical teamsters, to lunch at a Portuguese restaurant near the set of the German film. We were seated in a booth by the window, and I craned my neck for a look down Hudson Street. The trucks from our shoot were just blocks from here. A surge of guilt hit me thinking about our crew working out in the cold. They were loading in for their final day of filming.

We pitched Tom the new Blow Up slate as the "poor nephew to Open City Films." Open City wasn't much of a rich uncle, but it was on better terrain financially; the two initiatives couldn't be confused. Blow Up could be a training ground for crew members who might be testing the waters, and not yet ready to commit to a life in film or join the guilds and unions. These were tricky films to make. The financial risk had to be kept low or the whole philosophy was a bust. The number of teamsters on these films needed to be kept low too. Could he work with us, commensurate with these budgets? Tom listened and nodded, as he took in the whole story; it didn't seem in his character to make snap decisions.

Tom's eyes shifted over my left shoulder to the waiter's entrance. In a bit of a performance, the waiter spun the filet mignon above his head and rounded it down towards the table. The next part played out in slow motion. Tom rubbed his hands together and framed the landing of the plate with his thumbs. It was too late to stop him. By the time he realized the edge of the plate was just exposed cast iron, still cooking his filet, he had already grabbed it. There was a sickening hiss when the cast iron made contact with his flesh, singeing his thumbs. He was stoic but his face turned red and I swore I saw steam come out of his ears. Ice cubes and butter were flown in from the kitchen, and we triaged Tom's bubbling thumbs under a cold towel.

By Christmas, we had wrapped both the German film and the low-budget film. But after the holiday break I flew to Los Angeles where I jumped into pre-production on the next one. For now, I needed to unwind and trade stories with Gayle. I was still unsure how I had managed to make it through these two films without her.

Production managers, location managers, line producers, and producers like us trudged through a snowstorm for the annual Local 817 Teamster Holiday Party. The hotel ballroom in Lake Success was a real dress-up affair, and a way for the teamsters to say *thank you*. Most of us had ducked out of work early, pulled off our work boots, and slipped into heels on the ride over. We were each treated to a boxed gift that was wrapped with a thick blue ribbon. I held my gift under the tablecloth and broke the seal: a wine bottle screw, a beer opener, and a bottle cork. Each nickel-plated tool was emblazoned with double horseheads and the numbers *817;* a match for the key ring Harry had gifted me.

"Three ways to access alcohol. Nice!" said Gayle.

"I think there's a message here," I said. "Drink all you like—a teamster stays sober and gets you home safe."

"And don't even *bother* having your own car in New York City."

Tom waved me over and I approached as I wondered if he was still sore from the scorched-thumb incident. He gave Gayle a friendly hug, but he stopped short of a hug for me. Instead he held up both of his thumbs. They were still red but now scarred from the cast iron. I had a feeling we had burned the wrong guy.

| Chapter 15 |

THE DISASTER MOVIE

LOS ANGELES AND NEW YORK CITY, 2001

Like most New Yorkers, I had an infatuated relationship with Los Angeles. It's a fickle affair with a four-day lifespan.

I landed into ocean-spray, Jamba Juice, sun-soaked LAX. The wind was in my hair as my elbow rested out the rental car window. I felt relaxed and casual in the oversized sunglasses I rarely wore in New York.

A text popped up on my phone from Gayle: *Bob asked about you.* I had to pull over to recover.

Day two was a carbon copy of day one in the weather department. I joined the 6 a.m. line at Starbucks, faithful to the Eastern time zone. But within four hours, the reality of the day set in and it was clear I had overscheduled myself. With the 405 and the 101 traffic, there was no way I could make the second meeting on time, and the rest of the day's line up was already a flattened house of cards. There was no magical underground transport to whisk me around and I was at the mercy of the highway.

On day three, the ocean fog burned the Westside by late morning, revealing—you guessed it—another seventy-five degree sunny day. A better sense of navigation had settled in and I demoted the Thomas Guide to the back seat. Just knowing it was there gave me comfort, with its coffee stain rings and its dog-eared pages.

But by the fourth day, the palm trees had lost their novelty. The beautiful people looked like extras from a movie set, airbrushed and waxy. I missed my New York. This was not a home-after-four-days trip. LA would be my life for the next three months.

I turned east onto Sunset Boulevard, raising the volume on Dido's anthemic cry. Her voice cut into me, where an unreasonable homesickness was already festering. I rewound the iPod again and replayed the song.

After angling the rental down a precariously sloped alley, I entered the back door of Mali Finn's offices. Mali was an excellent casting director for stars, but I admired her most for uncovering raw talent. She was holding second call-backs in search of relatively unknown actors, so it was a glimpse into the cast she would assemble. On the floor, a chemistry read between our lead actor and one of these unknowns. We waited to see if there was some sort of spark between them; like stadium seating for a professional first date.

I waved to Mali and took a seat in the back row. I was eager to disappear into the process. When I leaned forward to hear a performance, my metal folding chair made a long painful scrape across the floor. My body shuddered; embarrassed to bring attention to myself. But Mali was unfazed, and the rude groan of a metal chair would not disrupt her flow.

Paul Quinn's *Never Get Outta the Boat* was the scrappy story of eight guys struggling through rehab in a half-way house. But even with this raw film invoking painful memories of drug abuse for several of the filmmakers, we earmarked the production kick-off with a party at a bar.

It was a sobering first morning on Venice Beach. The camera was hugged into an airtight box of underwater housing that allowed us to shoot through the salt water. Our actor timed a big wave and flipped his surfboard toward camera in a moment of escape on a movie that otherwise shoehorned us into a small ranch house in South Central.

We were three weeks into filming in the ranch house, and the testosterone count was high. Entering the back kitchen onto set was like navigating a minefield, but the emotions were mostly on screen. LA's spring heat wave had everyone sweating. The lack of air conditioning and a bit of method acting nudged the emotions even higher.

I walked away from set for a break with enough time to call Gayle and check in on the shoot she was managing for Wes Anderson, *The Royal Tenenbaums*.

"Bob had an accident on set," Gayle said before I had a chance to give her the gory details of my own set. "He fell over a balcony in Sugar Hill and slammed his head."

"Is he in the hospital?" I didn't know Bob well enough to send him a card. I couldn't call him or text him. There was no role for me to play. I had nothing to fix.

By now I had a long list of producing skills and talents on my resume, but none of these things would help Bob right now. I was needed in LA for another month. An aching pain settled into my throat, as if I had lost something; a nostalgia for something I never had.

✈

A garage band composed of crew technicians took up the open space in a raw loft space in Dumbo. I was Gayle's plus-one at a party celebrating the half-way mark of shooting.

Bob was standing in front of the band in support of a few of his crew. He appeared to be fully recovered, but I knew that already from my updates with Gayle. After a few beers, I worked up enough liquid nerve to say hello to him.

"These guys suck, right?" I said to him, as I nodded toward the band. It was my attempt at a joke. I knew it was his crew in the band. I tried not to shout. I spoke slowly while enunciating every word. But could he read lips? I thought about asking him about the accident and how he was healing, but that seemed too private. It was none of my business.

"I mean, this is your team…your grips?"

Bob nodded and smiled.

"I'm not sure you remember me…Gretchen from the German film?" I was doing that thing I'd done with Debbie Harry, pointing at my chest where an ID badge would be stuck to me.

"Yup. I know," Bob smiled and gave a gentle wink. But I wasn't sure. It might have been loft dust kicked up from the dance floor and stuck in his eye. He had done enough talking for now and he turned back towards the band. It wasn't abrupt or dismissive, it was just too loud for conversation.

I shrunk a little as I clutched my lukewarm Red Stripe. I couldn't maintain any sense of dignity standing there. I backpedaled over to Gayle and joined the circle of crew she had attracted. Bob would tell me later that he didn't remember winking, but it was the possibility of a wink that kept me hopeful for another six months.

On a freakishly clear-sky Sunday, September 9, 2001, Paul Quinn flew from Los Angeles to New York to show the LA film to us. My sister, Elizabeth, was visiting from DC and I left her studying the courtyard art at the World Trade Center while I walked up to our Tribeca office for the screening.

It can be a frustrating experience to watch a movie with its filmmaker. They're sensitive to every cough, every twitch, and every leg cross. You would be too if you poured two years of your soul into a mere ninety minutes of screen time. And this was a small audience; a friendly-fire group of four. The movie we watched would be the film we released. Paul had final cut so it was that simple; that was our deal at Blow Up. He had made precisely the film he wanted to make. We watched it through and then hit rewind to replay a few scenes. Any notes were with a light touch. The time for the big notes on movies like these had passed; back in the script stage. Paul gave us a playful salute and rolled his suitcase into a taxi towards JFK.

On Monday, September 10, I left my home in Williamsburg for Open City's Tribeca office, but I stayed on the E train one extra stop toward the World Trade Center. I did this when I needed a new book, but I was too lazy to haul myself to the library. Tribeca was lousy with the brilliant, curious, and famous people; celebrities with lofts filled with signed, first-edition books. But otherwise, the neighborhood was a literary desert. *Borders* was the only bookstore even close to Tribeca and I decided I needed a hard-cover dictionary in my office. Also, there was a new Deepak Chopra book out that I decided could change my life, help me stop running away, and find a Bob.

In the basement of the World Trade Center, Borders had both books set aside for me with my name on a bookmark inside the cover just like a small-town shop. It was a short five-block walk to our Hudson Street office on another ridiculously beautiful crisp day.

"Thank God for seasons. It's like movement; *progress*." I said to Tory when I opened the back window of the office. "I mean Los Angeles feels like *one season*, all year." My desk faced a dark courtyard, which was a haven for cooing pigeons that had no shame mating on my windowsill.

Tory changed out of her sneakers and unloaded a pile of scripts from her backpack. This was her fun weekend reading. It was fun for her because if there was talent in that pile, she would find it. On her mile plus walk to work, she dropped a quarter for a *New York Post* and read it cover to cover. She navigated around every curb, every sewage drain, and every designer dog from Chelsea—through the West Village and below Soho—flipping through the pages. I imagined tracking her journey on a Steadicam rig. It would show a seamless navigation through the city and be a walking advertisement for the *Post*'s dedicated readership.

I was stuck in LA when Tory had been married in a storybook New York City rooftop wedding. I missed the planning stages and all the thrilling nerves. But now she pulled out an album and flipped through the highlights for me. Her photographer had edited the images, and her stories put me up on that rooftop virtually celebrating with her. With the sequence of images mapped out in order, I'm sure I was there.

The New York City sky had never been so blue, each sequential September day more crisp and pure than the one before it. It was early Tuesday morning on September 11, 2001 and NPR's comforting line up escorted me through my morning routine. But just after 9 a.m., the local host interrupted the national news with a calm statement: *a small plane had hit one of the World Trade towers.*

That was absurd. Why was a small aircraft flying so low? In 1945, the Empire State Building was struck by a war plane and fourteen people were killed. It took a chunk out of the structure; as if King Kong had taken a swipe at it. But the building still stood, solid steel and granite standing firm on a full block in the center of Manhattan. History was proof this too would pass, wasn't it?

I took the pulse of the atmosphere on the street while the announcer built the story. Everything still seemed normal in my immediate environment. Traffic still moved on Bedford, a loud Queens-bound bus made its usual sequence of gasps and groans as it unloaded passengers. Hipper-than-thou commuters paraded toward the L train.

Then NPR died. I tried to tune back in to other stations, but WFMU and WFUV weren't coming in either. NPR was my morning lifeline; I could barely brush my teeth without having its cadences within earshot. I avoided TV in the morning, with all those perky morning shows hosts dragging the unwilling into their workdays. But today was an exception.

CBS was just beginning to broadcast images when Jason called.

"Stay where you are," he said. "Don't come into the office."

"I'm showered and dressed. I even voted!" I said. I had managed to vote around the corner, skulking out of my apartment in a pair of thinly veiled pajamas. The second part—getting to the office—would be easy.

"A plane really *has* hit the World Trade Center. A big one." He was being dramatic, I thought. "Gretch, I'm not being dramatic. This is real. Call Stephanie. I just talked to her—she might still be in the office."

Someday soon, I imagined, Jason would entertain a group of us over a dinner like he always did. He would recount how he overreacted to a small plane hitting the twin towers. We would all laugh when we pictured him pulling the kids into the car and heading north without a destination. Which is exactly what they did, they fled the city, because all of this was real.

Stephanie pressed herself against the office's front picture window, giving me the play-by-play from her view of Hudson Street. She was just five blocks away from everything. I heard fire trucks and ambulances flying downtown. Moments before our call, a devastating boom had shaken the office walls next to her. A rapid hard knock on my door forced me to hang up, and my upstairs neighbor Pam pulled me into the hallway and up to the roof.

Our roof wasn't the kind you would hang out on hot summer days. If you did, your feet would melt into the tar and besides, the landlord forbade us from going up there. But we would still sneak up there to share bottles of wine on warm summer nights. There was no barrier to keep us from falling over the edge. But even if we did trip, a dense crowd of hipsters would break our fall.

Up this high, we could see it for ourselves now: a thick stream of smoke where the small plane must have hit. Black smoke made a haunting trail across the New York Harbor and all the way to Brooklyn.

"It wasn't a small plane. It was a *727*. A real airplane," Pam said. "And another plane just hit the other tower."

"My god, what next?" I said, as I surveyed Manhattan's skyline uptown from the trail of smoke.

"I know someone who's there. She's running into the Battery Tunnel right now to get away. With a whole mob of people."

"What're they going to do with those towers?" I was incredulous, but I calculated that if they could use cranes to build something that high, they could use cranes to fix them too.

Human forms started to show up on every other rooftop. Hundreds of Brooklynites climbing up to their building's highest spot, in an attempt to see it for themselves and make sense of it.

"Let's go watch the TV," I said. "We'll get the whole story."

I started to go but when I turned back around for Pam, one of the towers disappeared, disintegrating under the pull of gravity. It could not be, was it just...gone? We ran down to my apartment and clicked through for a channel. We tuned into a network just in time to watch the second tower fall.

Rachel, Meg, Maria, Alex, and Andy came over. More of our neighborhood friends buzzed up. By eleven o'clock there were fourteen people staring into my TV set with their knees hugged up to their chins. They each gripped their cell phones for signs of life. There were two film directors, a couple of editors, three technicians, at least three musicians, and a muralist huddled in my apartment. With some equipment, we could have organized the group to film some sort of documentation of the day. But we were too busy thinking that this could be the end of the world.

We toggled back and forth through the four channels. I was probably the only apartment in Williamsburg without cable, and I had underproduced their experience. I bent the rabbit ears into the ABC-friendly configuration and clicked over thinking they would have better news. The reports about the planes at the Pentagon and Pennsylvania forced me to the other end of my shotgun apartment just to check again and confirm that the Empire State Building was still standing.

Still no word from my mother, but most calls were going to a busy signal. I resolved to stop trying her. She was safe in Massachusetts and far from this hell. But I hoped that she was trying to reach me.

The living room felt like a newsroom; a cacophony of TV, cell phone buzzes and rings, and one-sided conversations. Updates and rumors from the outside world were blurted out like currency. By noon, there was an excited energy of guilt mingling with mortality, and it coincided with the opening hour of the state liquor store on the ground floor.

I was the first in line to buy three liter-sized bottles of red wine. I pushed our collection of bills through the metal cash bowl toward the other side of the plexiglass. It was like buying wine at a prison canteen—not joyous, just serviceable. If I wanted to feel good about buying alcohol, I could go to the fancy wine shop and splurge on artisan cheese.

It seemed that stress absorbed alcohol. The liters of wine and six-packs of Brooklyn lager didn't last long. The front door rang again, and I leaned against the wall and buzzed whoever it was up indiscriminately.

It was a relief to finally step outside into the cool air and take in some deep breaths, but it seemed that all of Brooklyn was out on the street. Our nervous pack stumbled down to the Turkey's Nest; a local dive bar known for its barstool mix of Hasidic Jews, blue-collar workers, and East Village transplants.

All eyes were glued to the bar's TV screen, and I had been separated from my group. I was sandwiched between a guy with a camera slung around his neck and a rabid conspiracy theorist.

"You know, this changes everything," The camera guy said. His tone felt urgent, but somehow casual.

"It's awful. All those people…"

"No. I mean everything. How we travel…security," he said, still casual. "Making films. Everything's a new deal."

On the other stool, the conspiracy theorist overexplained how the whole thing was rigged, but I couldn't make sense of his logic. Beer and wine sloshed around in my head, as it searched for a happy place and came up empty. When my little red Nokia lit up on the bar, I grabbed it in relief and burst out onto the street. It was my mother.

"Thank God you're alright. I must have dialed you a dozen times." Twelve tries? On this day of the largest US disaster in modern history…twelve tries? If ever there were a time to exaggerate, this might have been it.

I shifted focus to Bob. What was Bob doing in this moment? How was he getting through this with his kids? Was he stuck in the city? Was he OK?

The group dissolved, but for the next several days we wandered our neighborhood. We bumped into each other like stray pool balls. We drank too much and pretended to feel protected by the roar of seven jets circling our skies. We tried to find ways to be helpful, but a ceremony of candles with the victims' names floating on the East River didn't save anyone. The city's soundtrack was muted.

All our efforts felt futile. Movies felt futile. Who would sit still for ninety minutes anymore? We were unsure whether we would have jobs or if the city would even exist in a day. We held a sandwich drive. We packaged food into brown bags to send down to Ground Zero, where hundreds of film technicians took their good will and equipment to erect lights for nighttime digging. They were still in search of survivors below acres of smoldering rubble.

I did other futile things like making a cheesecake and running it up to a firehouse in Harlem, the house of an old boyfriend's brother. I made another cake a week later, and swapped out the pan at the firehouse. It wasn't much, but it was something.

Being so close to Ground Zero, Open City was forced out of its Hudson Street offices. A week after the towers fell, I showed my ID on 14th Street. A policeman lifted a ribbon of caution tape, and I ducked under to the other side. Everything was cordoned off to allow emergency vehicles through. I navigated around burnt-out cars, fire trucks, and hollowed-out ambulances. It was like an active war zone. The air was thick and tainted with the severe smell of what I hoped was plastic. A smell sworn to memory.

From outside our office's ground floor window—the one Stephanie leaned against on 9/11 when we spoke—I could see a thick film of dust coating every surface. I flipped the light switches up and down. There was still no power below 14th street. There was also no phone service and no internet. In the back of the office, by the open window of the pigeon courtyard, my open laptop sat on my desk where I had left it. I turned it over and strange chunks of dirt—black like charcoal—trickled out from between the keyboards. It was a sickening sound. I slammed down the sash of the window, grabbed my laptop, and left for our West Village safehouse.

| Chapter 16 |

THE SCREWBALL COMEDY

NEW YORK CITY, 2001

We were offered a post-9/11 office at Goldcrest Films in the Meatpacking District where framed posters of the UK-owned company's productions lined the hallways: Pink Floyd's *The Wall*, *A Room with a View*, *Chariots of Fire*, *Local Hero*. It was like a who's who of British cinema.

Goldcrest's owner John Quested led us to an empty suite on the second floor. Well above six-feet tall with a full head of white hair, John was recognized and greeted by everyone in these halls. He was John Ford's first assistant director and he had worked with the British greats like Richard Attenborough and Ken Hughes. I liked the idea of working within a company owned by filmmakers. If we made movies under John's roof, we would be two degrees of separation from a classic like *Stagecoach*.

John held his hands overhead when the subject of rent came up. He refused to discuss it as he knew we were struggling to cover an overpriced Tribeca rent. We would work here rent-free. With this act of kindness, my faith in film-kind was restored. But I wondered when the sentiment would expire. New York City was the capital of money, with or without its towers. There would eventually be an invoice.

Tory, Stephanie, Robin the Office Manager, and I huddled close together in a bullpen. We were comforted by a set-up that forced us to work side by side. One staircase away from the safety of the street, and one block away from the Hudson River escape, life was reduced to the simplicity of single digits.

Gayle met me on Goldcrest's front stoop for a dinner date. On the walk over, I wanted to unload to her about our cash flow problems at work and the stress over losing an office. Even with all the films we had in motion, we were a company on the verge of folding.

"Missing" flyers of loved ones were still stapled to storefronts, subway entrances, and telephone poles. Any story I could tell Gayle about my own financial drama paled in comparison to New York's tragedy. On the sidewalks around us there were people still hopeful that a partner wasn't lost in the collapse, hanging onto the idea that instead they wandered down these avenues in a state of amnesia. It had been a full month since the towers fell, but human remains continued to be dug up and identified at Ground Zero.

"We need a new distraction. We need to forget for tonight," I begged Gayle for an idea. We couldn't fly off to Europe like we used to; we needed a local destination.

"At least you have a job to distract you—I haven't worked since 9/11," she said. Already the phrase *9/11* had been hammered to death by the news reports, but it still stung. Then, out of left field, "Do you still salsa dance?" Gayle asked.

"Sort of…not for a while," I said, "Salsa's like darts or bowling. With some wine, I can fool myself into thinking I'm good at it." I was already working up the courage.

"I know a place. On the Lower East Side…." Even off duty, Gayle knew a place.

The wine seemed to go down much smoother and much faster since 9/11. The liquor stores and bars were getting the upside of our collective crutch. Within fifteen minutes, it was decidedly an excellent idea to invite Bob to come salsa with us.

"Bob!" Gayle said into her cellphone. I covered my mouth like a conspiring teenager on a prank call.

"Gayle?" I could hear Bob's slow response.

"I'm here with my friend Gretchen. You remember Gretchen?" She said the last three words in slow motion. Something inaudible followed on his side, and then she told him about the salsa plan.

"Hm, tempting…" he said, then a long pause. "Honestly? I was just about to curl up with a book…." but *yes*, he'd drive into the city to dance with us.

I stepped on Bob's feet a few times when I walked him through the salsa steps, but we laughed and eventually found some sort of compromise on the stretch of floor on Attorney Street. For the first time since the attacks, I felt a sense of joy.

Later, we sat in Bob's car outside the Salvation Army store across the street from my apartment. A single bright security sign lit up the interior of the shop and highlighted the circular racks of sweaters all organized by primary colors. Finally, he leaned toward me for a kiss.

It was not the smooth start I had hoped for—the seamless romantic beginning to a new relationship—because there is always baggage. Even in the rocky November beginnings Bob drove me to the airport. It would be my first time in the air since September 11th. I didn't want to fly—in fact I would have been OK never flying again—but I was invited to Miami to speak on a filmmaking panel, and it was the right thing to do. In this new world, we were required to arrive at LaGuardia two hours ahead of flights which seemed like a colossal waste of time.

For years, I prided myself on how close I could cut the trip to the airport. I could arrive within half an hour, fly through security, stow my carry-on, and still find my seat before they pulled the boarding bridge up. But traveling by air—as that guy at the Turkey's Nest had predicted—was a new ordeal, and it would be like that for the foreseeable future. Our plane followed the Hudson River south, directly over the smoking embers of Ground Zero. It was a morbid view, and maybe even a violation to be in that air space.

The Miami panel's theme that was organized months before the twin tower attacks, was "How to Survive the Independents." The mission was to explore what we do without the studio's deep pockets and why the hell we do it. The moderator turned to Jake—whom I had invited from another New York production company called InDigEnt, a clever abbreviation for Independent Digital Entertainment. Jake was at least ten years younger than I was, but he had the self-assurance of a seasoned producer. I looked at him, and thought I could dissect and learn from his unabashed cockiness.

"How do you do it Jake?" the moderator probed. "How do you keep your budgets so low? Are you paying people enough to survive in New York?"

"Sure, we are," Jake wasn't defensive, instead he was generous with his stories. "We find films that we've got to make and then everyone's a beneficiary. If the film sells, everyone wins, and then we all recoup on an even playing field. Everyone from the lead actor on down to production assistant is an equal investor."

"Gretchen," the moderator shifted her attention to me, and I felt the dread at the sound of my name. Blood was in the starting blocks, and it was preparing to blush me. "You play a similar role at Open City and Blow Up. And on the Blow Up films, you can't pay your freelance crews a lot either. How do you compete with the bigger films?"

"I'd like to think of it like this: today's low-budget Blow Up crew is tomorrow's Open City crew, then maybe tomorrow's Hollywood studio crew." It hit me that I was speaking to a small crowd and my legs were standing still. My voice was not wavering. I had taken advantage of the free breakfast spread and the nutrition was paying off. "Blow Up can be a training ground, and a chance for a grip to find out if they want to be a film technician. Or she can experiment in the camera department or learn to hold a boom microphone before making the big commitment... before joining the union."

Miami felt like the other side of the earth from New York that weekend. The panel organizers treated us New York panelists with kid gloves. They were careful not to damage the walking wounded. After only two days along this postcard-perfect beachside city bathed in pastels, I felt like I was cheating on my city, and my gut twinged for home.

If the relationship with Bob had momentum in its early days, it was thanks to Ben Stiller and the Yankees. Not the individuals, but the institutions. Stiller's comedy *Zoolander* was our first real date, and Bob and I bonded over fake model struts and blue steel poses. A good comedy can be a window into the soul of your date. If they're willing to laugh until they cry, there's hope for a second date. I saved the ticket stubs and taped them to the inside of my desk.

The Yankees played their part by extending their season into November, which qualified them for the World Series even after the city came to a grinding halt. On that night, I approached a location assistant on the rigging set of *Men in Black II*, asking where I could find Bob.

"Is he in the subway?" I asked.

"Yeah. Welcome to my world. Where 90 percent of the job takes place underground," she said.

Bob and his team were rigging the subway station beneath the Museum of Natural History. They filmed plates for the movie, something they could do without actors on set. The actors, and any visual effects would be added later. Equipment like lights and stands could be painted out, like pasting a collage of moving images over each other.

As an outsider, I don't like visiting film sets. It feels like an invasion of privacy, an illegal peek into trade secrets of someone else's circus. It's also boring. If I'm on set, I want to serve a purpose and move things forward. Bob emerged from the subway steps and waved me over to his truck. He grabbed his canvas bag. He was ready to wrap and grab a pre-game drink with me.

I was not a serial dater. And if I was ever good at dating, I wasn't any longer. I was out of practice. Most of the relationships I'd had in the past—and, ultimately failed at—came out of introductions through mutual friends. There was an organic way of getting to know a person, socializing with a group, and letting things develop from there. These dates with Bob—the movie and now the baseball game—felt like I was joining the civilian world of dating. The grown-up world of planning and engineering a bond. It was so real that it made me nervous.

I blame those nerves for what came next. I dropped my purse into the bar's bathroom sink; it was the only surface in the room. It was one of those sinks with a sophisticated faucet, the kind that senses when human hands need water. And when I reached underneath to tie my shoes, the sensitive faucet mistook my purse for a pair of soapy hands. My purse stood in the sink like a bucket, retaining a full quart of water. I dove in for the only two things of value: the Yankees tickets and my waterlogged phone. I attempted cell phone CPR, and with no rice to dunk the phone in, I had to resort to the bathroom's hand blower. All this occurred while Bob waited patiently at the bar.

The Yankees fans were rowdy. It was game five in a best-of-seven series and we had endured the long line for bag inspection at the ballpark gates. Now the crowd's energy was unleashed when Paul O'Neill caught a pop fly to center field.

"Oh!" the ringleader of the bleachers yelled, as he cupped his hands around his mouth and blasted his lungs.

"Neill!" the crowd followed, and the speed ramped up with the exchange: "Oh"... "Neill" "Oh Neill." O'Neill finally took off his cap and waved it around toward his worshippers in the cheap seats. The crowd ate it up and O'Neill smiled. He turned his focus back on the next hitter and punched his fist into his glove.

Beer was not allowed in the bleachers, which was an indication that they tried it out before but made the call that alcohol and bleachers were a bad mix. But even without the beer, a competition between the box seats and our *bleacher creature* neighbors was brewing.

The guy in charge of the *Oh* in O'Neill started up on a new chant. *Fuck the box seats* with each word drawn out long and not too kid-friendly, but no one seemed to mind.

Maybe it was a ritual they played out at every game, but the box seats rallied and came back to taunt us, "We've got beer! We've got beer!"

And then the creatures responded with the last word. If they couldn't see us under a cloud of smoke, they could hear us, "We've got weed! We've got weed!"

I checked my phone, but it was at death's door. Its LCD screen gave a pathetic blink, on and off—then off for good. Fine, I let it go. I was sitting next to the only person I wanted to hear from anyway.

With each passing week, we could walk further downtown without police barriers to stop us, but the smell of burning plastic still got caught in my throat. Our production team stayed at Goldcrest until December when the caution tape across Canal Street was cut, power and phones were restored, and the authorities gave us the green light to return.

It was a bittersweet departure from Goldcrest; this new home away from home. But it seemed that this was the start of a collaboration. Goldcrest was creating the city's first fully digital postproduction facility, and we had watched it take shape. More editors and more talent came into the building each day. John still wouldn't allow us to pay rent. When our office manager Robin tried, he snuck into our room and placed the rent check back on her desk.

Was it too soon to see 9/11 in our entertainment? We all wanted the year 2001 to be over, but busloads of tourists still streamed down to Ground Zero. They would grab the chain link fence to stake a claim on this massive graveyard. And like all of commerce, entertainment hustled to take advantage of the zeitgeist.

By December, Ed Pressman introduced us to *The Guys*. It was a play staged at the Flea Theater—a Tribeca neighbor around the corner from us on White Street. The playwright, Anne Nelson, had met with surviving firefighters, and helped them write the eulogy speech that no one ever wanted to deliver. An audience of forty spread out across four lines of folding chairs qualified as an off-off Broadway packed house. Sigourney Weaver and Alec Baldwin took the stage, and the audience stowed away their playbills.

I was stoic during *The Guys* performance, and maybe even angry. I usually have a delayed reaction to any theater performance. The *aha* moment takes time to crystallize, but more likely, I was not ready to share my emotions with an audience surrounding me.

The play hit me by surprise. The first wave came as the L train hurtled under the East River towards Brooklyn. I shook around on the metal pole, swallowing deep sobs. Then my eyes involuntarily flooded and I had to recognize the impact of those eulogies, and the sheer volume of funerals and bagpipe whines over the past three months. I climbed the interminable subway steps and then my hallway stairs where I could let it all go alone in my apartment.

On the last step, I thought I smelled roasting garlic coming from behind my door. But it was just a fantasy, there was no dinner and no Bob cooking a meal in his chef's apron. He was back at his apartment in New Jersey. He had told me I needed to be patient; he was still working out some things in his life.

Patience for me took the shape of distraction with long days at work, and nights out with friends. I said yes to every opportunity. I wish I could say I hardly noticed the time, but that would be a lie. Each night, I rushed home to hover over my spinning AOL mailbox, telling me *you have mail!* On most days, there was an email from Bob.

The male lead for our movie adaptation of *The Guys* needed to be an expert tango dancer. He would deftly guide Sigourney across the apartment floor as she peeled back the layers of his character and the men he eulogized. But even with some movie magic and editing tricks, our lead actor needed to immerse himself in tango lessons for this challenging dance. We had two weeks to pull it off.

I tracked down Paul Pellicoro in his studio. From the subway kiosk, I could see the studio sign, *DanceSport,* in blue cursive neon popped out of the second-floor window overlooking Lincoln Center. Paul greeted me and I trailed behind his slight dancer's frame, through a group of ballroom dancers, to his office in a back room. A collage of autographed glossy photos from Winona Ryder, Robert De Niro, and Mira Sorvino decorated his walls. A larger gold-framed image of Al Pacino in *Scent of a Woman* took up a chunk of real estate behind his desk. Paul gestured around him as if to say, *isn't it obvious you've come to the right place?*

"Do you dance?"

"Salsa?" I said as if it were a question, meaning *does salsa count?* "I mean that's the only dancing lessons I've had, besides square dancing back in grade school." Square dancing did not count, I could tell by his response. "I took salsa in Brooklyn. They offer classes..."

"Oh right, free lessons if you come early to salsa night," Paul offered a knowing nod.

Salsa may have been low on his dancing rung, but when my friends and I had taken a few classes before my work in Costa Rica, I was voted *most improved*. Salsa was about letting go, a willingness to be spun around and stay married to the touchstone—the rhythm.

"Tango, of course, is not salsa," this could be a sermon he had preached to other potential converts; ones that were worthy of the upgrade. "Tango is *passion*...sensitivity...connectivity!" Paul pitched me on why he was great with instructing actors on the art of dance. He would teach Sigourney to master the tango, and she would thrive because there is nothing she could not tackle. She had beaten ghosts and slaughtered aliens, she had befriended gorillas in the mist, and now she would attack *The Tango*.

Paul pulled a book from his shelf, one of many copies of his tango opus, *Paul Pellicoro on TANGO*. He scribbled a brief note for me: *Thank you for hiring me. You're a nice person*. And he appointed himself the official dance czar of *The Guys*.

An insurance claim can be like dusting for fingerprints at a murder scene. It isn't until we projected a film print of the dailies that we noticed a focus problem on certain shots of *The Guys*.

"It's soft. All the 75 mm lens shots are soft." Jason stood by the screen in a performance for the insurance adjuster. He directed a laser pen on the actual point of focus that was far behind Sigourney's projected face. "See, it's back focus, it's not finding her face."

"Every lens was tested during the camera check out. We printed all the registration tests and none of them, not even that 75 mm lens, showed any issues." I added to the story for the insurance representative. We had a huge equipment liability—back focus affecting nearly every scene. What looked like precision focus through the camera's eyepiece was inaccurate. We would have spotted it if we had been printing and projecting dailies each night. But that convention had been discarded on most films, which saved money and time. Instead, we only watched the dailies that had been transferred to video, where focus issues could be glossed over.

We were awarded the claim, and in a case of déjà vu, we booked the same brownstone location in Harlem, reassembled the crew, and prepared to shoot the film a second time.

That night, when I took the steps to my apartment, it was not my imagination. It *was* Bob's roasted garlic that I smelled. Little by little, with each trip to see me in Brooklyn, Bob's toothbrush and his gear had marched up the stairs with him. Now he was here most weeknights, while he commuted to Silvercup Studios.

Bob knew his way around this galley kitchen better than I ever did, and he was a far better cook. He stepped out of the galley to greet me and nodded toward the drop leaf table, the place where we unloaded everything.

"Open it!" he said, possibly more excited than I was. It was a black case with a bow on it and I recognized the shape and the yellow *Dewalt* lettering on its cover. I smiled, not at all surprised that Bob's first material gift to me was a cordless power drill.

"Are you sure you're OK? Maybe you should see a doctor about that?" Jim Jarmusch cringed and cocked his head sideways when he asked about my face.

This was not a good first impression. My eye socket had puffed out to the size of a lemon, and my face was red and swollen. I thought back to what might have caused it. I had peeled and eaten a mango from the corner deli for breakfast, and this wasn't my first allergic reaction to mango skin. But this felt more reactive, like a bee sting or a spider bite gone mad.

"It's not as bad as it looks. I'm okay" I said as I touched the swelling, not at all sure how scary it looked. "I have some allergies."

Maybe it was my nerves again, or maybe I was starstruck. We were helping Jim produce *Coffee and Cigarettes* and I would be the point person from pre-production all the way through delivery. I flipped through a draft of the schedule I had put together that allowed for the sporadic availability of his cast. Jim and his producer, Stacey, had some comments and I scribbled them into the margins. I had done this countless times for filmmakers like Peter Bogdanovich and Nick Gomez. I should have been confident, but the eye infection made me visibly shake as I turned the pages. I looked to Stacey and took a breath. Something about her presence made me calm down and forget my disfigurement. She had the frenetic energy of the other redheads I had known, but I sensed that she was going to be a solid partner in this.

When Jim got up to leave, he made a funny face at me. Then I remembered my hideous eye and I put my hand up to cover it. "Yeah, maybe have someone take a look at that thing?" he said in an actual appeal for me to see a doctor. And then he was out the door.

Bob and I pushed our books against each other on the shelves in no particular order. Our libraries intersected with *The Perfect Storm*, *The Handmaid's Tale*, and *the Webster's Collegiate Dictionary*. By Easter weekend, we shared everything: our meals, the bathroom counter, and our illnesses. When the flu hit us, we sequestered ourselves to the couch for the weekend. We got up only to change over to the next VHS in the box set *I Claudius*. Watching television with Bob was an interactive experience—like a bonus commentary track. It's a play-by-play of what rigs are being used and what it's like to shoot complicated scenes in the rain, at night, and so on. It's like I was going to film school for free.

Bob recovered in time to return to set on Tuesday, but I spent the day sideways on the couch, resisting the temptation to stab a pair of scissors into my clogged ear. The intense pressure was only relieved when I pushed the palm of my hand against my ear, creating a suction-cup effect. The relief was only temporary. I dripped the pharmacy's solution into my ear canal and waited for the pop of relief and the pain to subside. But it didn't. The pain only intensified until I thought my head would pop off.

When Bob came home and saw the state I was in, he grabbed a pan from the rack. He warmed up a thimble of olive oil and gently poured it into my ear. Within moments, my ears gave a gentle pop, the pressure gone.

If you must be stranded on a desert island with one member of the crew, I hope you get the grip. Even without their trusted pocketknives and multi-tools, the grip is the one most likely to MacGyver into a coconut without spilling the milk. They are the most capable of building a raft from dry seaweed and ocean trash. It was no lie that Bob knew how to douse for fresh water while sourcing a stick and his strong will. And it was important to note that he had raised two kids and managed to keep them alive.

If I wasn't already convinced, I knew what true love was now.

Ami Z waited for me in the Ramada lobby wearing a rainbow beret over her salt and pepper curls.

"Did I tell you or did I not tell you?" She pointed to her hat and smiled; she was just as she had described herself.

While we filmed *Coffee and Cigarettes* on a sporadic schedule, we also developed another film, *The Assassination of Richard Nixon,* in San Francisco. Ami and the Oakland Film commission flew me in and put me up for a week. They promised to help me get the budget in shape and begin to secure locations and local crew.

We drove away from Jack London Square and into the grittier sections of Oakland. I had my eye out for an exterior that could stand in for the script's Black Panther headquarters; I knew this would be our more challenging find. Ami pulled over when I pointed at a garage I liked.

"The owner is from Brooklyn, would you believe it?" I said. I jumped back into the passenger seat with the owner's business card—one connection richer.

The more I learned about the escalated costs of filming in the Bay Area, the higher the budget climbed. I had been spoiled by free movie police in New York City. Here, the costs of a period 1970s film made sure that police, security, and locations were out of our range. Union rates for the area and idle days for a distant location would bowl this budget over.

We pulled up to the South Bay by the railroad tracks and Ami pointed across to Alameda, an island just south of Oakland.

"Manex is just over there," she said. *Like Oz,* I thought. Manex was the visual effects house that created "bullet time" for *The Matrix*. Now they were busy working on the sequels. It was tough for smaller film like ours to be held up against a Hollywood franchise.

Ami kept promising that I would have a meeting with Mayor Jerry Brown. The meeting would help open more doors. But as I hammered away at the numbers, I wasn't sure how he could help.

"Just missed him," Mayor Brown's secretary said when Ami and I checked in, "he's out on an emergency." Ami opened the mahogany door for a peek into the mayor's empty office as though she was trying to prove that he really wasn't there. I swore I saw the mayor's swivel chair rock a bit, and I wondered if he was hiding behind the drapes.

The film would star Sean Penn, San Francisco's local hero from the liberal left. Ami took a leap and assumed I was on board the fight to keep the US out of Iraq. She was right.

"You guys in New York, 9/11 was terrible for you. Just devastating." Amy said, "We feel it too, we're with you. But you know we're not going to put up with another Gulf War. Afghanistan is already too much. We'll protest."

"We will too, Ami," I said. I knew it wouldn't be the first protest for either of us. This wasn't the first time I had to defend New York while I was on location. Had the rest of the world only shuddered while we were violently attacked? As worldly as we thought we were, had New Yorkers been insensitive to the world's problems that came before?

I needed to fly back to New York for more filming on *Coffee and Cigarettes* and to prep another film. But first, I made a few important calls. One call was to introduce the director to Mali Finn so they could begin casting together in Los Angeles. The other call was to hire a line producer who would lead the charge in San Francisco while I managed New York.

Jim Jarmusch's brother, Tom, pulled together locations all over Manhattan and Williamsburg. He could forecast Jim's reaction to a space before Jim walked in the room. But for reference, Tom shot stills of all the location candidates and processed them at Flash Photo behind Canal Street. He pasted panoramas of spliced prints together, overlapped the images within manila folders, and identified them in sharpie. It was still the same wonky and rough process that Diana had used seven years ago on *Heavy*; not much had changed in that department. But these images were the visual cues we needed when we argued the pros and cons of a location.

Our hero location was an armory at the top of Fifth Avenue. We walked through this hulking structure together and Jim had mapped out where we could film three or four scenes within this one building. The production designer, Mark, would install black and white checkered floor tiles, and with a few more tricks he would transform an uptown armory into a downtown café. The cast availability aligned with the schedule and the scripts were mailed.

And then it all went pear shaped.

In our country's misguided attempt to avenge 9/11 with lies about weapons of mass destruction, the armory reverted to its original mission as a check-in center. The troops and reserves would report here before shipping out to Iraq in a week. The loss of our main location was tiny by comparison. We scrambled and reset.

Our next biggest challenge was a split screen shot, when Cate Blanchett would play opposite herself. She arrived at our Second Avenue stage and seemed to float across the set. The upscale version of Cate took a seat in our hotel lobby set, ordering a double espresso with steamed milk on the side. Her character was in town for a press junket, but she oh-so-kindly took time out to meet with her cousin.

This was the only scene we'd shoot in 35mm, because when Cate moved to the seat across the set to play her own cousin in a conversation with herself, we'd split the screen, and 35mm film stock had a much better "pin register" than 16mm, making it easier to align the two shots in post-production. We broke for lunch and a production assistant guarded the camera's lock down, otherwise we'd lose our precise positioning. Then we watched as Cate transformed her otherworldliness into her alter ego, a Williamsburg hipster.

It was the most perfect script I had read, but it wasn't my film to make. The Long Island Railroad train picked up speed after we left city limits. We flew through farmland, vineyards, and that final strip of land surrounded by ocean. In Montauk, Bob would pick me up at the station featured in the screenplay of *The Eternal Sunshine of the Spotless Mind*. I finished the last page and closed Bob's script copy before the train tugged into the end of the line. Charlie Kaufman's disorienting love story of hurt and regret crushed me. No logline or pitch could do the script justice.

We drove up to Montauk Manor, a Tudor mansion looming over town, where the crew was housed. I remembered the Manor from when I came to Montauk to recover from *Buffalo '66*. It had been abandoned then, and I had run around the grounds on foggy mornings, imagining ghosts knocking croquet mallets against the balls—a Stephen King sort of cliché. Now, the lobby's fireplace glowed against overstuffed couches and pristine white arches. Wood beams framed a sturdy ceiling. The crew sprawled around on the furniture as they enjoyed a day off. I knew the producers and many of the crew, but I took a hard right down the hallway to avoid a collision with any of them.

The keys to the Gator were kept in the ignition and Bob drove us along the beach where a huge crane was being built for a long shot on this stretch. Snow swirled around and mounted up in town, but it dissipated near the water. It was too cold for us to be on the beach, but next to Bob I was impervious to it.

Bob and the crew created ingenious in-camera smokescreens, shooting through plastic sheets framed in 2-by-4 portable doorways. The film would illustrate the loss of a memory—like the struggle to remember a dream—through a deteriorating cliffside beach house. It was not my movie, but I felt lucky to have a glimpse inside some of its inner machinations.

Soon after Bob wrapped *Eternal Sunshine,* we began to look like a normal Brooklyn couple. The kind of couple where Bob did the cooking and sent me off to the work after breakfast. We started to embrace the domestic cadence, until the director on the *Nixon* job called from Oakland.

"Can you come back?" the director said, a desperate twinge in his voice. "We need your help. The bond company's leaning on us, looking to cut shoot days. We can't cut scenes, but I think you'll have some ideas—some other ways to find it?"

As if I was the magic bullet; the fixer. Or as if the money was hidden somewhere, and I just needed to *find it*.

"Let me book a flight—I'll be there tomorrow." I kicked into gear, packing a suitcase and booking a ticket that would depart from LaGuardia at a rude morning hour.

I went through the motions of getting ready for another trip, always the team player ready to drop my life and show up. Bacon crisped up in the oven and Bob flipped a buckwheat pancake. I sat half-dressed at the table and something on my fork glistened. I incredulously reached for it and I realized it was a ring.

"I'll be a day late," I told the director with no apology. I had just accepted a marriage proposal and I was going to celebrate.

"Go, go! I mean stay; you've got to stay! That's huge," he said, but I wasn't sure his heart was in this reaction. "It's your first, right?"

"First wedding proposal? First one I can remember."

"Hah, right," the director said, "But get here when you can, OK?"

Dave Pultz, DuArt's color timer, hung up the phone in the lab's theater and turned to me and Fred Elmes, the cinematographer. The three of us were one reel into a five-reel projection of our first *Coffee and Cigarettes* print. On the screen, Cate Blanchett's image was now married together into one seamless frame. The lab's visual effects team had stitched the two shots together, and now posh

Cate leaned across the screen towards hipster Cate where their eyelines met.

"Irwin's giving a tour," Dave pointed at the phone receiver. "Do you mind if he pops in here with Dr. Ruth?"

"*The* Dr. Ruth? Sure!" I said. I stood up and took quick stock of my outfit. I ran my palms down my skirt and fastened another button on my blouse. I mean, it was Dr. Ruth—it just seemed like the right thing to do.

The owner of DuArt Film Laboratories, Irwin Young, had done many favors for our New York productions, and I was happy to do this small thing for him. Rumor had it that the hallways leading to this screening room were lined with original art from filmmakers. They were gifts to Irwin from those who ran out of money in post-production. Artwork in lieu of payment. That's how much he loved the business, and the filmmakers.

Irwin and Dr. Ruth popped in and Dave lifted the light levels so she could admire the screening room.

"Ah, very nice," she said, nodding. Irwin hunched over a bit, but he still towered over Dr. Ruth by a foot. Somehow Dr. Ruth took up the same amount of space.

"Gretchen's just been engaged!" Dave blurted it out, pointing at me, putting me on the spot. "Do you think it's a good thing, Dr. Ruth?"

She threw her head back and gave us her signature Dr. Ruth laugh. "I wish you many blessings," I think she said. I couldn't wait to tell Bob that Dr. Ruth herself had just anointed our engagement.

| Chapter 17 |

THE MOCKUMENTARY

NEW JERSEY, 2004

I bounced up and down on the wide pine floors.

"Are they too squeaky?" the agent seemed nervous, or maybe she was just annoyed.

"They seem good. Solid," I quit the bouncing act and rolled the carpet back over the exposed corner. The dated wall-to-wall carpet would be the first thing to go. "Every floorboard in my childhood home creaked. So even if they do squeak, it's like home."

It was my second trip to Essex County in New Jersey to test drive this early 19th century house. I wasn't scouting for another movie, I was leaving ten years of Williamsburg behind and Bob and I were searching for a home together. It had to have a place for a garden, a rental above the garage, and maybe room enough for a dog.

We were in a town with great historical significance, but when the Garden State Parkway ploughed through the center, its charm was bisected. The first film studio was built three miles from where I stood; a replica of it was still standing. In Edison's Black Maria, the alchemy of film surprised the world when the first film, *The Sneeze*, was made. But the real draw to this location was that we could be close to Bob's kids.

"What I'm worried about is the traffic." It was a rainy rush hour, a good night to gauge whether the streets were loud enough to penetrate the living room windows. The house had been under contract with another buyer, but it had fallen through. The sellers were hungry. Could it be too good to be true or was the timing just right for us?

"Traffic never bothered me," the owner shrugged. The real estate agent gave the owner a glare as if to say, *shouldn't you be in another room while I close this deal?*

Our offer was accepted on the house, and I finally accumulated enough savings to split the deposit with Bob. But I found closing on a house to be just as intense as closing on a film's financing: reams of paperwork, signatures, inspectors, bankers, and lawyers. All the entities wanted to push the closing date, but I wasn't having it. This was not complicated. It was just two parties, a few signatures, and one giant certified check.

"Congratulations," Bob said as we took our walk-through after signing our names on the dotted lines at least four hundred times. "You're a first-time homeowner of a two-hundred-year-old house with one oversized ball and claw bathtub."

"And a porch. And lots of other charming idiosyncrasies," I added.

"Yeah, charming idiosyncratic repairs," he said, fake wiping his brow in a foreboding way. "Let's hope it's not a money pit."

And then we eloped. We decided that the importance of a marriage outweighed the importance of a wedding.

What good is a big wedding if you're homeless? Each time I started to mark-up the wedding budget and the guest list, I felt like I was producing a movie. I avoided it until we ceremoniously ran the edge of this ominous list through a candle flame and we ditched it.

But I still managed to overproduce the elopement. We flew to San Francisco, and married by the Russian River. We drove down Highway 1 through Big Sur, and eventually made it to my sister's house in Los Angeles. It turns out that wine country, San Francisco, Big Sur, and San Luis Obispo are way too much to cover in one week.

Jason burst out of his office like a gambler claiming the winning wager.

"Yes!" he said. "Guys, come here. You'll never believe this!" Jason was not usually a fist pumper, but he was hopped up today.

Our first official film under the new banner was greenlit by Mark Cuban. We were already breaking away from the original mission: to make narrative features. This was a documentary Alex Gibney would direct, based upon the book, *Enron: The Smartest Guys in the Room*. There was just one simple email sent to Mark and his partner Todd Wagner, and we were given the go ahead within ten minutes. Has a green light ever been that easy? This was this exception that jumpstarted the entire slate. Boom, we were back in the documentary business.

It had been over five years since I had worked on a documentary. The last one was *Dancemaker*, where we followed Paul Taylor's dance troupe throughout rehearsals and on tour in India. Tom Hurwitz filmed the studio rehearsals in black and white 16 mm, floating under and around the dancers. I learned later that Tom was the son of a dancer and it made sense. The story was a testament to the bonds formed, the competition, and the rigor of a dance troupe. And it was nominated for an Academy Award. But even with the nomination, it never found a wide audience. I wondered if documentaries could be embraced and marketed successfully by distributors. Could they trust their audience's intelligence and allow documentaries to be seen as entertainment now? Alex had his work cut out for him.

The name of our new company was HDNet Films, a sister company to Mark Cuban's television station, HDNet. It was not a sexy name; it was square and silicone. We brainstormed a million better ideas for the company's name, but we needed to brand with the TV station and we could not be messing with brands. The initiative was to make films that were ready for pre-production. No big cast was required. The cash flow came 100 percent from Wagner/Cuban. The distribution would be Wagner/Cuban's recent acquisition Magnolia Pictures.

These budgets were low too, under $1 million. The rule was that we could only shoot in high definition; no film and no other medium. What surprised us was how hard it was to find good scripts with a producer and a director attached. Tory had made the initial connection with Mark Cuban and all her efforts had kept us afloat. Now we brought on Will, a former talent agent, to hustle and find projects.

We poured a round of cava and slid the glass doors open to toast to our first green light. Six floors below us, a drum ensemble pounded out a beat where all of SoHo gathered in costume for the Halloween Parade. The office was a modular communal space existing long before WeWork entered the scene with its ping-pong tables and bottomless beer kegs. The benefit of this space was that we shared the rent and the utilities. And we shared it with potential collaborators: a prestigious documentary filmmaker, a commercial production company, and the casting director, Cindy Tolan.

Within weeks, Tory had brought in a coalition of three filmmakers, and *The War Within* was our first greenlit narrative feature. Cindy came on board to cast the film and the proximity to her office was tempting. From a tiny space, she juggled clients like Mira Nair and Noah Baumbach prepping *Monsoon Wedding* and *The Squid and the Whale*. This was where Cindy's work in the theater kicked into gear, and she especially thrived when casting children.

"It's like catching lightning in a bottle," Cindy said when she found the right child for the right role at the right time. "If we waited any longer, we'd lose that magic."

And then something extraordinary happened. New York State approved a feature film tax credit. This meant New York could finally compete with Toronto and Louisiana. New York City piggy-backed onto the State's credit with their own local incentive, which encouraged us to do most of our filming within the five boroughs. We ramped up to six productions and I hired a full-time assistant and a post-production supervisor. We hired an in-house lawyer and we expanded into more modules. We swelled through the communal walls like water.

The incentives brought a barrage of films to the New York area and the trick became finding locations that could cheat for other regions. Staten Island cheated for coastal Long Island. The gorgeous campus of Lehman College in the Bronx stood in for the Ivy Leagues and a mansion in Todt Hill—from carefully positioned angles—passed as the Gold Coast of Chicago.

I started my day in Tottenville shooting boat-to-boat clam digging on the southern tip of Staten Island, but still within city limits. Before lunch, I drove to the edge of Jersey City to film a technicolor Eid celebration, then I headed back over the George Washington Bridge to meet another film's crew at the Bronx River Houses.

I squeezed next to the crew in a tiny West Village apartment on Zoe Cassavetes's *Broken English*, and then swung uptown for an on-screen confrontation at The Cloisters for another film. It was the same stretch of grass where Robert Redford had plotted with George Segal on an unmanicured hillside in *The Hot Rock*. New York City's film history was at every corner.

Outside the borough limits, Yonkers temped us because it was close and it had a wide range of looks, but we steered clear because the police tactics there felt more like they did in Oakland. If we stayed within the five boroughs, we had the traffic control division (TCD)—the officers dedicated to managing the city streets—at no charge to the production.

The green lights for new films came quickly. But the active films were just half the work. We vetted scripts, evaluated budgets and schedules, and sifted through a rapid influx of candidates.

The irony of the tax credit was that I now lived in New Jersey. Everything we filmed was east of the Hudson River, which put me behind the wheel of a car more than I wanted. I was not a multitasker. I was good at doing one thing at a time.

But the right side of my brain allowed me to digest the radio's news while I drove. I braked for the Holland Tunnel tollbooth, but this time I rolled down my window and screamed. NPR had just announced *Enron* had been nominated for an Academy Award.

A week after returning home from our honeymoon, Bob flew to New Orleans for three months of filming on *All the King's Men*. I stomped and cried into my shopping cart in the Trader Joe's parking lot. It wasn't fair to be alone for this first winter in a new, old house, haunted by its unfamiliar groans and creeks. It would rain sheets of ice so thick that it chipped shards of slate off the roof. The oil burner and the furnace would blow in the same week. And there was so much snow-shoveling.

I was newly married but had no one to come home to. I started to stay in the city later and later. Our office team was a tight knit group; we had to be. We played as hard as we worked. This meant late nights of long dinners and karaoke. We could go out dancing until 2 a.m. in an underground Meatpacking club and still push through the work together the next day.

The rapid-fire execution of films was thrilling, even if it felt we were on a mission to make *every* low-budget film out there. My bad habit of grinding my teeth crept back into my life. The ribbons of stress inside my cheeks—ribbons that had formed in Vietnam—returned. And the stress had another, more unexpected effect; I could not remember names the way I used to.

It wasn't therapy I needed; I tried that. I hated talking about myself across the room from a person who nodded and hummed her approvals and disapprovals. She scribbled on a legal pad, and her eyes fluttered heavily as if she was on the verge of sleep. To be fair, my mind drifted too—my eyes would pan over to the window and focus on her oversized potted palms. I took an imaginary pair of pruning shears and cut the wayward limbs. Damnit, I wanted to say to her, *say something constructive, something that will solve me!* The process all seemed so futile, and the progress was glacial and soul-crushing.

On the train ride home from my final abysmal therapy session, a man next to me opened his *New York Times*, and I leaned in to read a story about the Rock & Roll Hall of Fame inductees. Why had it taken so many years for George Harrison to be inducted? The article said that George had been the first Beatle to dive into Transcendental Meditation, and then he brought the band along with him. *Is Transcendental Meditation still a thing?* Apparently it was, but now it was abbreviated to less of a mouthful: TM.

I found a TM center and I signed up for a series of tutorials and courses. Maybe this would be the solution to rein in my busy head and quell my physical symptoms.

It wasn't immediate, and it wasn't earth shattering, but this form of meditation seemed to work. It had a calming effect on me, but it also felt like rearranging the metaphorical furniture in my head—although oddly it inspired me to rearrange the actual furniture too. Things just seemed to fall into place with more ease and less panic And when chaos did come my way, it was usually on the days I forgot to take the time to do it.

The question I always ask producers when they wrapped: *If you had it to do over again, what would you do differently?* Which made me think about the honeymoon I had overproduced. If I planned it again, we would have spent the entire week in the Deetjen's cabin hunkered down under the shade of Big Sur's redwoods. If that cabin had been good enough for Henry Miller to complete *Tropic of Cancer*, it was certainly good enough for us. I hadn't realized that what we needed was to just stay still for a few days. No one should return to life stressed out from an elopement.

I was wrong to think that the New York tax incentive meant that there would be less distant travel for me. I took the trips to Germany and the Czech Republic in stride, knowing how lucky I was to be globetrotting on someone else's dime.

Fluffy, fresh snow hit the pavement on our first day of filming in Berlin. Hal Hartley's *Fay Grim* built its grid within a brownstone lined block that was wider and somehow quieter than any New York street. Berlin had that feel of a studio backlot—ready to shapeshift into whatever the production threw at it. Pop-out double-decker buses served as catering trucks, cooking and serving in one efficient unit. The drivers of the larger trucks came to set in the morning and enjoyed breakfast. Then they returned at night after wrap. They took a second job or a long nap during the afternoon for all I knew. It all seemed so reasonable. So civil.

Parker Posey's dog stole the show on set, often lifting a leg on the location's oversized oriental carpet. Jeff Goldblum was quick to create a distraction, swooping in to chat up the owner.

Berlin was Hal's home, and he could make a film here with his eyes closed. His line producer Mike had put together a great crew. It just took one day of filming to know that they really didn't need me here, but another filmmaker did need me in Prague.

"Here, we'll eat like the locals," Ben Barenholtz said under the cool fluorescent lighting of a small shop in Prague's old city. He ran his hand over his bald head and tucked his napkin into his shirt. I imagined that he shaved his head that morning, but left enough time to manicure his white beard and moustache.

"I wouldn't have it any other way," I said, as I calculated the meal in front of me. It seemed that whenever anyone returned from a trip to Prague, they raved about the cobblestones and the food. They must have been talking about the fancier restaurants, the Michelin rated ones, not this food. I thrust a fork and knife into the dish and reminded myself of my iron stomach. But I struggled to make a dent. If you were to take a bone-saw to my forearm, remove a two-inch cross section, parboil it, and drop it on my plate, this would be what we were looking at. There was nothing green underneath it or on the side, not even a garnish.

We had walked here, towards this plate of meat, past the Estates where Mozart had conducted the premiere of Don Giovanni to an adoring audience. Almost two centuries later, Milos Forman had directed *Amadeus* at the same concert hall. The hall was bathed in a warm glow, set back from what looked like a staged wet-down of immaculately positioned cobblestones. They lived up to the hype.

Ben knew his way around Prague, and I was happy to have a guide. Born in an area of Poland that's now Ukraine, he escaped from the Nazis into the countryside at a mere eleven years old. Lucky for independent cinema, he survived and emigrated to the US. And then he made a life that became a road map of independent film lovers. He owned and ran New York's inimitable Elgin Cinema revival house in the late '60s and then segued into film distribution. He procured financing and offered support to emerging filmmakers like the Coen Brothers and John Sayles. When he had seen just a few minutes of *Eraserhead*, he gave David Lynch a place to stay in his New York apartment, which provided Lynch the space and time to finish his weird and awesome film. Ben had even made a brief appearance as a zombie in George Romero's *Dawn of the Dead*. He spun a good yarn, and I was a captive audience.

I told Ben about Bob's vivid memories from his Elgin Theater. As a teenager, Bob and his friends had slipped into Manhattan from Bay Ridge to watch Ben's infamous midnight movie screenings. They climbed to the balcony under a cloud of pot smoke. It was a thrill and an escape for a Bay Ridge kid.

"Yeah, I remember that crowd," he laughed. He pressed his palms together and raised them above his shiny head, like he was apologizing to the gods of movie theaters. "Those guys were loyal customers, what was I gonna do?"

We were not in Prague for the high-end food. This was a quick five-day trip to determine if a movie featuring singing mice puppets was viable. We didn't yet have the green light from Mark Cuban, but Ben had already been producing in typical Barenholtz fashion. He had already sourced enough money for Joseph, the director, to create the puppets and to film a proof-of-concept.

We drove north past the Kafka Museum—leaving city limits—and up to the top of the hill overlooking the city. Within twenty minutes, we wound around these old Bohemian country roads, and arrived at an abandoned factory. This was Joseph's makeshift studio. Joseph greeted us near the stone wall as we pulled in. He was ready to give us the tour.

This massive, concrete shell of a building was warmed by the creativity of Joseph's young design team—a cadre of thirty like-minded students and Prague-based artists rooted in the city's puppetry history. They were eager enough to work for just a stipend. Joseph walked us through the costume department, built stages, and set construction; each area was more impressive than the last. With the collective energies of this group and the leadership of Joseph's wild imagination, they were prepared to create not just one feature, but a series of innovative films.

Ben and I took the young puppeteers to dinner in a glass-sided annex near the Charles Bridge. After a few mild pilsners at the restaurant, our group walked to the middle of the historic pedestrian bridge and lingered near the walls.

"I know this sounds extreme, but puppets are what I can do. It's something I'm good at," a young artist from upstate New York held back tears as she confided in me. "I hope you'll figure out how to get Joe the money. Otherwise, I'm not sure what's next for me."

She hopped up on the ledge of the bridge with her co-workers, swinging their feet in unison and sharing cigarettes, with the glimmering backdrop of the city framing them. These young puppeteers reminded me of the Culinary Institute's chefs-in-training. The same creative dedication, the same drive and tunnel vision.

I had them in mind when I put together my notes and re-read the script that night. I worked to paint a strong picture of the progress in Prague. But Joseph's revised script was confusing. He still had too many stories to tell; all of them were busting out of the tight confinement of a feature film.

Within a month, the decision was final. We couldn't make the financing work and we had to pass on Joseph's film.

I was only invited to the Oscars by default. One of the *Enron* filmmakers couldn't use their ticket and I got the call. If I flew to Los Angeles that night, it was mine. I was so proud to be connected with the film. Alex Gibney had managed to take a huge financial disaster—a confusing abuse of power and greed—and boil it down to an entertaining and digestible story. People watched *Enron* and walked out of the theater feeling smarter; like someone cared enough to walk them through what the hell went wrong. And of course, we all hoped it might keep the powers that be from trying these schemes again.

I grabbed a sparkling black dress from the back of my closet, threw in a curling iron, and the company's American Express card. At this late notice, I gulped at the price of the plane ticket and booked a hotel room in Koreatown. I would bet you a trip to the moon that I was the only Oscar attendee choosing to stay in K-town for the Academy Awards. It was 2006 and the hip version of K-town—the version with the coveted real estate—was still ten or fifteen years in the future.

It was no Four Seasons, but the hotel was still an upgrade from my sister's living room. I would not be staying there on this trip. Guests at the Academy Awards do not sleep on slowly deflating air mattresses while the family's Great Dane supervises.

I pulled up the hotel window to bathe in some Los Angeles warmth and spotted a salon from my window. This would work.

"I have a proposition for you," I said as he swept up his last customer's hair cuttings.

"Go on," he said, now leaning against his broom.

"I have a big party to go to tomorrow. Actually, it's the Oscars." I paused for modest effect here, but he didn't seem to care about this. "I'm hoping you could help me with my hair and make-up."

He gave me a head-to-toe review and smiled, probably thrilled by the idea of fixing someone like me up, a *Clueless*-inspired makeover. "I know just the thing! I'll do the hair, and I have a friend who can do the make-up." *The* hair, *the* make-up. I saw now why actors like to work with wigs. If I could, I would screw off my head and leave it for him to decorate. I would walk the rest of my body back to the hotel and take a nap.

The following day was Oscar Day, and I returned to the shop for my renovation.

The only client in an otherwise shuttered Sunday morning, I was faced with myself under the salon lights. *This is me,* I thought, *no frills me*. That face I memorized; it was a face you could trust. It was nothing exceptional and nothing that begged for attention. My face and my whole look said *I get things done*. Tourists stopped me on the street to ask for directions, and to take their photo. I'm *that* person who looks like she's learned the rules, but won't bite if you ask her to explain them. Directors look at me and entrust me with their valuable money. I will make their movie happen. *Here, hold my purse while I dance*. Once at a screening reception, Alec Baldwin had turned to me to ask the probing question: *You look like someone who knows what's going on around here. Can you show me where the bathroom is?* I *did* know where that bathroom was, and I led Alec Baldwin there safely. Today was an exception though, because today I would get to dance. I would sashay right down that red carpet and past those larger-than-life phallic Oscar statues.

The make-up artist applied her final touches. She winked at me and twirled me around for last looks. I did not recognize the person in the mirror. My hair dangled with a full head of curls and my eyes exploded to twice their size. I was dolled-up in liquid liner and lashes. I looked like a contestant in a drag queen contest. But I played along. I held up a hair dryer—a stand-in for an Oscar statuette—and kissed the outer cone in profile, holding it above my Shirley Temple hairdo. My audience of two—my own, personal glam squad—applauded as they mocked the snaps and flashes of the paparazzi.

In the drive over to the Four Seasons to meet Jason and Joana, I adjusted the rearview mirror and pawed at my face, blending the excess eyeliner. The valet took the keys and relieved me of the driver's seat while I scrambled for a tip from my sparkling purse. And there they were in the lobby: Jason and Joana looking sharp in a tuxedo and a classy black dress. Petite and camera-ready, they were like that couple on top of a wedding cake. I posed with them for photos, feeling like an outsider; like one of these things just didn't belong.

The primary red carpet is reserved for real movie stars, not for documentary people. But Jason—the quintessential producer—found someone in charge who allowed us to walk on the main carpet as a group. We moved together as a tight blob of eight, like a sixteen-legged, shimmering black beast, grinning and tittering before the flashbulbs and TV cameras. Jennifer Aniston was ahead of us—perfectly at home on this carpet. She laughed with an E! host, three-quarter posed, and flipped her famous hairdo; she was unreal and gorgeous. George Clooney was behind us, to our left. Like carved-out-of-wax gorgeous.

Of our group, only Alex Gibney was singled out. He was the brightest star in our constellation, and the press knew it. Their collective charge pulled him forward to field their questions and engaged him for his Hollywood moment. But a heartbeat later the paparazzi's long lenses swung towards George, in hopes that this group of frozen smiles behind Alex would just move along to their seats.

We did not win an Academy Award. But when we lost, we threw back a few champagnes in the high-altitude section of the theater bar. Our nosebleed portion of the group wasn't invited to the hot Oscar party hosted by Vanity Fair's Graydon Carter. Instead, fourteen of us ate communal style at a nearby restaurant and I handed over a gold credit card. It was a feast sponsored by Mark Cuban.

At an after-party in the Hollywood Hills, I felt lost. I searched for people who looked like New Yorkers, but everyone seemed to be auditioning for a role. The sprawling outdoor grounds were dense with impeccable make-up, exaggerated poses, and gratuitous laughter. When the laughter died down and the air became hollow, they scurried off to the bathroom for another bump. It was the party that showed up for every audition, but never got the role. But why was I judging these people? How could I be so sanctimonious? I was there, I was one of them.

The morning's first light showed up on the front porch of the Four Seasons when a stack of fresh *LA Times* dropped on the bottom step. Those of us waiting for the valet grabbed a copy for the Oscar news and photos. Only in Los Angeles are the Academy Award results printed *above* the fold. I let out a small groan, with my face planted in the paper. Over my shoulder, someone leaned in to read my copy.

"How'd you do?" he said.

"We lost to the penguins." I folded up my paper and handed it to him. I couldn't immediately place him, but I knew I had seen him on the stage a few times during the ceremony.

"Oh right—you're the *Enron* film?" he said. It was Paul Haggis, the night's biggest winner with *Crash*. He shook his head, "You guys deserved to win."

Returning to Sundance that year, we premiered three films. I arrived late enough to land the top bunk. *Will I ever be old enough to get my own bed in Park City?* In the condo, we threw a party to celebrate our filmmakers. It quickly became one of those overpacked festival situations that you might enjoy for a bit, but are happy to leave early for a glass of wine in your own quiet condo.

Across the room someone shouted my full name. Loud and above the pulsating music. I knew who this was, but her name had been sucked out of my head by the thin mountain air. In this year alone, I had learned the names of over sixty crew members multiplied by seven films. That was at least five hundred names. Then the panels, the scripts, the emails, and the parties. I closed my eyes for a moment and reached down to pull her name from some deep pocket of my brain.

"Victoria!" there it is.

Not all the films we made for Mark Cuban were a success. I produced a documentary about the salacious night club—Plato's Retreat—and we named it *American*

Swing. But it wasn't the type of documentary that elevated your social status the way that *Enron* had. Still, I thought it was a time piece of New York in the '70s and early '80s; debauchery and infamy hiding in plain sight in the basement of the Ansonia on the Upper West Side. We premiered in Toronto and then the film found a small audience at the Museum of Sex. I sat in a folding chair for the screening; squished up against a glass case to my right. The directors introduced the film and I looked closer into the glass exhibit: a comprehensive collection of dildos.

Before three years were up, we had made sixteen films. But the final film would break the mold.

| Chapter 18 |

THE WAR FILM

AMMAN, JORDAN, 2007

When Brian De Palma asks you what you're reading, you should have an answer. Something that will make him think you're clever and well-read.

"Right now, what's on your nightstand?" he pushed for a book title and swirled the ice cubes in his cocktail as he set it down. There was a resounding boom when the glass reconnected with its coaster, where three recent rings sweated the landing.

I stopped myself before blurting out the first thing I was reading: a screenplay title, not a book. I looked around at the crew. There were six of us seated in the Grand Hyatt's lounge to hash out the agenda for the next morning's scout. Above us, two threatening glass-tiered chandeliers swayed. We were in Amman, Jordan in the spring of 2007 and the country was surrounded by regional wars. Our country had played a role in elevating these ravaging wars. Jordan— by some miracle and some competent leadership—was at peace, but it was now home to thousands of refugees.

We were here to film De Palma's *Redacted,* a story inspired by the war in Iraq. I was ready to dig in and solve problems when I landed. I wasn't expecting a personal interrogation.

"And don't give me the name of a screenplay," he said, "Scripts don't count! You are what you read."

He was right. But had he seen my luggage? My unpacked suitcase was thrown on my hotel bed and I ran an internal inventory of the reading pile I had crammed into it. I packed three half-read scripts, and an Anne Tyler book—because reading Anne Tyler in a foreign country is like curling up on an overstuffed couch. I had found solace with Anne Tyler during Saigon and I thought it might help me in Amman. There was also Queen Noor's memoir about her marriage to King Abdullah. That was a thick one, maybe I would hold off on reading it for my second trip to Amman.

Then there was *The Magic Mountain*. I had put it in my lap for the eighteen-hour flight from JFK to Amman. I was committed to making a dent in it. It was a perennial nightstand read, but I always hit a roadblock by page fifty. The book wasn't *Ulysses*, I don't know what my problem was. At Thanksgiving, Bob's friend had raved about *Magic Mountain*. She couldn't believe how we all had not read the book; it was her favorite. My competitive nature took the reins when it was time to pack, so I grabbed the book and stuffed it in with those flimsy scripts. I planned to trudge past page fifty. Instead it worked like a tonic, and I fell into a deep irretrievable sleep. I had to peel myself from my seatmate's shoulder and wipe the drool from my chin.

"The Magic Mountain," I said to Brian de Palma.

"Oooh, one of my favorites." Then he pointed at me, "We have a *real* reader here!" He said it in a sing-songy tone. Playful, with a side of menace.

But if you are what you read, I was a blueprint of films that might never be made. Scripts cluttered in and around me. And even if you stack them against each other, they can only build a flimsy house of cards.

Brian shifted the spotlight away from me and the parlor game, and my heart rate normalized. The conversation split into a few chatty sidebars and when the volume rose, Brian reeled the conversation back in.

"Whoa, whoa, whoa! Let's focus on tomorrow's scout."

Brian's film would be a media collage leading up to an incident that disgraced a US Army platoon and shattered the trust of the Iraqi people. The story mashed together video calls, self-shot camcorders, internet leaks, online gossip, documentaries, helmet cameras, and TV reporter stand-ups. For every camera, there was a different viewpoint.

Music nudged me awake. It was the call to prayer, piped through speakers and reverberating around Amman's Fifth Circle from the neighboring mosque. I took my twenty minutes to meditate, as a chance to recalibrate my jet-lagged body. I imagined the men at the mosque facing Mecca and I spun towards the front door, to register which direction was East.

In the elevator I rehearsed *good morning* in Arabic: *sabah el kheir, sabah el kheir, sabah el kheir*. I thought I had it down, but the words evaporated when Johnny, our cinematographer, caught the doors on the second floor. "Morning!" we both said instead.

Johnny and I met with Simone and Jen, the Canadian producers, for a quick breakfast in the lounge before the scout. Over eggs and toast, I learned about the challenges the production was up against just three weeks before filming. Among these obstacles was the bond company. After feeding them early with all the paperwork and all the insurance and assurances, the bond company had come alive with a new list of requirements for filming in Jordan. Had they now just now spun the globe around to discover Amman was smack in the center of the Middle East? I planned a late call with them, it would be 8 a.m. back on the East Coast. By then, I would know more and I could offer concrete solutions.

Bond companies are engineered to poke holes in the production, and I'm supposed to be engineered to anticipate them. But it's always easier if they operate on our schedule. Behind our table, a group of women in hajibs burst into laughter as they covered their mouths with their hands. It was an unbridled and spontaneous laughter; not the kind at someone else's expense. I shook off the weight of the bond call, and realized there would be a way through it. It was just a movie.

An armed officer monitored the entryway: "Personal effects and computer in the bucket. *Law samahat (if you please).*" Keys jangled and purses were placed on the conveyer belt as hotel guests navigated x-ray machines and body scans.

Leaving was easy, but entering the Grand Hyatt was as thick as airport security. Just a year earlier, Al Qaeda suicide bombers had yanked their cords in the lobbies of three Amman hotels—including this one—and killed over fifty-seven people. The rigorous scanning was a sobering reminder of how close we were to the region's struggles. Maybe the bond company had a point.

Our scout van rounded three of the city's circles and accelerated on the highway towards the outskirts of the city. Within twenty minutes, we were in an open field near a neighborhood of small concrete homes spilling down a hill.

"OK people," John, the first assistant director, said. We were the people. John had an uncanny way of getting everyone's attention without raising his voice. He turned on his heel in the sand and raised one hand. "We've got three of our primary locations within a kilometer of here. I'll walk you through the set-ups. Right here, this is our check point."

John pointed to the US Army tank that took center stage in this field. Jordan's film office had transported this behemoth to us and there it would stay for the next month. John mapped out the shot list for the checkpoint assault while three art department assistants filled sand-bags and piled them on the stack to form a barricade. It was now my second film involving heavy artillery, but if we kept these wars up, it would not be my last.

Stephen, the line producer, saw my face pale when we reached the hilltop above our third location. Below the road, a makeshift village sprawled. It was wider and longer than three football fields. Small tents stretched the span from end to end in this valley, abutted only by a steep hill on one side and a highway on the other.

"Everyone in this field, they're all refugees. Not just from Iraq, but from Palestine too," he said. Stephen had been in Jordan over five weeks and by now I suspected that he had acclimated to the situation, but he wasn't inured to it. "We've met Palestinians with their old house keys on a string around their necks. They think they'll be able to go home again."

Children that were holding hands in chains of twos and threes trailed our group as we toured their neighborhood. They watched us framing shots, forecasting the sun's arc, and choosing the plot where we would set up our Bedouin catering tent. The production collected their information on a legal pad, and aimed to cast refugees as extras. Then our twin vans pulled out for the next location, kicking up a cloud of dust. Behind the scenes, Stephen made a plan to interview the refugees on camera. He wanted to reveal how they were welcomed into Jordan, but left to fend for themselves. Their stories would be transcribed, translated, and subtitled for the DVD extras of Brian's film.

When the van rolled back into the city, Jen and Simone turned around in their seats toward me.

"OK there's something else we're dealing with," Jen said. "Those crates of military costumes and guns that shipped from Canada a few weeks ago? They're here in Amman."

"Bravo!" I said. "They had a world tour I guess."

"And now they're held up in customs on this side." The Jordanian film office had exhausted all their resources. They had worked with production to provide all the requisite letters and documentation. But still the uniforms and weapons sat in a warehouse, where they waited to be rescued. Without the military uniforms and armory, filming wouldn't be possible.

Scouting dust had turned to mud as it swirled down my shower drain. I took a moment to transform myself out of well-worn scouting gear and into a skirt and blouse. Then I ran through the stairwell, to join Simone, Jen, and Stephen for our royal mission.

At the base of what looked like an oasis of green hills, we presented our passports at a security gate, and we were cleared to drive to the next checkpoint. The drive felt like a lush jungle after a morning in the desert. We wound around to the top of the hill and pulled into a modest home that wouldn't have been out of place in a New Jersey suburb.

A gracious Princess Rym greeted us at her door, and Prince Ali joined us in the living room once tea was served. The royal couple's grace was matched by Jen and Simone's patience. *Just sit back and watch the pros,* I knew these moments of diplomacy were what all four of them were built for. We danced around the small talk about the lovely tea, the excellent local crew, and the attentive Jordanian film office. The future of filmmaking in Jordan.

Prince Ali set down his glass and asked the question we needed to hear: "Is there anything you might need our help with?"

"As a matter of fact, there is something..." Jen told the story of the customs backlog. A calm measured tale of one hiccup that could set us back thousands of dollars.

We were promised a few calls on the Prince and Princess' behalf. What had seemed impossible in the morning was now a solution only royalty could unlock.

In the developmental stages of *Redacted*, Jen and Simone had come to our office in New York. They sat around the conference table with Brian, and their presence already diffused any nerves. Their style was an effective tag-team; they could finish one another's sentences without somehow stepping on each other. They knew how to divide and conquer between casting, locations, story, managing a director's expectations, and delivering on a budget. And they knew how to listen.

We narrowed the location candidates down to Morocco and Jordan as a cheat for the open Iraqi desert. Brian's assistant director set off to scout, and we reviewed the photos. We tweaked the schedules and the numbers. We weighed the pros and cons. Morocco was too mountainous, which meant we would have to CGI out the backgrounds. And such rigorous visual effects work wasn't possible at this budget. Talented crew and equipment were based in Morocco and there wasn't yet much of a film industry in Jordan. But Queen Noor's film school had sparked an interest for young crews in the Amman area, and the film office had urged us to come; that was two checks in the pros column. The location photos came back from an area just outside Amman and the images clicked for Brian. And when we learned Jordan had an American tank on the ground the decision was solidified.

Then came the matchmaking.

Sometimes it's all about fortuitous timing and happy accidents. The casting director and I tried not to shout around the helium balloons of a two-year-old's birthday party at the next table. Paul Schnee and I were having a "general" meeting at Bubby's in Tribeca. It took a popping balloon and three kids shrieking for me to have my aha moment. Paul would be a great match for Brian. Brian wanted to cast unknown actors and one thing I knew for sure was that those with talent know how to spot talent.

When Paul and I had been drama majors in college, he was cast as the lead in the plays, chewing up the scenery in *Charlie's Aunt* and everything Shakespeare. He rehearsed off book while I handed off props in the wings. I struggled through acting class, but Paul thrived. From my vantage point, he was destined to be a great actor.

Then we brought in John, the assistant director that I had worked with on the Good Machine film. There are extroverted, barking ADs who command a set and there are the rare quiet ones. Both survive with a sense of humor; both can be effective. But when John moved his way through set to estimate timings, the crew felt charmed, not harassed. He split his time between producing and AD gigs. He only booked AD work for the right films. *Redacted* wouldn't be the lucrative job that would guarantee a down payment on a house, but it was an opportunity to work with Brian De Palma and a chance to travel to a place he might not otherwise go. After an hour-long meeting over coffee, the match was made.

Another key component to a strong finish was our post supervisor, Mike. He would stay in New York and set up our shiny new digital workflow. There was no more tape, now it was all zeros and ones. Digital capture meant we would have to count on drives to store all our work.

We ran a few tests and projected them in New York to compare whether Brian and Johnny liked the look of the night vision lenses. Night vision was something we could affect in post, so making the choice to bake night vision into the image during production would limit the options later.

The scouting group dined out in Amman at the crew's favorite Lebanese restaurant; it was two circles north on a dramatic hilltop. Useful news, useless gossip, and a hookah were circulated while we devoured plates of arayes, baba ghanoush, and labneh. When two more wine bottles landed on the table, the gossip revealed another story. We had lost some of our footage from the camera test. It vanished from the drive, and not a frame of it was salvaged.

The hookah smoke smelled of sickly cotton candy and something was caught in my throat again. But I knew there was no way they would repeat this mistake with the camera drives. I made a mental note to call Mike so he could come in as the heavy. He would enforce the iron-clad workflow, and present diagrams to be signed in blood if necessary. It was better to sacrifice something in the testing phase than to lose shot footage during principal photography.

I tried to keep on top of the technology, the terminology, and the trends. This was where my background in documentary filming and editorial usually gave me a leg up. But now all of it was changing so quicky, every month there was a new term to comprehend. Maybe if I could stay on top of it all, I could avoid obsolescence and stay forever young and relevant.

I resisted another glass of wine. I knew I needed to keep my wits about me for the bond company call.

By midnight it was the end of the bond's business day in Toronto. On my hotel carpet, there was a worn oval—like a miniature racing track—from my maddening pacing. The phone cord gnarled up, as if I could solve the problem by twisting it through my fingers and splaying it flat. The bond was insisting that filming in Jordan required terrorism insurance if we were going to move forward. I held an ice cube to my throat, to help calm a spasm there. I countered while arguing (mildly, for the fifth time) that we were not in a war zone and that it was Morocco who was being rattled by a string of suicide bombings. Morocco had been at the top of the bond's original list of film-friendly, insurable countries, but now it was the American Consulate in Casablanca that had boarded up and evacuated. Yes, Amman's proximity to the Israeli-Palestinian conflict and the war in Iraq was palpable, but Jordan was *not* at war. Jordan was keeping its shit together and taking in the casualties of all this warfare.

My argument just seemed to prove the entire world was more volatile. It wasn't too late to bind terrorism insurance, but it wasn't going to be affordable. If the film was going to have its plug pulled, it could come down to this.

After a series of calls and a search back through our initial communication, the bond agreed to let go of their last-minute requirement. When I finally hung up, I let the phone coil snap back into place.

Brian's film would go on.

On Sunday, when production was in a stable place on its down day, I hired a car to take me to the Dead Sea. We drove west, passing miles of encampments; a reminder of how close the refugees were to their original homes. I walked through a series of steps down to the water's edge. Then I stepped into the Dead Sea; the same void of water I had pointed to on the spinning globe as a kid. Back then it was a mystery, and something to find someday. And now I was in this salty water, floating on my back effortlessly. Hours could pass in this weightless universe. Across the sea to the west were the hills of Jerusalem, The West Bank, and Israel. It all looked so peaceful from this hallucinogenic floating bath. The films we made could get close to sharing the clashes and the casualties of these wars, but any reality of the pain and unrest was still unfathomable to someone like me.

It had been a good three-year run with sixteen films in the can. But the green lights had slowed down and it looked like Mark Cuban was ending the HDNet Films experiment. Brian's film would be the last feature and just a few of the documentaries were left to complete. I was postponing the inevitable search for a new job.

The orange phone message-alert blinked as it lit up my hotel room when I returned from the sea. It couldn't be good news. It was either the bond company—maybe they had changed their minds—or it was home. Bob's voice sounded strained when I reached him in the emergency room by his father's bed. His father had suffered a heart attack. My next move was obvious; I called the airline to change my ticket for the first flight home.

| Chapter 19 |

THE SUSPENSE THRILLER

SPAIN, 2008

Going from a steady job back into the freelance world is like jumping off a diving board into a pool, but without any idea of what lies below.

A helicopter hovered over Bill Murray's head then disappeared as it floated to a landing in the Almerian sands. There was only one black helicopter in the European region and I had wrangled it. I enlisted the help of Mark Cuban's HDNet helicopter pilot. The pilot had been all over the world as he filmed the news from a bird's eye view. And even though he couldn't travel to us, he knew someone with the right equipment. I was no longer working for Mark Cuban and I was no longer making films with Jason and Joana. Instead, I was a freelancing producer making a film with Jim Jarmusch in Spain.

After a clean take on the landing, Bill Murray cracked another joke and riled the crew up. I wandered off set and pulled out my phone. I was anxious for a call that would determine my future.

"I think we're seeing the end of The Mark Cuban Experiment," I blurted out to Stacey four months earlier in New York. Saying it out loud felt like a betrayal. But this was Stacey, I could trust her to keep it under wraps.

Over three years and sixteen films, Mark Cuban and Todd Wagner's HDNet Films was a machine. We had shaken the bushes for producers and talent. We considered every viable script that could be filmed within our habitat. We employed and trained thousands of crew members and we were the poster child for the New York City tax credit. But now it was coming to an end, and I needed to consider my own future.

"Really?" You could see the wheels churning behind Stacey's eyes, the gears engaging. She was always a few steps ahead of me. "What does that mean for you. What'll you do?"

"We're still completing the slate," I shrugged "Finishing the De Palma film and a couple others." In truth, I was terrified about what came next, about rejoining the hustle of freelancing.

"We're scouting in Spain—Jim's next movie is with Focus and the whole thing will film there," Stacey looked up. "And...we need a producer. Someone to produce with me."

"OK, well you've got my attention now," Focus Features was the real deal. They would finance up front and they'd put muscle behind the distribution.

"You wouldn't have to do the post this time, I'd do that." I liked that idea. "You'd go to Spain, deal with the scouting, the casting, all that. I can't come to Spain until we start filming.

Then as if on cue, Jim appeared. He leaned against the restaurant's staircase railing, committed to a brief hello without taking a seat. Two fans approached Jim, and he turned to chat with them. With his shock of white hair and his height, it was always just a matter of time before someone spotted him on the streets of New York. Jim engaged with them, curious about an album they had apparently just cut. They launched into a rapid-fire list of their favorite Jarmusch films: *Stranger than Paradise*, *Mystery Train*, and *Down by Law*! The first guy pulled a paperback from his back pocket and folded back the cover, sacrificing it for Jim's autograph. Within a few minutes, they were exchanging numbers and planning to see a set of live music.

"This happens to him all the time," Stacey laughed and shook her head. "He talks to everyone." I remembered this rapport, this funny repartee between Jim and Stacey. Maybe leaving one family—the one with Jason and Joana— for this one was the best possible timing.

"Let's do it," I said. "Let's go to Spain!"

Stacey and I pulled out a map of Spain and a calendar on our first research flight. The core of production would be in Madrid, but as our main character travelled throughout the country, so would we. After a few weeks of filming in Madrid, we flew south for ten days in Andalusia. Then we took a train west to Seville for another two weeks and returned to Madrid by high-speed rail where we would wrap.

On paper, the film was a piece of cake. I had just one film to focus on with one director and one distributor. I had been juggling so many films at HDNet Films—some at an arm's length, others in painstaking detail—so it was confounding to think of this as a singular mission. Could all the scattered energy that I once deployed before now be distilled? Would it be exponentially better? There was nothing but Jarmusch and this strange trip in Spain.

After a full day in the production office, I returned to my hotel room for dinner before a second shift. I dedicated the second shift to the East Coast time zone and the third to the West Coast. Three stations came in on the hotel TV: two channels of Spanish news and some sort of German pornographic show on the third channel. I clicked it all off, poured a glass of wine with a slice of Manchego, and watched the *Point Blank* DVD a second time—a film Jim had drawn inspiration from.

Ellen Lewis—Jim's casting director since *Dead Man* and one of industry's sharpest— called with news of verbal commitments from two new cast members, and now I could tag team with each of their agents to pinpoint the details. Nine hours behind us in Los Angeles, I aimed to reach each agent after their breakfast dates but before their lunch meetings.

"I don't *have* him," the agent's assistant said. *Don't have* is what they're trained to say. I pictured the assistant grabbing the lapels of his boss's Tom Ford jacket, *I've got him now*! "I'll add you to his call sheet," she said instead.

The dreaded agent call sheet; the assistant would roll from one call to the next, ticking names off a list. Invariably, the call would come to us on the East Coast when we were sitting down for dinner. At this rate, we were nine time zones ahead; another two days could pass before we connected. I recited my Spanish cell number to encourage a call back that day, *before the lunch appointment, if possible*. I was polite as hell—because that's my style, but also because today's assistant is tomorrow's super-agent.

At 1:00 a.m. the phone lit up with a 310-area code. I answered, acted wide awake, and began to negotiate.

Then next morning, I streamed NPR on my computer. I was homesick for news from the US. New York City was on fire with the collapse of Lehman Brothers and now Bear Stearns. The financial world was tanking. These companies had been steady investors in the independent film world; where would the money come from now?

I tried to tune out the noise. The next night, before another round of calls back to Los Angeles, I pulled up an iTunes episode of *Lost*. I savored the final episodes of this bizarre show. And it was a sacred respite because it had nothing do with Spain and nothing to do with the bursting housing bubble.

Jim's cinematographer, Chris Doyle, was back and forth to Spain, as he directed his first film in Poland. Warsaw would need him at several key moments during pre-production, but we resolved to make it work. He was a fantastic cinematographer. He thrived on any challenge we threw him. If we had a night "walk and talk" down a busy Madrid street with two characters, Chris had a plan with a simple China ball tethered to a boom. When Jim wanted to shoot wide exterior night shots on the Almeria coast, the solution would be construction work lights, visible in the shot as part of the story. Chris and Jim were in sync

The scouting team sat at an outdoor bar surrounded by Madrid locals—Madrileños—and Chris ordered another round of shots for everyone. They leaned across the table to hang on his stories; dramatic scenes in Poland and

Wong Kar-wai in Hong Kong. *Chris was perfect,* I thought, *was there a catch?*

Chris returned to Poland for the final phase of his own film while Jim, the production designer Eugenio Caballero and I scouted Madrid's museums. Eugenio was still reeling from his production-design Oscar for *Pan's Labyrinth* and we felt lucky to have him.

We hit the ground running early Monday when the Prado was only open for school groups. We had a tour of two giant wings to ourselves. The click-click of our guide's heels echoed off the hallowed galleries of Velasquez, El Greco, and Goya. I walked ahead and around the corner where Bosch's *Garden of Earthly Delights* triptych spanned the wall. It was a massive sight; a cautionary tale of life's temptations.

It was the Reina Sofia Museum that won Jim and Eugenio over. Its Greek columns opened to an outdoor courtyard and its roomy galleries showed off the multiple shapes of Juan Gris's guitars. We had the luxury of being alone in the museum, like a glimpse into the private lives of the wealthy.

Scouting and research continued at night in a flamenco club. The performer stomped the floor and clapped on the cabaret stage, while demanding eye contact from her audience. We were entranced by her red costume that swirled above our heads and her deep, sultry voice.

Back at the Muralto Hotel we reviewed the list of locations we saw. Jim and I sat in the back lobby with Eugenio as he strummed a sequence of chords on his guitar. Two months ago, Bob had been teaching me one chord a week during methodical lessons that were slow enough for me to digest. But now Eugenio handed me the guitar and I couldn't remember a chord. I held up my hand and ran my thumb over the finger pads on my left hand. The callouses from my starter guitar string's pressure had disappeared; my fingers were now only suited for the keypads of a computer.

Flying in for a landing on Almeria's seaside on Spain's southwest coast, I expected to see a glimpse of the Mediterranean and then nothing but green hills. We should have been seeing whitewashed homes on lush rolling cliffs—like the images our scout Suzannah had sent us. Instead, it was like Wite-Out liquid had redacted a full third of the landscape. Acres and acres of earth were shrouded in white tents, each tent was the size of a dozen wedding tents.

"It gets worse each year. Every season there are more acres covered in these plastic greenhouses." The Spanish line producer, Patricia, seemed obliged to explain. But millions of fruits and vegetables grew underneath these eyesores—Europe's produce basket. "They're not going away; they feed most of Western Europe."

Politically active and proud, Patricia was a firm manager. She only needed to say *no* once for a crew member to understand. There was no grey area, no room for misinterpretation. So when she apologized for Spain's weak spots, or when she pronounced wifi "wee fee," something inside of me melted for her.

We travelled far north and east of these tents to our locations. Into the countryside, we drove through fields escorted by the clockwise cartwheels of towering windmills. An oversized billboard featured a cowboy lassoing a stray bull under large block letters: *Bienvenido Mini Hollywood*. This was the home of Sergio Leone's old Spaghetti Westerns. But we passed it by and drove to a town of stucco homes and wide slate rooftops that cascaded down a mountaintop. These Andalusian villages were pitched high and were walkable through a staircase maze and narrow streets, but impassable to our vans. It was the café at the highest point that Jim chose. The art department snapped reference photos in the spot where Gael Garcia Bernal's character would make a dramatic entrance; he would part the doorway's jangling beaded chains—Andalusia's answer to the screen door—with both hands.

Jim stepped back in the high desert to admire an empty home. With just one foot in the main room, he turned towards Suzannah with a giant grin; this was it.

"I knew you'd find it," he said. "I knew it was here somewhere, and that you'd find it." Eugenio and Jim planned how to inhabit the space, but still retain the coolness of its abandonment.

With a sliver of daylight left, we veered off the highway of wind turbines. Mini Hollywood called our name.

"It was the end of the Spaghetti Western era and the extras saw it coming," a guide said, leaning against a barn behind the main drag. We blended into his tourist group. "The extras took control of the set pieces after the filming of *The Good, the Bad and The Ugly* and capitalized on Almeria's tourism industry. The set pieces you see here now? It's all available for filming again," the guide said, giving us a wink. "With a little tourism on the side."

The town saloon and the church were real buildings with interior sets, furnished with barstools and pews.

They were the exception. Most of the structures were just facades, propped up with two-by-fours. A strong wind or a deliberate punch with an angry fist and they would be flattened.

In Seville, we mapped out several locations behind the walls in the Old Town district. West of these walls and across the bridge, we were introduced to a gem on Cartuja Island. A deteriorating structure that showcased the city in Expo '92 would stand in for a stage where we could build a set for the film's final confrontation between Isaach de Bankolé and Bill Murray.

In Seville—as in each Spanish city—there was a Museo del Jamon; a shrine to Ham. Ham was taken very seriously everywhere here. We broke for lunch, happy to find a restaurant that was committed to preparing a vegetarian option for Jim. A creamy gazpacho with mix-in toppings was presented to Jim by the chef himself.

"So, no jamon, si?" Jim looked up to the chef and prepped his spoon for a stab.

"Si, si, no jamon," the chef said.

Relieved, Jim took a bite.

"Except in the broth," the chef smiled, holding up his index finger. "Of course, pfft! Jamon only in the broth!"

I stood at the edge of the set finishing a phone call, watching Tilda Swinton cross the café plaza in a full head of curlers. We made it to principal photography, but before I could exhale to take it in and absorb the hurdles we had forged to get here, a bird dropped a giant crap on my head. I looked up to see the bird cackling down at me, as if identifying him would help. This was his turf and he didn't want our crew camping out in his back yard and screwing up his day. I couldn't remember whether birdshit in the hair was a good or a bad omen, but I knew I needed to get it off, so I ducked underground to our holding area. The café's black and white tables were shoved off to the side and piled on top of each other, sequestered there until they got their own space back. Sometimes I think all we do in the movies is displace the world's things.

Torres Blancas sat as a concrete bastion that oozed tears when it rained. It looked more like another relic from the World's Fair or an architectural experiment in the Eastern Bloc. This hulking apartment tower—with rounded walls in every interior and exterior—was Madrid's tribute to retro-futurism. It was a disorienting trick of a building and it had been preordained as a principal location for Jim's film. Named for the opulent marble exterior it would eventually receive, the bones of it had been built, but then they ran out of money. Even without its final touches, it functioned as a home for hundreds of people. We wound our way around its dark circular halls and staged our scenes. On the roof, our actor braved the cold March air for Jim's movie as she swam the length of the pool. It was another glimpse into a lifestyle and a view of Madrid we would never see otherwise.

I paced between wildflowers and boulders in an Andalusian field, where two period train cars had been towed to a hilltop of a private collector's olive farm. The owner—a locomotive enthusiast—wasn't afraid to hover around the frenetic activity of grips and electrics. In fact, he embraced the opportunity to talk tech with them and he grilled them on their gear and their methods of cart-ing their gear through the rough terrain. Eugenio had been ingenious with our show's minimal resources. He was frustrated that we couldn't give him the green light to build the train interior on a stage, but he would made good work of this practical location.

The fact that we were veering off course was actually a good thing. We were going through 35 mm film stock like water. What we saved in clever filmmaking, had all gone into Fujifilm and to the lab. On the other end of the cell phone in London, the bond company representative used an expletive to describe our liberal use of film stock. She had wanted us to shoot digitally, and did not understand that Chris Doyle would not stray from his beloved film stocks. I pulled my phone from my ear while she was ranting. I was sure she just said *this is a fucking disaster*. We had seen actual disasters; I had even been responsible for some of them in my career. This was *not* a fucking disaster. These were scare tactics; a hard nudge for me to right the ship.

There were two job possibilities for my life after Spain. I had one option to work with an established film company, and another option to work with a team that I had worked with before. The second option was riskier as it involved venture capitalists. But as I watched one bank after another fall down, I wondered whether either of these options was viable. It was probably better to go with the original offer that had a proven backer and a track record. I thought the job was mine for the taking.

Until it was not. The call came in as scheduled, but not as expected.

"See the thing is, the job doesn't exist any longer," they said on the crackling line from New York. "We're not going to focus on production anymore. It's too expensive." They were going to let the reckless investors—the insanely overworked producers—make the films, then pick them up like broken soldiers from the battlefield. Distribution was where the money was.

I marched around the field across from set as I punched numbers into the phone for a better answer from the less stable option.

"It's all happening, you have to trust me."

"In this climate?" I pushed, because there was no time to dance around this. "Aren't the investors a little gun shy?"

"You've got to be patient. It could be months. It could be a year, but they're committed."

Waiting six months to a year to work again would be a luxury. At home, Bob was trying to retire from grip work; it was a career for the young and able-bodied, or at least for those who planned to still move their bodies in retirement. One of us needed a job. I had been working since I was thirteen and I didn't know who I was without the work. And now I didn't know who I was without film production. I wanted more films like Jarmusch's and I wanted to oversee lots of films, not just one at a time. Was anyone out there ready to finance them?

I hovered over the accountant's printer in Seville on our final day of filming as it churned out the bottom line of the cost report. I prayed for any projected savings so I could quickly repurpose them. We did a thorough examination of the numbers, and the proof was on the page: we'd finished principal photography with contingency to spare. This extra money allowed for green-screen visual effects, and music to be covered in post-production. If there had been too little money left, it would be irresponsible, and would leave post-production in the lurch. If there was too much money left, I would be second guessing myself and wondering if I should have allowed the stage build for that train after all.

A crowd formed and filled the streets of Seville. Wood, wax, and wire were sculpted together and coated in gold; then lifted above by the crowd. This was not in celebration of our wrap, or of our cost report's solid bottom line. It was Seville's Holy Week where the residents carried giant crosses and marched through the streets in massive processionals. A funereal crowd delivered these sculptures to the church. Stacey and I ran from one procession to another—each with its own theme—until we reached the last march that celebrated the Virgin. Coated in silver, the likeness of Mary held her son to her chest and wept for him. I watched in awe at the convictions of this crowd. It was as if their collective reverence would offer resolve; that they needn't worry about their futures because it was in some higher power's hands.

"Can you believe this?" Stacey folded back the paper on the café table to show me an image. "This huge crane collapse on the East Side?"

"My god. New York cannot catch a break," I read further into the copy. "Four bodies were carried out of the building...."

The Seville sky was a sharp blue canvas, just like September 11th, seven years ago. As I studied the images in the article I knew I was ready to return home and mourn with the rest of New York City.

I dressed the part. I boarded early for the perks. I built a nest around my spacious plane seat: a pair of noise-cancelling headphones, an iPod, a novel (no screenplays), slippers, an eye mask, and a pillow. As a wrap gift, Jim had treated me to a business upgrade for the flight home and I was going to savor it. Then my phone rang and disrupted the dream.

"Independent film is over. It's dead." No *hello* or *how are you,* Adam just launched into it.

"We've been hearing that tired tune since the '90s," I said, as I leaned back into the crunchy beans of my neck pillow. *"Independent film is dead. Long live independent film!"*

"This time it's different. And with this writers' strike? It's dead, dead." I caught the huff of an Eighth Avenue bus rumbling behind him. "You should get off that plane and stay in Spain. Stay in Europe where they still care about film." That was easy for him to say, I thought. With European parents, Adam could now apply for dual citizenship. Coproductions in Spain and Italy would swoop up his multilingual skills in a heartbeat. For just a moment, I wished I'd been born to more exotic parents.

"Not an option," *can I just skip the flying part, close my eyes, and be whisked home*? "Movies survived the Depression—they can survive this. People will always need the distraction of films."

"Hollywood makes the blockbuster distractions," he said, "We make the weird independent ones. Remember?"

"I've gotta go," I laughed and lied. "We're about to take off and I want one of those free mimosas."

"Sure, have your mimosa. And come on home. But don't expect to find work."

As a freelancer, the pressure to be working is always on, even among friends. *What are you working on?* The answer qualifies your worth. I worked up to a blithe but practiced: *Nothing right now—taking some time.*

The forecast was scary. The current climate was tragic. Bob told me that six homes just foreclosed on our block in New Jersey. Vines and weeds crawled up the walls and swallowed them. Every week, another house folded. And now my own house was underwater, its value outweighed by the mortgage we owed.

The deterioration of Wall Street had been rapidly accelerated during the making of this one movie in Spain. What next? Would our plane retract its wheels from the JFK tarmac, unable to land into the abyss? Would the apocalypse creep up through the asphalt and gnaw away at the cow fat and bones that glued it together? Would we ever land?

Trays of mimosas started coming. Not the plastic base-and-flute expendables they had in coach, the real crystal. I reached for a glass and pretended to savor it, already thinking about how a second one would feel. A CNN reporter bleated out crisis updates on the seatback monitor in front of me. If I never worked again, I would probably never see the bottom of a free mimosa glass again. But I turned the second drink down, playing the tape forward, imagining the static it would create inside my head. I finally let myself feel the tug of home, knowing that Bob would meet me at the airport.

Just before takeoff, the pleated pants of an American businessman stopped at my row. A matching jacket to those pleats was folded into a neat square and placed flat in the overhead bin. Then the suit himself took his seat next to me and nodded towards my TV monitor. He held his aisle-side hand out and a champagne flute floated into it.

"They're all complaining about overpaid executives," he said to me—a wink-wink—businessperson to businessperson. "I say we execs have been working hard all our lives. We *deserve* the money."

He made me think of a director I had worked with once who turned his pockets inside out at the end of each shoot day, throwing out the loose change along with the lint. Quarters, nickels, whatever, just tossed it all in the trash. It was unimaginable to me, but to him it was just excess baggage that was weighing him down.

My seat mate raised his mimosa to me and the monitor, but this was not my toast.

In John Le Carré's final interview—the one Errol Morris captured for his documentary—he said his life had been a series of embraces and escapes. Now, I felt the same way about the film industry; I felt the same way about life.

A familiar set of chords piped through the plane's speakers. I couldn't quite place it. Was it the muzak version of Steve Earle's *The Revolution Starts Now?* I clicked off the TV and let my ears suck into the headphones. I shut out the muzak, the suit, and The Crash; I tried to sleep,

But I kept one eye open through the flight, and when my seatmate laughed as he watched *Be Kind Rewind* on his seat back screen, I knew he couldn't be all that bad.

| Chapter 20 |

EPILOGUE: THE STANDALONE SEQUEL

NEW YORK CITY, 2008

My plane did land at JFK that day, and what followed was the longest stretch of unemployment in my career. Not just for me, but for plenty of others too. The smaller studios and production companies tightened their belts and eventually this period would be coined the Great Recession.

I am still convinced that there are only two degrees of separation between every job and person I've worked with in film. When I walked up Washington Street in the West Village for a meeting with Nick Quested—the owner of Goldcrest—I realized it had been seven years since Nick's father John had sheltered us after 9/11. The building had since grown into a compact eight-floor studio. With their sister company in London's SoHo, they were an international force of film sales, post-production, development, and film financing. Production was the only part of the equation that Goldcrest was missing, and now they were ready to resolve that.

After a trial run on James Ivory's film in Montreal, we agreed that it was a match for me at Goldcrest. We created a business plan and flew to the Toronto Film Festival to meet with producers and announce my new role as head of production. We met with anyone who would still get behind independent features: executives from the mini-majors, international distributors, financiers, and even a new company who beamed movies out through the internet.

Fifteen years later, we have endured through union strikes, a pandemic, and another promise that no one wants to watch grown-up films. But we're still making them.

We make them differently now with more digital and technical support and fewer trees. We migrated to serial storytelling and to small screens. Yes, you can shoot a live-action film in your pajamas, edit it, market it and distribute it without leaving your apartment. There are as many styles of filmmaking as there are colors on the spectrum. But we still collaborate, we still get a dopamine rush on that first day of filming, and we still grow silent when we hear the word *action*.

Those compelled to tell stories—stories that get your heart racing amidst this cast of characters—might just find home in the cult and the carnival we call filmmaking.

Your call time is 5 a.m.

ACKNOWLEDGMENTS

The stories from this book cover so many years of my life, it's difficult to include everyone who belongs in this small block of acknowledgements. But I have the most gratitude to Jason Kliot and Joana Vicente for giving me a shot when I wasn't on *The List*.

A big thanks to Janice Shay. Also, to Deborah Englander, Caitlin Burdette, and the rest of the team with Post Hill Press. I am the beneficiary of the excellent work of James Faccinto and Sara Mulvanny. I am so grateful for the early read from Sarah Rainone and the later looks from Elizabeth DeNoma, Jaimee Gunther, and Amenya Makuku. There was constant, unconditional support from Rachel Liebling, Tibi Scheflow, and Meg Reticker.

This book had its own cheering section with Bobby, Evelina, Scott, Christian, Harry and Ellis in the front row. My mother Susan, sisters Jennifer, Elizabeth and Carolyn and their families have been a great inspiration too. If not for the generous and sage advice of Sandhya Jain-Patel, Christine Walters, Kerry Fulton, Cynthia Lopez and the NYWIFT board and staff, I would not have persevered. And thank you for the wisdom and wit of Nick Quested, David Kennedy and Domenic Rom.

I'd be remiss if I did not thank New Jersey Transit for its delays, providing me with long stretches of uninterrupted commuting time. It's amazing what you can accomplish on a comfortable train with your laptop and your anonymity.

This book is dedicated to those who think they've been taken out of the running, who think because they're not born into something, that it's out of reach. It is not. But you have got to break down some walls to make it happen.

Most of all, I am grateful for Bob, who never doubted I could do this.

ABOUT THE AUTHOR

Gretchen McGowan is an award-winning producer and the head of production for Goldcrest Films in New York City where she has overseen titles such as *Cat Person*, *Carol*, and *Restrepo*. Gretchen independently produced Jim Jarmusch's *The Limits of Control*, helped to make his iconic film *Coffee and Cigarettes*, and has made over sixty films across the globe.

www.ingramcontent.com/pod-product-compliance
Ingram Content Group UK Ltd.
Pitfield, Milton Keynes, MK11 3LW, UK
UKHW021651190726
13853UKWH00001B/203

9 798895 654484